Accession no.
36183896

WITHDRAWN

IRISH POETRY UNDER
THE UNION, 1801–1924

This book retells the story of Irish poetry written in English between the union of Britain and Ireland in 1801 and the early years of the Irish Free State. Through careful poetic and historical analysis, Matthew Campbell offers ways to read that poetry as ruptured, musical, translated and new. The book starts with the Romantic songs and parodies of nationalist and unionist writers – Moore, Mahony, Ferguson and Mangan – in times of defeat, resurgence and famine. It continues with a discussion of English Victorian poets such as Tennyson, Arnold and Hopkins, who wrote Irish poems as the British Empire unravelled. Campbell's treatment ends with Yeats, seeking a new poetry emerging from under union in times of violence and civil war. The book offers both a literary history of nineteenth-century Irish poetry and a way of reading it for scholars of Irish studies as well as Romantic and Victorian literature.

MATTHEW CAMPBELL is Professor of Modern Literature at the University of York. He is the author of *Rhythm and Will in Victorian Poetry* (1999) and the editor of *The Cambridge Companion to Contemporary Irish Poetry* (2003).

IRISH POETRY UNDER THE UNION, 1801–1924

MATTHEW CAMPBELL

University of York

LIS - LIBRARY

Date	Fund
9.3.15	1-che

Order No.

258 5224

University of Chester

CAMBRIDGE
UNIVERSITY PRESS

CAMBRIDGE
UNIVERSITY PRESS

32 Avenue of the Americas, New York, NY 10013-2473, USA

Cambridge University Press is part of the University of Cambridge.

It furthers the University's mission by disseminating knowledge in the pursuit of
education, learning and research at the highest international levels of excellence.

www.cambridge.org
Information on this title: www.cambridge.org/9781107044845

© Matthew Campbell 2013

This publication is in copyright. Subject to statutory exception
and to the provisions of relevant collective licensing agreements,
no reproduction of any part may take place without the written
permission of Cambridge University Press.

First published 2013

Printed in the United States of America

A catalogue record for this publication is available from the British Library.

Library of Congress Cataloguing in Publication data
Campbell, Matthew (Matthew J. B.)
Irish poetry under the union, 1801–1924 / Matthew Campbell, University of York.
pages   cm
Includes bibliographical references and index.
ISBN 978-1-107-04484-5 (hardback)
1. English poetry – Irish authors – History and criticism.   2. English poetry –
19th century – History and criticism.   3. English poetry – 20th century –
History and criticism.   I. Title.
PR8769.C36   2013
821.009′9415–dc23   2013015858

ISBN 978-1-107-04484-5 Hardback

Cambridge University Press has no responsibility for the persistence or accuracy of
URLs for external or third-party internet websites referred to in this publication
and does not guarantee that any content on such websites is, or will remain,
accurate or appropriate.

For BJC

Contents

Acknowledgements

This book was conceived, written and finished with the support of the Universities of Sheffield, Notre Dame and York. I am particularly grateful for all the support I received at Sheffield, and the periods of research leave and conference support which enabled me to try out much of this material. I also received invaluable research support from the Leverhulme Foundation and the British Academy. A period as O'Donnell Professor at the University of Notre Dame was vital in eventually bringing much of this material together.

Ray Ryan at Cambridge University Press first saw the value in this project and stuck by it over the years. For his support many thanks are due, and to the anonymous readers who provided such helpful insights in its final stages.

Earlier versions of Chapters 4 and 6 appeared in *Class and the Canon*, edited by Kirstie Blair and Mina Gorji, as well as in the *Tennyson Research Bulletin* and *Victorian Literature and Culture*. Parts of Chapters 4 and 7 appeared in *Irish Studies Review* and *Bullán*. I am grateful to the editors for permission to republish.

Many friends and colleagues and students have helped in many ways, material as well as intellectual. I particularly wish to thank Tim Armstrong, Matthew Bevis, Kirstie Blair, Terence Brown, Rachel Buxton, Jacques Chuto, Claire Connolly, Neil Corcoran, Matthew Creasy, Roy Foster, Nicholas Grene, Eric Griffiths, John Haffenden, Hugh Haughton, Alex Houen, Daniel Karlin, Margaret Kelleher, Jim Kelly, Angela Leighton, Hamish Mathison, the late Breandan Ó Buachalla, Adrian Paterson, Michael Perraudin, Adam Piette, Adrian Poole, Justin Quinn, Christopher Ricks, Neil Roberts, Philip Roberts, Marion Shaw, Erica Sheen, Sally Shuttleworth, Jim Smyth, the late Kathleen Tillotson, and Angela Wright.

Maeve Campbell and Hannah Campbell lived much of this and Paula Campbell, as ever, was always there. Valerie Cotter has read every word, many times over, and without her insight and love this book would never have been finished. This book is dedicated to Brian Campbell, lawyer, artist, existentialist-golfer, gaeilgeoir, book-lover and language lover.

CHAPTER I

'The Synthetic Irish Thing'

In his 1959 essay, 'From Monaghan to the Grand Canal', part autobiographical fragment and part jeremiad on a moribund Dublin poetry scene, Patrick Kavanagh recalled that his early work was praised because 'all agreed that I had my roots in the soil, was one of the people and that I was an authentic voice.... There's always been a great market in England for the synthetic Irish thing.'[1] Kavanagh's rhetorical slide, from authentic to synthetic, will be familiar to recent readers of Irish literature and history from a variety of critical and political positions, readers who have found that authenticity itself is a synthetic construct and that the hybrid, the bogus and the counterfeit lurk at the roots of modern Irish culture. Such accusations attended the matter of Irish writing from at least the controversy surrounding the publication of the Scot James Macpherson's Ossianic fragments, fabricated as they were from Irish mythological texts, and the *Irish Melodies* of Thomas Moore, in which newly written English lyrics were joined to Irish airs. Among the results of these inventions was a conflicting version of Irish Romanticism, cast either as what Matthew Arnold called the 'Titanism of the Celt, his passionate, turbulent reaction against the despotism of fact', or for William Hazlitt, the conversion of 'the wild harp of Erin into a musical snuff-box'.[2] Resistant to such stereotyping, the young William Butler Yeats praised an entirely different tradition which was rooted in the example of his immediate predecessors, the cultural nationalists Thomas Davis and James Clarence Mangan, and the Protestant patriot Samuel Ferguson, a small canon of critics and poets which would form the inspiration for his cultural revival: 'The grass is always green for them, and the sea merely blue, and their very spontaneity has made them unequal. But a wonderful freshness and sweetness they have, like the smell of newly-ploughed earth. They are always honest companions; no one of them wrote out of mere vanity or mere ambition, but ever from a full heart.'[3] As someone who knew what it meant to follow a plough through less-than-fertile Irish land, Kavanagh might be right to

I

pour scorn on the spurious organicism of the synthetic Irish thing, particularly given that 'Davis, Mangan, Ferguson' all lived in the city. But over the course of the nineteenth century, as these powerful ideas of rootedness and antiquity met the demands of print culture and performance, it was Irish poetry that established itself as one answer to what Declan Kiberd has called, borrowing a phrase coined by Timothy Brennan to account for the emergence of the contemporary postcolonial novel, 'The National Longing for Form'.[4]

There were a number of ways that the synthetic recovery of Irish culture from the end of the eighteenth century was achieved, from the 'false sublime'[5] of English prose versions of ancient Irish poetry to the translation and repackaging of the remnants of the courtly bards or peasant poets and balladeers of a 'Hidden Ireland' for the English-language reading classes. In both cases, the matter of the Irish (or the 'Celtic') was edged into a home which might appear to belong to an alien, English. 'By the forms of its language a nation expresses its very self,' Arnold said in his 1865–66 Oxford lectures on Celtic literature, in terms we might mistake for those of a Young Ireland polemicist, counselling the preservation of Irish. His language came from a place he called England, and when he asked himself what that place was, he found himself tempted by one possible answer, which might not have looked like Victorian England at all: 'A vast obscure Cymric basis with a vast visible Teutonic superstructure'.[6] Finding that the Cymric basis persisted in language and culture in Wales (the *Eistedfodd* was revived in 1860), and that the last speaker of Cornish was still a living memory, such thoughts enabled Arnold to say that Celticism was at the root of a broadly conceived British culture which is distinct from, and indeed superior to, its European relatives.

More than language, Arnold says it is 'literature' which is the key to a people, and family resemblances within the language of that literature establish for him a poetry written in the synthetic language of a modern United Kingdom of Great Britain and Ireland. Poking around the roots for origins, Arnold reiterated something discovered by many who had compiled and translated the documents rescued from British and Irish antiquity, literary forms which for all the classical and Christian traditions of their superstructure had in the obscurities of their etymology something older, possibly pre-Christian, certainly pre- and anti-Reformation, and were somehow working in different, unaccommodated ways at the foundations of the British state. Like Kavanagh's rootedness and authenticity, to adapt one version of an ancient Britishness stripped of its superstructure, the Celtic looks like 'the thing itself: unaccommodated man'.

That may be no more than 'a poor, bare, forked animal,'[7] but it provided a powerful version of authenticity in a state of nature as a riposte to the modernising industrial society of the philistines.

The story of Irish poetry written in the English language throughout the nineteenth century is that of the unaccommodated searching for the thing itself. The method is a subplot, of sorts, of the deliberate stripping of English poetic form to its roots and the grafting of different literary and linguistic forms, prosody, syntax and style onto it. Those metaphors of 'root' and 'graft' are inherently problematic ways of describing things which are cultural and not organic – culture as if it were organic – and much fun was had in post-Romantic Irish literary criticism about the use and abuse of such terms, of which much will be said later. Suffice to say here that recovering poetry and music and language from the past resulted in coming up with something new in poetry written in English. The dominant method was through translation of various sorts, even when, as with Macpherson, there was no discernible 'original'. Notoriously in Arnold, geographical, anthropological, linguistic and what we would nowadays call racial terms swap places promiscuously in his conception of the origins of Celtic literature. This is not the place either to reiterate the charges or to defend Arnold, but we could make a slight historical leap back to this problematic terminology to adapt and then to reverse Arnold's terms for the geography, anthropology and politics of England for the emergence of a distinctively Irish culture in an anglophone nineteenth century.

For the purposes of Irish literary history, an obvious replacement of Arnold's 'vast obscure Cymric basis with a vast visible Teutonic superstructure' is simply to shift it west, finding an obscure Gaelic basis with a visible English superstructure. This might then be to describe something in Ireland comparable to Arnold's modern British state. It might also describe something unified, with one history in language and culture layering over and thus replacing the other. Thus in one Victorian formulation, we end up with Alfred Tennyson's King Arthur in 1842, surrendering the Celtic epoch to its replacement, however vague that might be: 'The old order changeth, yielding place to new.'[8] But Gaelic Ireland was never so resigned to its fate, and Ireland remained, as many observers pointed out through the eighteenth and nineteenth centuries, not one place or people but two or more: Irish, English and Anglo-Irish sometimes existing in a place that Daniel Corkery called 'Irish Ireland', a 'peasant' place, distinct from a place called English Ireland.[9]

If there is a view of the Gaelic which might be thought to be the opposite of Arnold's view of the Celtic, it is that of Corkery, published in 1924 at the end of the Civil War which had followed the establishment of the

Irish Free State. He reconstructed a divided culture sunk in degradation after Britain's 'Glorious Revolution' of 1688. Working from a phrase of Samuel Madden picked up from Corkery's bête noire, the unionist Victorian historian W.E.H. Lecky, he saw that from a description of a divided English/Irish, Protestant/Catholic eighteenth-century Ireland as 'a paralytic body where one half of it is dead or just dragged about by the other', he could offer one of a number of definitions of his theme: 'The Hidden Ireland, then, the land that lies before us, is the dead half of that stricken body; it is the terrain of the common enemy, ruled by deputies of deputies of deputies, and sunk so deep in filth and beggary that its people have been thrust, as torpid and degraded pariahs should, beyond the household of the law.'[10]

We cannot separate Corkery's 'Hidden Ireland' from the crucial function it played in the early years of a Free State keen to pursue the *Kulturkampf* of de-Anglicisation (and its relative failure, which is another story). But two more versions of Arnold, albeit crossed with Corkery, might look something like this. Over the course of the Irish contact with its English neighbour, an English and Protestant superstructure was imposed on the Gaelic and Catholic basis of the culture. This Gaelic basis suffered an attempted eradication after the defeats of the Jacobite cause and the Union of England and Wales with Scotland in 1707, a process accelerated by the Penal laws of the early eighteenth century. Add the subsequent suppression of Jacobite rebellions in Scotland in 1715 and at Culloden in 1746, and the decline might have been thought to be terminal. Nevertheless, towards the end of the eighteenth century, a confident English-speaking culture, benefiting from the learning promoted by a settled ascendancy class, met again the old Gaelic basis, which was in its turn becoming newly visible, assuming a superstructure in which the seeming ruins of the Irish language and Irish music were shored up by English translation. This was manifest in one way by poetry and song, in the contact of English poetry with Irish lyric and melody. But it also coincided with a new politics, of rights and revolution, inspired by events in America and France. It is difficult to underestimate the confluence of art and culture with this new politics, no matter how uncomprehending of each other their adherents might originally have been. An emblematic moment occurred in the middle of the Belfast Harpers Festival, on 13 July 1792, when two Protestant figures, Edward Bunting and Wolfe Tone, could be seen in the same hall, one a diligent nineteen-year-old student writing down the nearly lost music of a fairly ramshackle collection of elderly, mostly blind Irish harpers, and the other using the occasion to

organize United Irishmen and Volunteers for the next day's celebrations of
the third anniversary of the fall of the Bastille, all the while complaining
of the musical accompaniment which exacerbated his hangover: 'the harpers again, strum, strum and be hanged!'[11]

One possible site of the origin of what the nineteenth century would
later call nationalism was thus also a site of recovery, making a historical
connection with something thought lost, and beginning the process of its
restoration – albeit printed in the English language or in notation for the
pianoforte. Melody and style were translated, adapted, written down and
relearned to be joined with a new subject matter. In Arnoldian terms, the
superstructure assumed the basis; in Corkery's terms, the sunken began to
recolonise the terrain. The renewed antiquarian interest in the recovery and
translation of ancient Irish texts, court and folk poetry, melody and song,
as well as the persistence of Irish-language poetry and English-language
ballads, meant that the resultant synthetic form of Irish poetry in English
came into the light as something new but still based in a project primarily concerned to rescue and complement the cultural remains of those
who had remained unaccommodated with the Ireland of Ascendancy and
Union. These remains were composed and performed by a people whom
Corkery memorably called

> the residuary legatees of a civilisation that was more than a thousand years
> old.... With that civilisation they were still in living contact, acquainted
> with its history; and such of its forms as had not quite become impossible
> in their way of life, they still piously practised, gradually changing the old
> moulds into new shapes, and whether new or old, filling them with a con-
> tent that was all of the passing day and their own fields. What of art they
> did create in their cabins is poor and meagre if compared with what their
> fathers created in the dun and grianans of queens; yet the hem matches the
> garment and the clasp the book.[12]

The poetry beginning to be written in Ireland could also gain from such a
late-Romantic formulation of tradition as the persistence of the traces of the
old in the new writing for a new audience in speakers of another language.

Corkery's case is exemplary for an Irish literary criticism sensitively
attuned to the nuances of Irish historiography. His work has been much
revised since Louis Cullen used it as the basis for a revisionary movement
in Irish history.[13] The critique of Arnold has for some time been a starting
point for the counter-revisionist turn of Irish postcolonial and nationalist
criticism.[14] But one thing that neither Arnold nor Corkery can be accused
of is the static mourning of the merely nostalgic. Bearing in mind the sincerity of Corkery's complaint against the destruction of the literary and

linguistic culture of his forebears, and its seeming opposite, the no less sincere modernising educational mission of Arnold's Oxford lectures, both critics offered versions of culture in process, in adaptation, reorienting the 'Celtic' or the 'Irish' to the new. They described a becoming of sorts, even when they were content with the evanescent and the parochial – 'the passing day and their own fields' – which would eventually emerge for a poet like Patrick Kavanagh as end enough for poetry.

This book is interested in retelling a part of that story again, by looking again at the ends and the beginnings of Irish poetry. Nineteenth-century Irish poetry in English was for most of its life trapped inside an arranged marriage – most would say a forced marriage. For all that Great Britain and Ireland constitutionally tied the knot in the Union of 1801, as we can see from the place-changing of Arnold's and Corkery's terms in the preceding sketch of literary and linguistic history, that knot can look fairly difficult to unravel in longer stretches of the relationship between English and Irish poetry. 'History encloses him so straitly that even his fiery moments do not set him free from it', James Joyce said of James Clarence Mangan, 'the type of his race', Irish poet.[15] Figures for the unravelling came very slowly and frequently with an apocalyptic import, as in the two spools disarrayed for the last judgement in English poet Gerard Manley Hopkins's Dublin poem of the *dies irae* of the end of Empire and time, 'Spelt from Sibyl's Leaves'. Irish versions were even less certain: the closest William Butler Yeats's end-of-the-century poem 'The Valley of the Black Pig' comes to a liberating apocalypse is at its threshold, 'Master of the still stars and of the flaming door'.[16] Even Joyce, a writer who chose escape, ended his only significant poetic sequence, *Chamber Music*, abandoned on a shoreline, blasphemously quoting the crucified (and un-resurrected) Christ, 'My love, my love, my love, why have you left me alone?'[17]

The becoming of the moment of liberation was wary of both birth and rebirth, and it is important that the hindsight cast back from subsequent Irish history, of cultural revival, insurrection and (partial) political and cultural independence, not be allowed to over-influence readings of poets acutely aware of their subject status, caught between origins and originality. At the very least, to tell the story of nineteenth-century Irish poetry, we cannot avoid matching it with another, more frequently told one, following recent historians and critics from a number of ideological positions in revising it a little to allow in the broader British poetic story. Taking a lead from the work of the historian of Britain J.G.A Pocock, three-kingdoms or four-nations models of British history have been crucial for historians of Enlightenment and Romantic literature. Witness Robert Crawford's account of a 'devolved' English literature located back into its institutional inception in Scottish universities and Edinburgh printing houses, or John Kerrigan's appropriation of Shakespeare's 'Scottish Play' at the beginning of a seventeenth-century archipelagic English.[18] There has been a long-held revisionary view of the Irish locations of the composition of Spenser's British epic for Elizabeth, *The Faerie Queene*. By the end of the eighteenth century, a Bardic nationalism, to use Katie Trumpener's phrase, might be seen as widespread across a devolved English literary scene, so much so that Maureen McLane, attempting to establish a 'transhistorical, transmedial' reflection on poetry after historicism, locates a paradigm in Anglo-Scottish balladeering 'the persistence and transmutation of a poetic and musical phenomenon as it encounters new media and new historical situations'.[19]

But the four-nations paradigm has slipped from the literary history of the newly expanded United Kingdom after 1801. The slippage has been from the study of nineteenth-century Ireland, centred as it is around the catastrophes of the Great Famine and emigration and governed as it has been by the hindsight of eventual rebellion and independence. It has also suffered from the oft-noted repression of the Famine in the Anglo-centric and imperial preoccupations of studies of Victorian culture.[20] For nineteenth-century Irish poetry, however, the archipelagic examples were strong, whatever their dubious authenticity: *Ossian*, Bishop Percy's *Reliques of English Poetry*, the medieval forgeries of Thomas Chatterton, the great commercial success of the renovated songs provided by Robert Burns in his collaboration with a number of Scottish publishers and European composers, Walter Scott's *Minstrelsy of the Scottish Border*, and ultimately William Wordsworth and Samuel Taylor Coleridge's *Lyrical Ballads*, a particular form of Romanticism for which a new poetry was founded in the old forms of country and orality. For all that literary history usually posits that Yeats, writing a century after Wordsworth, is at the beginning of a revival of original Irish poetry written in the English language, in MacLane's terms, the 'persistence and transmutation' of English and Scottish ballad-collecting and 'the new media and new historical situations' of the reprinting and translation of the Irish ballad and lyric were to result in much original Irish poetry in English in the nineteenth century.

The poetry which followed the example of Romanticism we might broadly call 'Victorian' – no matter how problematic that term might be in relation to Ireland. The strongest detractor of the poetry of nineteenth-century Ireland has been Thomas Kinsella, for whom the loss of Irish resulted in his own singularly divided Irish modernity, inheritor as he saw himself of a 'Dual Tradition'. Developing arguments made in an influential lecture first given in New York in 1966, Kinsella blames the 'poetry of general dullness, a great supply of bad verse' written by Irish adherents who were following British Victorian forms, the example of which was 'minor and bad verse, from a succession of poets content with established modes and forms and making small changes, in a changeless tone, inside narrow bounds'.[21] A generation of scholars has learnt to read again Victorian poetry since its great belittling by the modernists among whom Kinsella was a late developer. But bar the markedly dissimilar approaches offered by Robert Welch or David Lloyd, fewer have tried to read again Victorian Irish verse.[22] That involves reading against the grain, in many ways celebrating, if that were possible, its baggage as synthetic, forged, stolen or mere translation. Then again, what of 'Tam O'Shanter', 'The Rime of the Ancient Mariner' or 'The Lady of Shalott'? These are synthetic British products which were partly recovered mythic or oral tradition, but mostly invention. If the American folklorist Richard Dorson refers to these British poems as 'fakelore', his definition of it might yet be turned to positive account: 'a synthetic product claiming to be authentic oral tradition but actually tailored for mass edification'.[23] In Ireland, the needs were of a 'mass audience' further split by the change of language: in Kinsella's terms, 'the change of vernacular from Irish to English was leaving a majority audience divided from its past.'[24]

The Irish poetic turn to bring its own traditions – in mythology, epic, court poetry, Jacobite lyric, folk melody or ballad – into print at first sought simple academic pleasure from its earliest practitioners, perhaps coinciding with the desired immersion of Ireland in the greater United Kingdom and its world-spanning empire. Aping Percy, Charlotte Brooke could call her 1789 collection of translations *Reliques of Irish Poetry*, but that publication – the first serious attempt to find English poetic form for Irish-language aristocratic as well as peasant poetry – was to founder because of two ultimately related circumstances. The first might be suggested by the date of the year of its publication and the events in France which were to draw Britain into an alliance with the forces of reaction against the revolutionary spirit unleashed across Europe. The second was Brooke's own version of the Great British family:

> The British muse is not yet informed that she has an elder sister in this isle; let us then introduce them to each other! together let them walk abroad from their bowers, sweet ambassadresses of cordial union between two countries that seem formed by nature to be joined by every bond of interest, and of amity. Let them entreat of Britain to cultivate a nearer acquaintance

with her neighbouring isle. Let them conciliate for us her esteem, and her affection will follow of course. Let them tell her, that the portion of her blood which flows in our veins is rather ennobled than disgraced by the mingling tides that descended from our heroic ancestors.[25]

This passage is familiar to many historians of Irish Romantic culture, promoting the 'cordial union' of culture between Britain and Ireland in order to follow the ultimately successful union of England and Wales with Scotland earlier in the century. It might be discrete not to look too closely at the metaphors Brooke employs: one feature of the critical discussions in this book will be to question the poetic unions attempted in practice and in theory by a succession of Irish poets and critics. But another will be to look at the metaphors that are used, and the inevitable vocabulary of hybridity, grafting, marriage and issue. Brooke's intention is genial, but her metaphors of sisterhood, shared blood and mingling tides suggest a marriage which might be rather too close in terms of shared family characteristics.

Brooke's method to effect this union was translation, and if the semi-incestuous metaphor implicit in her account is not entirely under control, neither was the translation. A translation which cannot register difference in the translator's language cannot suggest something new. But at times she could admit a more than family distance, a yawning gulf unbridgeable by translation.

> A chinn duibh dhílis, dhílis, dhílis,
> Cuir do ceann dílis tharam anall;
> A bhéilín meala, a bhfuil boladh na tíme air,
> Is duine gan chroí nach dtabharfadh duit grá.

> [Lay your head, my own (my own, my own)
> Your head, my own, lay it here upon me.
> Honeymouth that smells of thyme
> He would have no heart who denied you love.][26]

This is the ending of an anonymously composed Irish folk song, usually referred to by its Irish title, 'Ceann Dubh Dílis' ('My Own Dark Head' or 'Dear Dark Head'), as it appears in Kinsella and Sean Ó Tuama's classic 1981 collection, *An Duanaire 1600–1900: Poems of the Dispossessed*, along with Kinsella's modern translation. Printing the stanza in 1789 in a Gaelic font, Brooke's gloss simply went thus: 'I need not give any comment upon these lines; the English reader would not understand it, and the Irish reader would not want it, for it is impossible to peruse them without being sensible of their beauty.'[27]

Seventy-six years later, Samuel Ferguson was to publish his attempt at just this feat, of translating the untranslatable:

Cean Dubh Deelish

Put your head, darling, darling, darling,
    Your darling black head my heart above;
Oh, mouth of honey, with the thyme for fragrance,
    Who, with heart in breast, could deny you love?
Oh, many and many a young girl for me is pining,
    Letting her locks of gold to the cold wind free,
For me, the foremost of our gay young fellows;
    But I'd leave a hundred, pure love, for thee!
Then put your head, darling, darling, darling,
    Your darling black head my heart above;
Oh, mouth of honey, with the thyme for fragrance,
    Who, with heart in breast, could deny you love?[28]

This poem appeared as one of Ferguson's *Lays of the Western Gael* in 1865, in a volume which finally gathered together his 1830s translations of Irish court and peasant poetry with more recent work on translated and original versions of Irish myth and epic. The volume served two functions. The first was primarily patriotic, to continue to redress the great correction of the Ossianic from the mystical, the sentimental and the defeated into what Peter Denman calls 'Ferguson's hard-edged vision of the simplicities of a heroic Ireland'.[29] More pertinent to this poem, and the poetry discussed in this book, the *Lays* also removed Ferguson's versions of Irish-language song and lyric from their original polemical context, as an appendix to another corrective or revisionary act. This was the young Ferguson's sharply critical review of the tastelessly anglicised versions of seventeenth- and eighteenth-century Irish poetry collected in James Hardiman's 1831 *Irish Minstrelsy*, accompanied as they were by a sectarian and O'Connellite critical apparatus.

A much later translation, Ferguson's 'Cean Dubh Deelish' functions thus as something which has been placed at a deliberate distance from its 'source'. It was published in the 'Versions from the Irish' part of the *Lays* without an original for comparison. In Hardiman's collection, texts in an Irish typeface faced the English versions, and Kinsella and Ó Tuama were later scrupulously to follow this procedure in *An Duanaire*. In one sense, giving version or adaptation and not literal translation, Ferguson appears to be asking us to read an English poem on its own terms, and what a strange thing that is. Brooke must have been wary of the challenge of translating the first line alone, where 'dílis' can mean in English alternately 'my own', or 'dear', or perhaps both. Hardiman's translator, Thomas Furlong, had avoided this problem entirely, offering the first line as, 'Oh! Sweetest and dearest of maidens behold me.'[30] But the repetition of the word *dílis* in the original line presents a further challenge. Of course, to sing, 'Put your head darling, darling, darling' might be perfectly acceptable, but no melody is given on Ferguson's page either. Dislocated as much as translated into English print, a song lyric without a tune, the line achieves the strangeness of the new while still echoing a fugitive, and by this stage text-less, old.

By the faintest suggestion, the reader guesses at the trace of another language and music sounding through the English of an original poem, an English nevertheless slanted back into the conventions and accents of its Irish origins. Shifting the word 'above' to the end of the second line certainly helps with the rhyme (with 'love'), but that rhyme has been won by changing the word order of English. Similarly, 'Oh, mouth of honey, with the thyme for fragrance' and 'Oh, many and many a young girl for me is pining' brilliantly exploit the early caesura after the exclamation ('Oh') to lengthen their vowels through the strangeness of an imported foreign syntax and prosody that now seems careless of rhyme. 'Oh, mouth of honey, with the thyme for fragrance' is both unrhymed and a challenge to English scansion (either: / | / x / x | x x / | x / x; or / | x x / x | x x / | x / x). Syntactically, the lines sound like Irish-English with the word order shifted again; a redundant article is introduced to give an Irish accent speaking English in the market town, the field or the pub: '*the* thyme for fragrance'. The very close repetitions of the first and last four lines are of course in the 'original' if the reader were to be given it, but here they add to the sense of the poem's extraordinarily intimate adoration, a consummation perhaps denied in the poem itself but nevertheless about to happen. Such anticipation might be risky, but still familiar to readers of English Romantic or Victorian verse. What would be unfamiliar in the English poem would be the image of competing girls advertising their sexual availability to the poet: 'Letting [their] locks of gold to the cold wind free'. Rarer still would be what looks like a three-stress foot at the end of the line (in classical scansion that rare thing, a molossus): 'cold wind free'. This was a trick picked up by Yeats in his supposedly founding Irish-English lyric of twenty-five years later, the 1890 'Lake Isle of Innisfree' with its' 'bee-loud glade' or 'deep heart's core'. In Ferguson's hands, the folk song turns to art poem, a synthetic formal achievement but one nevertheless catching the frankness, the ache and the voice of an original in the forms of another language, like the loved one in the song, where a certain intimacy is about to give way to a longer embrace.

Ferguson's version of 'Ceann Dubh Dílis' presents us with one challenge of the nineteenth-century Irish poem in English. Even bearing in mind its status as a translation concerned to sound linguistic and cultural difference in its metric and lexis, the poetic achievement suggests difficult questions for a criticism. We need to seek for more than just history in accounting for its success. Angela Leighton concludes her discussion of Yeats's antinomial sense of 'form' (partly a ghostly spirit and partly the energetic organisation of the individual poem) with a discussion of his short 1916 poem of the persistence of love, 'Memory'. The word form is used fairly precisely there as the grass nest of the mountain hare that continues to bear the imprint of the hare once it has gone, just as the poet retains his feeling for lost lovers. This arresting image has attracted other Irish poets and poet-critics, Michael Longley and Peter McDonald, for whom 'form' is a symbol of presence remaining in the face of its consistent erasure felt either actually in loss or meta-poetically, given its frequently fraught critical relation with its usual bedfellow, 'content'.[31] Leighton says this, beautifully, about form as a fugitive but also remnant, which we might use to think about Ferguson's 'Version from the Irish': 'The hare has gone, and with it, content, matter, story, emotion. But the form remains. For form is simply the rhythm of what came and went, and was saved in the various forms of language itself [...]'.[32] For Leighton's 'what came and went' we might also remember Corkery's diminution of theme, 'the passing of day and their own fields'.

The achievement of Ferguson's 'Cean Dubh Deelish' is just one of these 'various forms' of language, a lost, anonymous peasant-author found almost by accident to be inhabiting the right words for the right feeling in a poem translated into another poetic language, itself full of the possibilities of its own various forms. As Leighton says elsewhere, adapting Theodore Adorno's notion that 'luck and play' have much to do with the successes of writing, the achievement represented by a poem like Ferguson's will not easily be brought into 'a philosophical nutshell, once and for all, but only along the way, in the part gamble, part-guesswork which each singular, differently formed work inspires'.[33] Singularity is, of course, paramount here, and its downside might be the inability to incorporate the different readings that different poems need with the method also required to read them with some sort of coherent critical-historical narrative, whether or not the protection of a philosophical, or indeed political, nutshell is required. The Irish reader of poetry will have Yeats's admonition in mind: 'The poet is never the bundle of accident and incoherence that sits down to breakfast.'[34]

Although Ferguson's poem is no fragile thing, its delicacy does need some protection from temptations to over-read its significance, to lend a coherence to its becoming in phases of loss and rediscovery. It may be that giving up utterance to singularity may remove both content and context from such early blossoms of Irish poetic form. One redress might be to turn back to the kind of large cultural or political history outlined in the earlier pages of this introduction. But there are middle ways. Susan Wolfson, for instance, suggests an approach to reading for form in the face of materialist criticism, in terms in which history can be a little more than 'what came and went'. Referring to the preoccupation with organic forms in British Romanticism to which all of these debates in Irish aesthetics about rootedness and authenticity are indebted, she says that 'attention to form can articulate issues often felt to be inimical: not only the factitiousness of organic coherence, close designs and cognitive totality, but also the construction of forms in relation to subjectivity, cultural ideology, and social circumstance.' One of the best-remembered symbols in a Romantic poem is the 'companionable form' of the fluttering film of soot in Coleridge's 'Frost at Midnight', a simile for the sceptics, 'a toy of thought'. As Wolfson says, looking for organic form and union in symbol we find instead Coleridge's 'critical probing into the poetics of unity ... exposing the unity vested in the privileged form of the symbol as an illusory or factitious (however intensely desired) effect of poetic form'.[35]

For Wolfson's 'factitious', we can substitute something that appears to be working at a lower level in Irish poetry under the Union: Patrick Kavanagh's 'synthetic Irish thing'. His formalism is no less aware that the attention to style – or his preferred word, 'technique' – might still be productive in reading something that is by turns political or historical critique, parody, burlesque or even forgery. For Kavanagh, 'Technique' is 'a method of being sincere. Technique is a method of getting at life.' Whatever the wilful paradoxes of artifice and life – method sincerity, the authenticity of technique – and the tempting of stereotypes of mere aestheticism that go back to Arnold (the Celt 'runs off into technic, where he employs the utmost elaboration, and attains the most astonishing skill'[36]), the synthetic Irish thing emerges as a necessity, something that must be created in order to sustain artistic growth. Technique is employed in the service of both the 'intensely desired' but nevertheless factitious poetic union of sound and sense, and the intense desire for the synthetically rooted and ultimately procreative, the new:

What are our roots? What is our material?
    Real roots lie in our capacity for love and its abandon. The material itself has no special value; it is what our imagination and our love does to it.
    Lying at the heart of love we wander through its infinities.[37]

In his own disarming way, Kavanagh switches from a rooted cynicism to an aspirant romanticism, rubbing the poetry of loneliness and sterility against that of creativity and love. Wandering through the infinities of love involves a happy surrender to 'what came and went', and it is important that a historical narrative not be allowed to smother the small-scale delicacies of the Irish poetry that came before him, which he saw as its future.

This book is about the beginnings and not the end, or at least Kavanagh's feared end, of lyric Irish poetry in the English language. If it finds that the roots of anglophone Irish poetry are hard to excavate, it also shares Kavanagh's ambivalent example of the 'love' that led to its creation. Synthetic or authentic, pure or hybrid, original or translated, organic or cultured, political or amatory, male or female, Irish or English: these opposites will frequently reveal themselves to be nothing of the sort, and change conceptual places promiscuously in the pages that follow. Seeking the infinities at the heart of love, in longing and desire for loved one or country – and frequently one through the other – the Irish, and indeed the English, poets discussed in this book might be led more to the uncertainties of Kavanagh in the attendant formal conditions of false translation, distorted melody, savage parody, repetition and stasis, exile and defeat. Kiberd's 'National Longing for Form' was phrased in Arnold's Celticism as an art that 'seems to make up to itself for being unable to master the world and give an adequate interpretation of it, by throwing all its force into style'.[38] If Kavanagh wants to say, *contra* Arnold, that technique might not be the way of mastery and adequate interpretation, but simply a 'method of getting at life', then it is perhaps pushing things a little to follow Kiberd to the triumphant emergence in the postcolonial or liberatory moment of the literary and dramatic revival of the early twentieth century. But style is not born fully formed, and the linguistic shape and poetic forms of revival were at first tempered in the synthetic, bogus and the hybrid.

The characteristic note sounded early in the nineteenth century by Thomas Moore, in his handsomely rewarded publishing project of setting English-language lyrics to Gaelic court and peasant melodies, is of seemingly irrecuperable loss giving way to partial revival, the ancient giving way to the new. Moore's lyrics, like much Irish poetry in English written between his time and Kavanagh's, was tempered by a recently contracted relationship, a relationship that over the subsequent century or so from 1801 was governed by the strain of the cultural consummation of the United Kingdom of Great Britain and Ireland. Many critics of the Irish novel have seen that constitutional arrangement reflected in the metaphors of Irish fiction in its various genres. Concerned with allegory rather than symbol, coded rather than socially descriptive narratives, nineteenth-century Irish fiction tells national tale in the forms of romance or gothic rather than realism. In fictions as generically disparate as Maria Edgeworth's *The Absentee* or Sydney Owenson's *The Wild Irish Girl*, the marriage plot is one of rapprochement and partnership across a cultural difference recognized and then dissolved.[39] But the union of Irish and English in poetry, sometimes violently resisted, sometimes fervently wished for, was a forcing together in the technical struggle of the national forms of 'ballad and story, rann and song', to adapt William Butler Yeats's 1892 manifesto for the brotherhood of Irish poets, 'To Ireland in the Coming Times'. There were Irish experiments in epic, and if the international market created by Macpherson for the larger synthetic brand, the 'Celtic', was eventually to be exposed as founded on a hoax, its main nineteenth-century apologists were initially French – Ernest Renan[40] – and English – Arnold. The eventual achievement in Ireland was not epic, but one in which despite the preponderance of small-scale forms, technique could result in something often chillingly celebrated as a sort of power by Yeats, the most notable proponent of a lyrical mastery that enabled Irish poetry to get at life. Whether rooted or uprooted, wandering through the heart of love or in a language and milieu desperate to overcome its loneliness and rejection, the achievement of that Irish poetry was to forge the synthetic from the old and the authentic. In the many conflicting senses of the word, Irish poets sought to establish the original, as rooted in origins, but also as growing into the new.

Poetic synthesis was the product of a literature deliberately making differing poetic versions of itself in the English language, as much as reeling under the stress of the unforeseen mixing of Irish and English cultures. Ireland's long history within the 'four nations' or 'archipelagic' British Isles recast itself in the long peace of the nineteenth-century United Kingdom. The better-known British story, as recounted by generations of students of Victorian literature, is of victory over the French followed by reform, science, empire and the novel. The Irish story is of defeat in rebellion, Union, nationalism, Famine, rebellion again and the ballad. For Irish historians of a variety of methodological and political hues, Ireland was never *in* the United Kingdom, it was *under* the Union.[41] Or, as W.J. McCormack has asked, 'If nineteenth-century Ireland is fundamentally relatable to England, and to Britain generally, why is it that in the area of cultural production the relationships are suppressed more often than expressed?

The central issue here concerns Ireland's complex role as metropolitan colony within the United Kingdom.'[42] The historians' extrication of Ireland
from the postcolonial – or at least post-colony – metaphor of amalgam-
ation inherent in the word 'Union' suggests a continued subjugation. To
be a colony 'within' a Union also suggests the continuance of two parts of
the colonial process, the coloniser having become settled colonist and the
colonised a recently defeated insurgent.

No matter how the majority population in Ireland was religiously
and politically opposed to that union, when it heard again the recovered melodies of the harp that once sounded through Tara's halls,[43] they
were accompanied by English lyrics. Those lyrics might have contained
allegorical matter when composed by Moore or stronger political point
when circulated by Young Ireland polemicists or scabrous street balladeers. Translating Irish music by adding English lyric, they still told of sectarian and political difference. At the same time, a minority sought in
the Union the succession of their 'ascendancy' status in the culture of a
unified Ireland. Writing as a Belfast Protestant poet Ferguson asked, after
200 years of his family living and owning land in Ireland, that he be,

> No rootless colonist of alien earth …
> A stranger in the land that gave him birth,
> The land a stranger to itself and him'.[44]

Those lines come from 'Mesgedra', one of Ferguson's poems on mythical pre-Christian Irish material. It is a 'Lay of the Western Gael' given an
English-language outing in a poem that ends up seeking joint citizenship
(or more properly joint subjecthood) between Irish Catholic and Ulster-
Scottish Protestant in Queen Victoria's United Kingdom.

Gaelic, English, Scottish, Danish even – by 1801 a large majority of all
of those waves of colonists who still lived in Ireland were English speaking, although they shared the memory of the linguistic and cultural difference practiced by a surviving Atlantic few. Nevertheless, as this great
language change appeared to be consolidated, Ireland under the Union
was an unsettlingly creative place. If English poets who wrote Irish poetry,
or at least poetry on Irish subjects – Arnold, Tennyson, Swinburne or
Hopkins – could never quite figure why there was resistance to the project
first envisaged by Brooke – of assimilation into the new literary language
of the United Kingdom – those Irish poets who brought Irish-language
poetry and the remnants of the songs of an ancient Gaelic culture before
the newly literate print-fixated audiences in Ireland, Britain and America
frequently surrendered the shape of the originals to the demands of the

English language. In turn, the resultant lyric and poetry began to sound distinctly different from the poetry of England, as the example of Scottish balladry and the new forms of post-*Lyrical Ballads* British Romantic poetry met those remnants of peasant and courtly melody in newly conceived synthetic constructions of the bardic. By accident as much as design, the poets of the earlier period of the Union – Moore, Ferguson or Mangan – offered a variety of technical solutions to Kavanagh's quandary. Practicing a species of translation, they retained the rooted while longing to follow the abandon of imagination within their odd English-Irish, United Kingdom relationship. As McCormack says, unable to avoid the organic metaphor, the later nineteenth-century product was not from pure stock: 'The Anglo-Irish Renaissance, the Irish genius for words, is not solely a product of native soil.'[45]

This book will look at the technical products of those Irish roots and English soil, English stock and Irish graft, Gaelic melody and English lyric, English poetry in Irish accents. Organic metaphor and cultural form unavoidably cross-fertilise in the history of this discourse, presenting us with the rooted and hybrid, authentic and bogus by turns. If the overall impression is of the widespread adulteration of metaphors from nature themselves, as much as the culture they seek to represent, then that adulteration comes in the broadest sense from both a European post-Romantic literary culture aware that it is working with the mixed set of linguistic and artistic possibilities revealed in and justified by history, and the processes of adaptation and borrowing endemic in the passing on of the songs and lore of the 'folk'. The most powerful theoretical recipe for this mixture of high and low cultures has been offered by those critics who gather variety into heteroglossia, and beyond that, into the discourse of hybridity noticed in so many postcolonial cultures across the world. Avoiding the slippage into organicism a critic such as Wolfson sees in a Coleridge-derived poetics, Jahan Ramazani, for one, has urged a distinction between 'organic hybrids' and 'intentional hybrids'. If the latter are 'strife riven and dialogic', still, 'the term "hybridity" itself suggests too neat and complete a union of disparate parts'. Either way, the result can be both singular and new, as Ramazani says, 'a poem that would have been unimaginable within the confines of one or other culture'.[46]

A leading critical voice in the application of this discourse to nineteenth-century Irish poetry has been David Lloyd, who finds that the nationalist project to create new ballad forms was central to the subsequent creation of a higher genre, the epic. He sees this happening just as European literature was turning from the epic to the novel. The union that Irish cultural nationalism sought was not with Britain, but between all Irish people, in order to create the monologic from what Lloyd calls 'exactly the "national myth" that [Mikhael] Bakhtin envisages as having collapsed when the novel supplanted the epic'. Anterior to epic, a resurgent Irish lyricism could prepare the ground, no matter that in other places it had already been – to follow the horticultural metaphors – 'supplanted'. Lloyd's aim is the critique of nationalism as much as of Irish poetry, but his description of adulteration is instructive in the area where Irish ballad, stalled epic and modernist novel come together in the pages of James Joyce's *Ulysses*:

> [T]he processes of hybridization active in the Irish street ballads or in *Ulysses* are at every level recalcitrant to the aesthetic politics of nationalism and, as we can now see, to imperialism. Hybridization or adulteration resist identification both in the sense that they cannot be subordinated to a narrative of representation and in the sense that they play out the unevenness of knowledge which, against assimilation, foregrounds the political and cultural positioning of the audience or reader.[47]

Perhaps this asks just too much of street ballad, if not that much of Joyce, saturated as his work is with synthetic Irish lyric in its sentimental and burlesque forms. Recalcitrance, unevenness and an opposition to assimilation are among the distinctive technical or formal properties of many nineteenth-century Irish poems, as written by Irish and English poets, whether anti-imperial or anti-national. It is important not to depoliticise those qualities, but to read them closely might provide a richer prospect than Lloyd allows. For one thing, to recreate the circumstances of the writing of these poems is to feel again the contingency of their composition, the accident by which some succeed and many fail, the exciting prospect that some innovations offered, the dead end of others.

This is a matter for poetry, and the reading of poetry needs to be reclaimed, just as the poets needed to reclaim their own sense of creative autonomy and originality in their anxieties about authenticity and hybridity that went in parallel with those of union and its repeal. To adopt a word of hiberno-English origin used by Seamus Heaney to describe British-Irish poetic relations, the English poetry of nineteenth and early twentieth-century Ireland is 'through-other' with that of England and Scotland and Wales, in Gaelic as well as English. Its through-otherness is something that we disentangle at our peril. The critic can no more go back to the origin than Ireland could return to the bardic sophistication of its Golden Age. Wishing for such ideas, the Irish poet under union is more than likely to end up with James Clarence Mangan, imagining thirteenth-century Connacht, but ultimately finding himself confronted with the skeleton of the Famine victim. Mangan's best poems follow this mix of temporality and imagination into odd post-Romantic corners, through-other with Ireland and England, Irish and English, English and German, French and Persian, West and East, bogus and original. They exemplify one version of the through-other that might suggest the modelling of a new poetry emerging out of difficult times, which is the subject of this book. The word will return in Chapters 7 and 9, but for the purposes of introducing how it might inform the readings of poems in this book, I have little to add to Heaney's stating of the matter:

> [A]ny account of the Irish poet and Britain must get past politics and into poetry itself. [...] It is not only a poem's political concerns and paraphrase-able content that need attending to. A précis of the content, for example, takes no account of the literary echoes and allusions which can be fundamental to its poetic energy. In a poem, words, phrases, cadences and images are linked in to systems of affect and signification which elude the précis maker. These under-ear activities, as they might be termed, may well constitute the most important business which the poem is up to and are more a matter of the erotics of language than the politics and polemics of the moment. Which is to say that poetry moves things forward once the poet and the poem get ahead of themselves and find themselves out on their own.[48]

Heaney's words were first delivered to an audience in Aberdeen in 2001, 200 years after the act of Union. Spoken in a new century facing peace of a sort, they request that by listening out for the 'under-ear activities' of individual poems we can hear the genuine subversiveness of poet and poem 'out on their own'. This book tries to keep Irish poems under-ear, not forgetting that they make their way out from under the sign and history of union.

Not all poets of nineteenth-century Ireland had the goal of nation or empire in mind, and, in Kavanagh's terms, many simply sought to wander through the infinities of love, their achievements maybe simply to record what came and went. Of course that love had to be expressed in the newly coupled forms of the Irish-English lyric, unavoidably synthetic or hybrid or through-other as that might be. For some it might even have been a species of adultery, but the product did hold out the possibility of the new. Towards the end of Ireland's 120 years in the United Kingdom, in the year of his violent death, Thomas MacDonagh could look forward to the return of cultural confidence in what he calls 'The Irish Mode' in English poetry. There is little attempt either to cling on to linguistic purity or the provincial identity of the colonised, as he concludes:

> Later, when we have expressed again in English all the emotions and experiences expressed already in Irish, this literature will go forward, free from translation. Through the English language has come a freshening breath

from without: with the Gaelic Renaissance has come a new stirring of national consciousness: these too have been the great influence in all new literatures. At that I can leave it, at that freshening and that stirring of it.[49]

Writing in 1916, there is neither monologism nor hybridity here, just the stirring of the new. MacDonagh's cultural freshening was to end for him at the wrong end of a firing squad: style and action, technique and life are often dangerously run together in Irish history. It is an observation on a smaller scale, but MacDonagh knew what was at stake in an Irish poetry in English, which freshened and stirred the Irish synthetic stew.

CHAPTER 2

The Ruptured Ear: Irish Accent, English Poetry

A Wandering Rhythm

In his first published novel, *Murphy*, Samuel Beckett leads his hero into the British Museum, where he is accosted by a former acquaintance, Austin Ticklepenny, 'a distinguished indigent drunken Irish bard'. Ticklepenny is working as a nurse in a mental hospital, a position he has been forced to take in order to afford his therapy. His Irish-German doctor, Dr Fist, has told him 'Giff de booze ub or go kaputt'; but drinking, it emerges, is not his main problem:

> Dr Fist wrote from Dublin explaining that the curative factor at work in this interesting case was to be sought neither in the dipsopathy nor in the bottlewashing, but in the freedom from poetic composition that these conferred on his client, whose breakdown had been due less to the pints than the pentameters.
>
> This view of the matter will not seem strange to anyone familiar with the class of pentameter that Ticklepenny felt it his duty to Erin to compose, as free as a canary in the fifth foot (a cruel sacrifice, for Ticklepenny hiccuped in end rimes) and at the caesura as hard and fast as his own divine flatus and otherwise bulging with as many minor beauties from the gaelic prosodoturfy as could be sucked out of a mug of Beamish's porter. No wonder he felt a new man washing the bottles and emptying the slops of the better-class mentally deranged.[1]

Beckett's satire has long been held to be at the expense of the poet Austin Clarke, staunch anti-modernist and defender of the innovations of the Irish poetry of the Celtic revival. In the 1930s, Beckett saw in Clarke an end of a century of experiment with 'gaelic prosodoturfy' in English, something which had resolved itself merely in the stopped rhymes and heavy internal assonance of a poetry that imbibes the Celtic much as it would a pint of porter. Ticklepenny is made to shoulder the twin national diseases of drink and poetry, where poetry is the cause of the alcoholism and the cure is blessed relief from poetry. Beckett takes his place in a long line of satire on the poetry of his native country stretching back to Swift via Francis Sylvester Mahony (who will be the subject of Chapter 3). Common to this satire, it suggests a cause for national neuroses, and in so doing suggests just how a seemingly pedantic technical matter – the prosody of Irish poems written in English – might sustain greater mass delusions that warrant the intervention of another of the satirical objects of *Murphy* – psychoanalysis.

Clarke deserves a fairer hearing than Beckett gives him. He had suffered a very real breakdown and incarceration in a mental hospital during the first year of the Irish War of Independence in 1919, a breakdown eventually recollected in his long poem of 1966, *Mnemosyne Lay in the Dust*. He had briefly succeeded to the lectureship in University College, Dublin, which had been held by his old MA supervisor, poet and critic Thomas MacDonagh, executed for his part as one of the leaders of the 1916 Easter Rising. One source of guilt for the republican Clarke was non-participation in insurrection. Another cause, seemingly smaller in scale, was his confession of an initial deafness to the sound effects MacDonagh and William Butler Yeats were hearing in a new poetry written in the English language. Writing in 1951, in his pamphlet *Poetry in Modern Ireland*, Clarke confessed that when, as a student, he first met what he called 'Celtic Twilight poetry', it seemed 'incomprehensible.... I groped through a mist of blurred meanings, stumbled over lines in which every accent seemed to be in the wrong place'. Yet after his first sonic acquaintance with these Irish accents in English poetry he later came to feel that, 'it was pleasant to escape awhile from the mighty law and order of English poetry into that shadowy world of subdued speech and nuance [...] So, abandoning for a while the fundamental commonsense of English poetic tradition, our poets set themselves free for curious mental experience, and rendered themselves liable to many intermingling influences'.[2]

Beckett's 'class of pentameter ... free as a canary in the fifth foot', won despite the poet's habit of hiccuping in end rhymes, is more than just a prosodic Celtic contrivance. The blurring of meaning, the stumbling of the reading voice and then the escape from English law and order are not just effects of 'fairy music', the features of which Clarke relates in terms borrowed from Yeats and MacDonagh before him: 'delicate wayward rhythms', 'slow-delaying rhythms' or even 'evasive rhythms.'[3] If the sound of the poems frees the poet for 'curious mental experience', it is an experience beyond 'fundamental commonsense'. That is something gained by abandoning, 'for a while', the English poetic tradition.

But it also allows British stereotypes of the lawless, irresolute, procrastinating Celt to simmer away in the Victorian background, whereas in the mid-twentieth-century foreground there was a violent and in many ways unfinished political history.

This is a matter of poetry under the Union as much as poetry playing its part in a project for political and aesthetic liberation. If the political circumstances of Clarke's early career are what we would nowadays call those of decolonisation, the poetic response was not quite what might be expected. Post-independence Irish artists did not in the main adopt a mode of social realism like their contemporaries in the new Soviet Union – although there would always be a large audience for the satire and rhetoric of the street ballads and marching songs of the insurgent moments of 1798 or 1848 or the Fenians, which had been gathered in collections such as *Paddy's Resource* or *The Spirit of the Nation*, and were still to be printed throughout the twentieth century. The best mid-twentieth-century example is 1916 volunteer Colm Ó Lochlainn's *Irish Street Ballads* (1939), in which comic and love lyrics outweighed those on political or historical topics.[4] Irish epic was a continuous preoccupation, but Clarke and Yeats saw tragedy and defeat as much as nation-building in its mythology. Clarke describes a lyric culture of deliberate obscurity, a poetry of evasion which nevertheless prizes simplicity of subject matter, innovating while it claims authenticity from antiquity. It moves in expression between sound and sense in two languages, two sets of literary conventions and two places that were, until 1921, one (the United Kingdom of Great Britain and Ireland) and were then to become two (Saorstát Éireann/the Irish Free State, and the United Kingdom of Great Britain and Northern Ireland). If the language of both that kingdom and its divided parts was English, so was that of the new Irish poetry in English. In many ways that new poetry strove to be Irish-English, and the means of doing that was as much a matter of sound as subject matter. Given these circumstances of a poetry attempting to come out from under a linguistic as well as political union, the issue is continuously described by its contemporary critics and adherents as being foremost a matter of poetics, an aesthetic matter in which poetry sought a consolidation of sonic form as it crossed back over from English into Irish.

As can be seen from Beckett's satire, this has not always been an aesthetic that has been welcomed into Irish literature. Beckett elsewhere complained that a modernist Irish poetry had to react against 'the antiquarians, delivering with the altitudinous complacency of the Victorian Gael the Ossianic goods'.[5] Early in his career, the contemporary poet Seamus Heaney, who might be thought to share in a poetic project exploring its unions and disunions in a mode tied to locality and accent while aware of international linguistic and cultural possibilities, expressed impatience with the way the matter has been phrased in Irish poetic criticism. 'Discussion of what tradition means', Heaney said in an interview with Seamus Deane in 1977, 'has to move from a sort of linguistic nostalgia, a puerile discourse about assonance, metres and so on, to a consideration of the politics and anthropology of our condition'. Heaney was speaking in violent times, and about a later history of the United Kingdom than will concern us here, but he remained even then committed to locality and engaged (with Deane and others) in the indirect resistance of a residual Corkeryism: 'my own poetry is a kind of slow, obstinate, papish burn, emanating from the ground I was brought up on.'[6]

In an important essay about the history and inheritance of nineteenth-century Irish poetry and its translating traditions, poet and critic Bernard O'Donoghue has shown that there is more than 'puerile discourse' to Heaney's own use of assonantal music. As Clarke phrases it and Beckett mocks it, this is a latter-day example of a crossing over from the supposedly strict rules of an English prosodic-musical system into the supposedly liberating folk rhythms of Irish poetry, music and accent. All of this is performed in the rhythms of an 'Irish-English' language, but in English poetry. It achieved, at least in poetic diction, what O'Donoghue has called 'a new vernacular to be used in original poems'.[7] Like Yeats before him, Clarke presents the prosody of the Irish poem in English in two lights, either as the 'submerged' Irish poem coming up for air now and then on the surface of the English lyric or as an invention or experiment of his own as suggested by contact with an international set of poetic examples. Elsewhere, Clarke invokes the experiments in prose poetry and submerged rhyme by the French poet Paul Fort, or the multi-syllable end rhyming of Spanish ballad poetry. According to Robert Farren in his classic post-independence 1948 study *The Course of Irish Verse,* the alliance of an essay on English metre by the revivalist poet William Larminie and its enthusiastic approval by poet and editor AE (George Russell) was responsible for pointing early twentieth-century poets towards a poetry of assonance with examples from both Spanish poetry and Gaelic metre. It is one purpose of this book to suggest that there was at least a century of prosodic innovation in Irish-English poetry before the revival, but Larminie thought he had heard something new for English poetry, 'the creation of a body of metres having in them the promise of the future, rich with unexhausted possibilities'.[8]

The promise of the future of poetry becomes mixed up in a teleology of independence that works through the seemingly puerile in this discussion of the sound of poetry, an aesthetic argument which looks political as much as anthropological. As with all of these experiments, although grounded in a discourse of ostensible authenticity, the creation of a synthetic poetic language is a conspicuously impure process. What Larminie heard in the strict rules of 'old Irish verse' was not something that could simply cross over into English. For the importance of the concord of consonants in Irish verse and their subsequent elaborate classifications, he suggested, 'it would probably be found that something similar would be desirable in employing assonance in English'.[9] 'Something similar' is neither a replication nor even a translation, in the meaning of 'to carry across'. Thus Larminie finds that English and Spanish verse provides examples of such 'similarity'. Such criticism trades authenticity for a peculiarly Irish modernist paradox, where the desire to found discussion of the metre of the Irish poem in English on the 'submerged' metres of the indigenous traditions of Gaelic poetry also engages with a positively European set of similar examples, and has concurrent 'British' or 'archipelagic' examples to contend with. The sound of the poem is the product both of an unavoidably 'poetical' Irishness and a widespread regional modernism, in which the new international language aspires to the impenetrable and non-translatable.

By the 1920s and 1930s the Scots poet Hugh MacDiarmid could make the case for Synthetic Scots as a vernacular language for poetry by invoking the breakthrough of the vernacular in Dante's *De Vulgari Eloquentia* and the more recent examples of the invention of Landsmaal in Norway or the revival of Catalan as well as what James Joyce was doing in his unfolding 'Work in Progress' (later *Finnegans Wake*). Whatever hopes the international socialist MacDiarmid held for Joyce's *Vision of World Language*, he also held that, 'We are not moving towards a world language, but in precisely the opposite direction; and much of the most vital work in all European literatures is untranslateable into any other medium and, indeed, unintelligible save to a few experts in its own country.'[10] Despite what Matthew Hart has said, borrowing from David Lloyd's account of the 'minor' poetry of James Clarence Mangan (offering perhaps the closest Irish analogy to MacDiarmid's experiment), the Irish version of this was not, like synthetic Scots, an 'impossible' innovation. Its relation to standard English remains grammatically and lexically clear, and is connected with nineteenth-century experiments in seeking similitude of prosodic effect to do the job of translation, the setting to melody and antiquarian and etymological discovery that are among the subjects of this book. For Hart, MacDiarmid's 'breakthrough is predicated on a paradoxical determination to recover the national language and remake it all at once'. It will thus become a 'Nationalist Internationalism'.[11] If such internationalism had fewer advocates in Ireland (the honourable examples of Beckett and Joyce aside), Irish poetry still shared a concern with recovery and remaking, and was thus at one and the same time authentic and artificial. Its particular syntheticism was very much part of an attempt to make something that was its own thing, both originating and original.

The first great retrospective critical construction of this poetry is in Thomas MacDonagh's *Literature in Ireland*, published in June 1916, a month after its author's violent death. MacDonagh's notion of an 'Irish Mode' in English poetry is still one of the most finely tuned prescriptions for the poetry that emerged from nineteenth-century Ireland. He said that it was written by those who have 'no literary memories in English', who are 'still at the simple beginnings ... still at lyric babblings.' He tells us that, 'To read correctly Anglo-Irish poetry one must follow either Irish music or Anglo-Irish prose speech.' Later he adds, slightly less securely, that 'Gaelic measures ... too, have had their effect on Anglo-Irish verse,'[12] but no claim for the replication of Gaelic metres is made. If the aesthetic achievement looks deliberately small scale, the larger claim is for a poetry that must be written for sound and shy in print, dependent on music and performance or accent and speech. MacDonagh's first critical book had been a study of one of the few successful experiments with quantitative verse in English, by the renaissance poet Thomas Campion, whose syllabic verse allowed him to think again about the 'chanting' of his friend, W.B. Yeats:

> It is this chanting quality in his verse and in the verse of some others, joined to a wandering rhythm caught from Irish traditional music, that has informed a new species of verse. It is chant-verse, overflowing both song-verse and speech-verse. For not only does something of the word reverence of chanted speech unstress the lyric beat of this poetry, but something of the musical quality of chant lightens and changes the weight of its speech verse.[13]

The wandering rhythm, the unstressing of beat, the changing of weight: this is poetry which overflows both song and speech, something MacDonagh grasps in older English and classical quantitative verse forms. It is reclaimed for those creating an original poetry in Irish-English, promoting syllabic quantity over marked accent or stress. Thus, paradoxically, the musical effects of 'word reverence' overflow grammatical sense.

The contrast between the usual synthetic means of describing English-language metre as accentual-syllabic and various experiments either with a quantitative syllabic poetry or an accentual metre was something that vexed many Victorian and early twentieth-century poets and theorists of English rhythm. Larminie's article was a fairly late addition, and was received rather less enthusiastically in England than by AE and his acolytes. For the great Edwardian historian of English prosody, George Saintsbury, Larminie 'rather rashly discusses the antiquity of assonance in Irish poetry, and advocates its substitution for rhyme in English, with a sort of go-as-you-please rhythm behind it.'[14] After the example of Campion, experiments with the length of English syllables in classical metres were rare, and perhaps more pertinent for Irish poetry and the rhythmic innovations of modernism, the stress metres of Gerard Manley Hopkins were presented by Robert Bridges as excavated from the example of old English, and experiments in accentual verse by Shakespeare or Milton.[15] MacDonagh tells us that these debates came to his notice through Yeats's reading of Coventry Patmore's *Unknown Eros*, and his highly influential 'Essay on English Metrical Law' of 1878.[16] Yeats's own experiments in chant-verse were not to outlive his collaborator and fellow performer of the verse, the English actress Florence Farr, and such 'texts' that remain of it, in the form of recorded readings, are scant, although, as in the case of Yeats's 1932 BBC recording of 'The Lake Isle of Innisfree', rightly celebrated. As Ronald Schuchard's study of the Yeats-Farr experiments shows, the influence on modern poetry was marked, as indeed was the fact that it was the revolutionary MacDonagh who gave an account of them. Ezra Pound reviewed *Literature in Ireland* on its first publication in *Poetry*, and if he didn't quite read MacDonagh's insights on metre as a justification of vers libre, he could not avoid their liberating aspects, 'analyzing the breaking from false shackles in a quite different manner'.[17] What in MacDonagh might appear to be a mere technicality – the contrast of English and Irish accentual verse – emerges as a greater contrast between the English and Irish given the unavoidable biographical pressure of MacDonagh's violent death.

Although MacDonagh could posit that 'metrical quantity proper does not exist in English', he could also assert that 'what may be called central English verse, in order to emphasise the stressed, under-emphasises the unstressed'. By comparison,

> Irish frequently allows for the clear pronunciation of several syllables between stress and stress. Such Irish verse is not rigidly governed by the law of mono-pressures; it is generally found in songs, the tunes of which have

a good deal to do with drawing the metrical feet dancing out of their bars. The less pronounced hammering of the stressed syllables is more noticeable in Irish prose speech; and on account of it English as we speak it in Ireland has a much more deliberate way of pronunciation, a much more even intonation, than the English of the English.[18]

This shifts between an ear trained to listen to the music of poetry and one alert to the anti-colonial purposes to which that achievement in the ear might be put, an aesthetic victory of Irish-English over 'the English of the English'. However problematic we might find this account in terms of prosody or phonology, it is part of a powerful retrospective construction of a synthetic Irish verse marking its difference from English poetry primarily in terms of sound. It serves a number of functions; on the one hand the sort of deliberate affront to Alexander Pope's dictum that 'the sound must seem an echo to the sense' that might be familiar in Romantic or modernist poetics, and on the other an equally modern or Romantic courting of a deliberate primitivism supposedly based in antiquity while tending towards the abstraction of music. In the introduction to their *Broadsides* anthology of 'Anglo-Irish Ballads' in 1935, Yeats and F.R. Higgins work from an understanding of the quarter tones of Japanese music, which 'permit speech to rise imperceptibly into song' in their description of something closer to home, the melismatic performance of the *sean nós* singer cast unavoidably into the modes of the music of antiquity: 'If what is called the gapped scale, if the wide space left unmeasured by the mathematical ear, where the voice can rise wavering, quivering, through its quarter-tones, is necessary if we are to preserve in song the natural rhythm of words, one understands why the Greeks murdered the man who added a fourth string to the lyre.'[19] MacDonagh's fine distinction between Yeats being 'tune-deaf' but not 'tone-deaf'[20] is borne out by this wilful restriction of musical possibility and promotion of wavering, quivering chant over melody.

'Language Fades before Thy Spell!' Moore and the Music of Irish lyric

This book is concerned mainly with the century or so of Irish poetry in English written up to that of Yeats. Much of that poetry was written with music in mind, either as the song source of Irish-language lyric, or as an English lyric written for an Irish melody. Melody was held to be the pure gold of Irish music, the wordless spirit of a melancholy nation:

> Music! Oh, how faint, how weak,
> Language fades before thy spell!

> Why should feeling ever speak,
> > When thou canst breathe her soul so well?
> Friendship's balmy words may feign,
> > Love's are even more false than they;
> Oh! 'tis only music's strain
> > Can sweetly soothe, and not betray![21]

Thus, Thomas Moore in the lyric to his song 'On Music' in the third number of his *Irish Melodies* in 1810 supplanted language with music, nevertheless finding that music speaks true despite the great betrayal at which Moore's lyrics merely hint.

Harry White engages with another version of these sonic differences, quoting from Seamus Deane's prizing of poetry and popular song in Irish writing before Yeats, which might also be read as a gloss on Moore's stanza:

> But long before Yeats had written a line, a 'reconciliation between the English language' and the 'essential spirit' [quoting Deane] of Irish music became the primary objective of Irish poetry. In this objective, the lyric impulse of Moore's *actual* engagement with music was overtaken by the powerful attraction of Irish music (already present in Moore) as an image of Gaelic culture to be re-created in the metaphors and sounding forms of a new verbal music [White's emphasis].[22]

For White, Moore's music is something renovated and reconstructed as an ideological signifier for Irish national revival. However, his reference to Moore's '*actual* engagement with music' reminds us that its beginnings were in Moore's seeking for metaphoric and sonic form. At issue is 'a new verbal music', as White puts it, and he suggests a way of negotiating the tricky critical sands of deconstruction into which it might sink.

All of those problematic phrases of Deane or MacDonagh – 'essential spirit' of Irish music, 'central English verse', 'the English of the English' – might be thought to collapse under the weight of tautology, and it is difficult to avoid the inferences drawn from such phrases that this might be a self-enclosing discourse. Adapting David Lloyd, Leith Davis has said that for Moore to assert 'an Irish identity reliant on an ideology of nationalism [...] was identical with an imperial ideology in its attempt to posit "a transcendent realm of essential identity"'. For Davis or Lloyd, Irish music is described as an accomplice in a mystifying nationalist discourse, reliant on tautology and thus blind to the differences that will inevitably deconstruct the project. In their sights is a nationalist critic such as Terry Eagleton, who can call music 'a kind of discourse beyond signification'.[23] In relation to Moore, Eagleton can say, 'The music of Moore's lyrics is the untranslatable spirit of the nation, a distilled essence of national yearning which resists

verbal embodiment.'[24] Davis responds that music, 'does signify much: it is
overdetermined rather than indeterminate'. These are circular arguments,
bedevilled with debates about authenticity and essentialism on both sides,
and with rather less to say about music or poetry than nationalist ideology
and its critique. It is not entirely a naive response to suggest a pragmatic
way around such arguments in both the terms and practice suggested by
White and Deane. For White, this can be done by attending to the actual
engagement with Irish music in songs by Moore; for Deane, by confronting not tautological enclosure but the divisions and contradictions which
in turn enable artistic process:

> We may say that Moore's elegance was frequently reduced to enervation;
> we may say that his words do not live without their accompanying music,
> or that the music is violated by the artificiality of the words; we may laud
> or regret his influence on Irish nationalism. Yet, ultimately, the kind of
> issue raised by Moore's poetry, or, more particularly by the *Irish Melodies*
> and some of the *National Airs*, lies at the heart of Irish writing for more
> than a century afterwards.[25]

We can try to hear again what was in its time, 'a new verbal music'. Doing
so, we can grasp how Irish poets writing in English up to and including Yeats benefited from the example of what White calls (adapting T.S.
Eliot), Moore's 'auditory imagination'.

Something such as MacDonagh's Irish Mode emerged from the development of a sophisticated poetic form founded in writing for music. This
form may have been intimately involved in its own processes of becoming
and achievement, but in creating such synthetic forms, Moore and others knew exactly what they were doing. That formal process was attuned
both to the expression of loss and its recovery, and was linguistically
and musically at once translation and new, simultaneously form and its
own content. White suggests that we make a 'useful distinction between
Moore's auditory imagination and those conventions of musical symbolism which prevail in the tradition which Moore "single-handedly" established'.[26] Thus, any reading of nineteenth-century Irish poetry in English
and its inheritors must attend to the emergence into form of this poetry as
grounded in the striving for sonic effect and the synthetic construction of
that effect as in itself a matter of content as much as form: Irish metre and
English verse; Irish music and English verse; Irish versus English accents;
to say nothing of the role of the 'music' of speech and a performed accent
in English-language verse. If this means a primary attention to poetry
itself, lyric qua lyric, then when reading the political or historical purposes
of this poetry we need to recognise that the figurative uses of poetry and

music created and then recognised by writers from Moore to MacDonagh were initially grounded in just such a set of aesthetic questions in which the form of the verse was also matter for its own meaning.

MacDonagh's main example of the Irish Mode was Yeats's 'The Lake Isle of Innisfree'. The poem shows an English-Irish speech through its metrical effects. This is MacDonagh's account of the poem's Irish rhythm:

> This general movement, changing from a slow beat to an easy rise and fall, happens constantly. I sometimes think it expresses, whether in accentual verse or quantitative, the mingled emotions of unrest and pleasure that comes with the break up of winter, with the south wind, with the thought of the shortness of life and the need to make haste to explore its good and simple joys – the desire to leave the unlovely, mingled with a vivid conception of the land of heart's desire.[27]

Matters of linguistics and prosody unavoidably make their way into a broadly Arnoldian Celticism as the subject matter in these extracts: sentimentality ('mingled emotions of unrest and pleasure'); the reaction against the despotism of fact ('the desire to leave the unlovely'); formal irregularity ('the metrical feet dancing out of their bars'); the weather ('the break up of winter, with the south wind'). MacDonagh claims linguistic difference within the same language, contrasting 'what may be called central English verse' with that spoken by the Irish. In the difference of accent he finds sounds of metrical and poetic difference that may in themselves tell of unassimilable cultural and political division.

This is a criticism writing from a position of political radicalism, for all that it presents cultural difference as more a matter of poetic than political import. The poetry can emerge as anger, half-recognised satire, in-joke, and the unresolved ambiguities that arise when one or more languages and poetic traditions are often rubbed roughly up against each other. Take this example, a stanza from a poem written by the nationalist poet, translator and Cork schoolmaster Edward Walsh, published in the newspaper of the Young Irelanders, *The Nation*, in 1844. Walsh rhymes Irish with English and English-Irish with both outrage and humour in a macaronic monologue version of the new Irish love song:

> I've heard the songs by Liffey's wave
>   That maidens sung –
> They sung their land the Saxon's slave,
>   In Saxon tongue.
> Oh! Bring me here that Gaelic dear
>   Which cursed the Saxon foe,
> When thou dids't charm my ruptured ear,

Mo craoibhin cno!
And none but Gods; good angels near,
Mo craoibhin cno![28]

Ruptured by English his ear might have been, but Walsh's English-language poem allows an Irish-language endearment (*Mo craoibhin cno*, 'my little cluster of nuts or nut brown girl') to rhyme with its 'Saxon foe'. The word *sassenach*, Scots Gaelic and Irish Gaelic for an English person or 'Saxon', would have been available to the Irish-speaking and Irish-writing Walsh. He translates it back into its English original, and although the etymology is Middle English and before that German and Latin, the *Oxford English Dictionary* tells us that it is only in the nineteenth century (in Scott's *Lady of the Lake*) that we get an instance of it meaning Englishman or Lowland Scot. Once Walsh gets the word back into English it does not quite appear to belong. He uses it to achieve near-rhymes and double-syllable rhymes for both English and Irish: 'maidens sung/Saxon tongue', and 'Saxon foe/*craoibhin cno*'. Strictly speaking, in the passive mood the maidens' song *was* sung, and here it should be: 'the songs ... /That maidens *sang* – /They *sang* their land'. Sang would not rhyme with tongue, of course, but the poem speaks in an Irish-English demotic, a marker of class and dialect. Containing both the *ur*-sociolinguist's joke and the poet's macaronic rhymes, the stanza is a moment in little of the emergent Irish poem in a new language. In that place it retains music and song, the Irish language and the not-quite-mastered new language of English in what at the time (1840s Ireland) might have appeared to be the last whisperings of complaint against the foe in whose language this poem has been compelled to appear.

'*Mo craoibhin cno*' might be exactly the sort of poem expected from mid-nineteenth-century Ireland. Impatient with the narrowing of tone into pathos by Moore or Samuel Ferguson, for Walsh the putative love song gives way to political satire. Published first in *The Nation* newspaper, it was reprinted by the editor of that paper, Charles Gavan Duffy, in his 1845 *Ballad Poetry of Ireland*, a book which was reviewed enthusiastically by Thomas Davis as not just rooted but racy of the soil: 'In possessing the powers and elements of a glorious nationality, we owned the sources of a national poetry.'[29] It is important not to underestimate the quality of the critical work of Duffy and Davis, inflected by polemic as it was, and Walsh's poem tells of the sort of rupture the writers of *The Nation* sought to heal. One source of balm would be new poems written for a new English-reading mass audience, grounded in Irish music and speech but also seeking confidence in English print.

'A people without a language of its own is only half a nation', Thomas Davis said in 1845, and the calculation is typical of him: not the whole story but half of it. Nevertheless, the consequence of the imposition of an alien language is that those in the nation exist 'adrift in the accidents of translation', and their expression is merely abridged:

> To impose another language on such a people is to send their history adrift among the accidents of translation – 'tis to tear their identity from all places – 'tis to substitute arbitrary signs for picturesque and sugges-tive names – 'tis to cut off the entail of feeling, and separate the people from their forefathers by a deep gulf – 'tis to corrupt their very organs, and abridge their power of expression.[30]

If White suggests that the trope of poetry as music represented a way for Irish art to compensate for the paucity of its classical music tradition, then we might also argue, after MacDonagh, that Irish poetry sought in music, speech and performance a means of re-mooring that poetry to those big nouns in Davis from which one of its possible audiences had been set adrift: 'history', 'identity', 'names', 'entail', 'feeling', 'forefathers', 'organs' and, ultimately, 'expression' itself. Davis cheekily echoes one Irish prede-cessor of a different political persuasion – Edmund Burke, apologist for the entailed inheritance and the legitimacy of the unity of Great Britain from antiquity.[31]

As suggested in Chapter 1, accident can produce compensations in the conditions of feeling adrift or being merely abridged. Davis had elsewhere complained of 'great gaps in Irish song to be filled up',[32] and the critical tradition that his polemic sponsored has persisted down to the account of nineteenth-century poetry, briefly discussed in Chapter 1, by modern-ist poet and translator Thomas Kinsella, who characterised himself as an inheritor of this sense of abridgement, of a 'gapped, discontinuous, poly-glot tradition'.[33] The accident of Irish poetry in the nineteenth century was the eventual discovery of a means in lyric to fill those gaps, ultimately securing continuity in discontinuity in a synthetic form which may be by turns polyglot or musical or gapped. As one of the foremost critics of nineteenth-century Irish verse Robert Welch has said, with regard to Samuel Ferguson:

> He simply does not have access to a language capable of representing the broad conspectus of experience and of relating past and present in a con-fident awareness that there is such a thing as coherent tradition. It is in these assumptions and confidences that Victorian authority is grounded, but for an Irish Victorian there would be, continually, for all the desire to heal and compromise, a profound sense of rupture, unease, and strain. In

the twentieth century, ironically, poetic authority is grounded in just these discontinuities: 'we sing in our uncertainty', wrote Yeats.[34]

In one sense, as explored in Chapter 4, a Unionist poet such as Ferguson writing Irish poetry under the Union sought healing and compromise in poetry itself. But this was also a desire to heal an accidental as much as contrived set of ruptures and disunions, in the imposition of union or opposition to it. Moore's reluctant separation of the lyrics of the *Irish Melodies* from the tunes to which they had been set (simply to secure copyright in the face of unauthorized American publication) produced an effect in print unforeseen by writing for musical performance. Presenting the lyrics of his *Melodies* in the 1821 edition, Moore complained of their 'divorce' from the airs, and pleaded that he 'should with difficulty have consented to a disunion of the words from the airs, had it depended solely upon me to keep them quietly and indissolubly together'.[35]

To return to the example previously quoted, the stanza from Moore's 'On Music', this lyric became separated from its melody, a popular eighteenth-century air, 'The Banks of Banna', in 1821 and in subsequent printings of Moore's *Poetical Works*. Thus, we find it in print and not performance as a submerged iteration of a theme of faithfulness and betrayal now divorced from the tune that would be needed to make sense of it. Remove what White calls 'Moore's *actual* engagement with music' and we are left with music figuring faithfulness in a 'poem' not a song lyric. The absence of music adds to the original lyric's dread of disunion and betrayal – no matter that the compensation music had offered for this was its original theme. The poem that emerged from this divorce of lyric and melody was not composed with this in mind, but was now printed by accident: the semantic consolation in this creative disunion is that a further ambiguous treatment of the theme is suggested. Welch is one of the sternest critics of the Moore project, and he says of the last stanza of 'On Music':

> Feeling becomes disembodied. There is no language for it. Music, for Moore, was associated with the centres of feeling, and Irish music in particular seemed to him to derive its 'tone of sorrow and depression' from the core of Irish experience. There being no system in which to represent that experience, to embody it, music offered a mood which could float free from the constraints of the actual.[36]

Emerging from the contexts of these differing critical inflections of 'actuality' in White or Welch are the verbal and sonic, as much as lexical, textures of Irish poetry under the Union. By accident as much as design, its various disunions and betrayals achieved significant form in English-language poetry.

If the content remains an ambiguous, sometimes secretive thing, particularly in Moore, he never quite allowed himself what Welch calls a 'system' of representation. Moore's poetry engaged with the 'constraints of the actual' by its very free-floating nature more fully than Kinsella or Welch or even Thomas Davis could allow. This need not be melancholy – as Chapter 3 will show – music was used for satiric and bawdy purposes as well, telling, as such things did, of political and moral difference and controversy. Such verse did not come from a consensual project, given that its various participants would probably never quite agree that it was a project at all. Either embedded in song or in differing printed media, through sonic and lexical allusion or by means of translation or metre or etymology, with a residue of Irish-language verse or the attempt to catch an Irish accent speaking English: the history of the unions and disunions of English-language lyrics with Irish music was eventually to emerge as MacDonagh's synthetic Irish Mode.

For George Saintsbury this was set in motion by Moore, as a poet who alone 'seems to be what the musical prosodists would have all poets – a person who was "bilingual" – who could express himself indifferently in notes and in words, or in the two blended.' By 'indifferently', I suppose Saintsbury means without difference. But he then goes on to say that 'the results of this were double', meaning on the one hand the perfect musical and prosodic accommodation of Moore's bests songs, and on the other, a poetry 'where the prosodic music [...] is accommodated in its own despite to its own loss, and in fact occasionally to its temporary destruction'. The example given is 'Eveleen's Bower' (from the second number of *Irish Melodies*, 1808), where Moore introduces what Saintsbury calls 'outlaws', extra-metrical syllables. Take the first two stanzas:

> Oh! Weep for the hour,
> When to Eveleen's bower
> The Lord of the Valley with false vows came;
> The moon hid her light
> From the heavens that night,
> And wept behind her clouds o'er the maiden's shame.
>
> The clouds pass'd soon
> From the chaste cold moon,
> And heaven smil'd again with her vestal flame;
> But none will see the day
> When the clouds shall pass away,
> Which that dark hour left upon Eveleen's fame.[37]

Not mentioning, or perhaps not hearing, the problematic three syllables and final extended vowel in the heroine's name ('Ev-e-leen', not 'Evelen' or 'Ev'len' or 'Éve-lyn'), Saintsbury draws attention to the prosodically marring extra syllables in the sixth and ninth lines: 'And wept behind her clouds o'er the maiden's shame', or 'And heaven smil'd again with her vestal flame'. Sung, and given the original setting to what Moore and his arranger John Stevenson called an 'unknown air' in the *Melodies*,[38] the song demands a melismatic slur over the offending and other syllables. Spoken, and allowing 'heaven' two syllables in the second instance, the lines certainly tend to prose.

Add in a stock folk song theme of innocent peasant girl seduced by the wicked Lord of the Valley, a knowing Romantic ballad symbolism of virginity and femininity figured through snow and moon and the classicist allusion to the girl's 'vestal flame', and we can see that Moore certainly knew the complex creation he was making:

> The white snow lay
> On the narrow path-way,
> When the Lord of the Valley cross'd over the moor;
> And many a deep print
> On the white snow's tint
> Show'd the track of his footstep to Eveleen's door.
>
> The next sun's ray
> Soon melted away
> Every trace on the path where the false Lord came;
> But there's a light above,
> Which alone can remove
> That stain upon the snow of fair Eveleen's fame.

The ingenuity of the final images in the lyric leave us with the melting of one 'trace' in the snow, the Lord's footsteps leading to Eveleen's door, but also with what has been left behind and cannot be erased by this world, the unmelted 'stain upon the snow of fair Eveleen's fame'. The poem suggests a memory of disgrace only removed by redemptive grace after death, 'the light above' of heavenly knowledge obviating the human 'stain'. The political allegory would not be lost on Irish or Scottish readers, accustomed to the figurative uses given to deceitful seduction in their ballad traditions. Catholic readers would also understand a shame in which confession (regardless in this instance of the ethics of complicity and 'false vows') ensures the removal of its stain. Moore might have been an outlaw to poetic musical rules in his use of the extra-metrical, but the song lyric when removed from the song stands as a residue of folk song, of Jacobite and Catholic allegory and of the knowing construction of the delicately balanced art object. 'Temporary destruction' might be the view of the Edwardian English critic Saintsbury, but the subsequent prosodic influence of reading – as opposed to singing or hearing such a lyric – could present immense opportunities for those successors who found they might now create an Irish poetry that can tell a story hidden in a national allegory that sounds different from the English in which it finds itself.

Moore's masterpiece, if such a small thing might be described thus, is 'At The Mid Hour of Night', where we can see the immense artistic benefits of this emergent lyric mode. It was published in the fifth number of the *Irish Melodies* in 1813, set to an air called 'Molly My Dear', which Moore found in Smollett Holden's 1805 *Collection of Old Established Irish Slow and Quick Tunes*.[39] In 1861, its lyric had been one of five Moore poems printed in Francis Turner Palgrave's *Golden Treasury*, and it is given as MacDonagh's first example of his small anthology of 'Original Poems' of the Irish Mode in *Literature in Ireland*. In the *Broadsides* introduction, Yeats grudgingly allowed that 'this poem, and perhaps one other, are the only poems of Moore that have the poet's rhythm':[40]

> At the mid hour of night, when stars are weeping, I fly
> To the lone vale we lov'd, when life shone warm in thine eye;
> And I think oft, if spirits can steal from the regions of air,
> To revisit past scenes of delight, thou wilt come to me there,
> And tell me our love is remember'd, even in the sky.
>
> Then I sing the wild song 'twas once such pleasure to hear!
> When our voices commingling breath'd, like one, on the ear;
> And as Echo far off through the vale my sad orison rolls,
> I think, oh my love! 'tis thy voice from the Kingdom of Souls,
> Faintly answering still the notes that once were so dear.[41]

Despite his antipathy to Moore, Yeats's praise of this lyric persisted across his own critical career. The lyric was printed along with 'Oft in the Stilly Night' in Yeats's 1894 *A Book of Irish Verse*, given its better-known title, 'The Light of Other Days'[42] (that is the 'one other' lyric that has 'the poet's rhythm'). Both poems – as poems, not song lyrics – 'express what Matthew Arnold has taught us to call "the Celtic melancholy", with so much of delicate beauty in the meaning and in the wavering or steady rhythm that one knows not where to find their like in literature.'[43]

Over forty years later, Yeats gave instructions on how to perform this 'wavering or steady rhythm': 'The stress falling on "mid", or "weep", on "lone", on "warm", syllables not sufficiently isolated to sustain it, compels us to speak "mid hour" "are weeping" "lone vale" "shone warm" slowly, prolonging the syllables; it is as though the stress suffused itself like a drop of dye.'[44]

Yeats cannot bring himself to scan the lines conventionally: the examples of Patmore or Larminie and his own chant-verse experiments had inoculated him from that mistake. The extraordinary critical synaesthesia of verbal stress as suffusing dye, where tempo is conveyed as an uncontainable saturation of space, says much about both Yeats's auditory imagination and the effect that writing for song has on a subsequent performance of Moore's verbal music as spoken poem. Moore's instructions for performing his lyrics were for an emotive vocal performance, to be sung as if spoken, and thus the 'tune-deaf' Yeats heard something unavailable to one who can sing. Like most modern readers, Yeats encounters them in music-less print and not as performed song. To mix the spatial and aural metaphors a little more, the happy accident is that something new has occurred to the sonic palette of English verse.

Accident it may or may not be, but this adjustment, this alternating 'wavering or steady rhythm', was formulated by Moore himself as he grasped the evanescence of the performative in both the rhythm and the subject matter of his lyrics.

> There is but one instruction I should venture to give to any person desirous of doing justice to the character of these ballads, and that is to attend as little as possible to the rhythm or time in singing them. The time, indeed, should *always* be made to wait upon the feeling, but particularly in this style of musical recitation, where the words ought to be as nearly *spoken* as is consistent with the swell and sweetness of intonation; and where a strict and mechanical observance of time completely destroys all those pauses, fingerings, and abruptnesses, which the expression of passion and tenderness requires. The truth of this remark needs but little enforcement to those who have ever heard a song of feeling and delicacy paced along in the unrelenting trammels of an orchestra.[45]

Moore had crossed back from song to the spoken just as MacDonagh and Yeats seem to be pushing the spoken towards song. In both accounts, by Moore and Yeats a century or so apart, time plays the part of the impatient bridegroom, who should '*always* be made to wait upon the feeling', and the eventual consummation of the union is best experienced as stop-start: 'those pauses, fingerings, and abruptnessess, which the expression of passion and tenderness requires.' In one way this is a travesty of the sprightliness of the usual performance of the Irish traditional tunes, replaced as they have been by the 'drawling, dead, doleful and die-away manner' that so appalled Edward Bunting, earnest collector of many of the melodies from which Moore dusted their 'authentic dross'.[46] It is also in the manner of an Arnoldian and later Yeatsian 'Celticism', where the style is the subject matter, procrastinating and unpunctual, wandering and indirect. Its influence could be felt further as one touchstone for the Victorian taste Yeats officially abhorred. For Tennyson, the reason for pressing this lyric on Francis Turner Palgrave for inclusion in the *Golden Treasury* was that he 'much admired its long drawn music.'[47]

Leith Davis, for one, invokes the racial discourse of Saxon and Celt in such a musical construction of Celticism, viewing such metaphors of bride and groom, union and marriage, the resolute and the indirect as political and sexual opposites, where the political is problematically figured through gender difference.[48] But this would be to replace the feeling and delicacy of this lyric with that unrelenting orchestra, totally inappropriate to the small victories of Moore's lyric, where form must be figured through the subtleties of its own performance. 'At the Mid Hour of Night' can be sung equally by a male or female voice, because the speaker has no obvious gender. It may not even have body, so uncertain is it of union on earth as in heaven. Borrowing from the melody, Moore achieves in English a rhythm of ethereal changeability, moving delicately through the aspirations, and indeed fantasies, of its brooding speaker. This speaker yearns for a disembodied state in which he or she can commune with the dead, a communion achieved in the lost past that the very rhythm of the lyric itself attempts to recreate. The second stanza sings its own 'wild song', leading into a singer's trick in its second and fourth lines. The commingling voices of the living and the dead, 'breath'd, like one, on the ear'. The ceasurae in this line make both the singer of the song and reader of the lyric pause for breath, as that little dying in the line brings the singer/speaker closer to the dead and allows the separated lovers a sonic communion in the line's final anapaest, 'on the ear'. The effect is then repeated, but this time into an imagining of voice:

> I think, oh my love! 'tis thy voice from the Kingdom of Souls,
> Faintly answering still the notes that once were so dear.

The strong direction for pause given to performer or speaker by the exclamation mark sets the lyric up as a conceit in which Echo is allowed to figure immortality. The wishful present tense 'I think ... 'tis thy voice' is matched with the direct address that was the abruptness of 'oh my love!' Sound echoes through the poem as the response of the dead, even as the end line returns us to the time and tense of a song simultaneously over and ongoing: 'Faintly answering *still* the notes that once *were* so dear'. In a way this is a grammatical nonsense, but in another the 'wild song' of an ancient melody travels back across history in the recreation of a lost physical closeness, leaving us with the sonic persistence of a past historic. The sounds of a dying language and musical culture echo through the sounds of the language that have taken its place.

The case of Moore is the closest we might come to Davis's source of national poetry, the point from which the Irish-English synthetic lyric began to be formed. By the time of Walsh and Mangan, full-scale translation projects were well underway, and before the catastrophic irruption of famine into the cultural resurgence of the 1830s and 1840s, a conserved Irish language could be heard in a text such as Walsh's '*Mo Craoibhin Cno*', or even in the street ballads of cities that had been English speaking for more than a generation. As Walsh's poem also suggests, the characteristic argot of Hiberno-English, like that of Scots in the eighteenth century, also found a place in printed Irish poetry. Moore, however, added in one crucial component that was to change the prosodic structure of the Irish poem in English, as suggested by the Gaelic melodies to which he adapted his lyrics. This mixing of Irish tune and English Romantic poem attracted the first followers and critics of the new synthetic Irish thing, and enabled his successors to explore the mode needed to present English versions of Irish-language poems.

The Submerged Poem: Ferguson and the Amhrán

Austin Clarke praised Daniel Corkery's *Hidden Ireland* for demonstrating the range of subjects in the last remnants of a Gaelic literature that had little option but to write in a suppressed style, often conducting political debate only through allegory and song. The 'hidden' of the title reverberates in formal ways through his account of the prosody of Irish poems now written in English. In addition to praise of the blurred, shadowy, wayward and evasive, Clarke posits what he calls 'submerged rhyme' as a characteristic of the innovations of the poetry that he himself strove to write in English. This, he says, he learned from his contact with French and Spanish poetry as much as Irish:

> [I]t was not until I met Paul Fort in Paris and studied his use of submerged rhyme that the experiment seemed to me possible. The assonantal patterns of Gaelic prosody are intricate, but in the simplest form the tonic word at the end of the line is supported by an assonance in the middle of the next line. The use of such patterns in English is limited but they can change the pivotal movement of the lyric stanza. In some forms of

early syllabic Gaelic metres, only one part of a double-syllable word is
used in assonance, a system also found in the Spanish ballad metres, and
this suggested experiment in partial rhyming and muting. For example we
can have rhyme or assonance, on or off accent, stopped rhyme, (e.g. ring,
kingdom; breath, method), harmonic rhyme (e.g. hero, window), cross-
rhyme.[49]

The rather dry account of caesural and internal rhyme here, 'the tonic
word supported by an assonance in the middle of the next line', becomes
the scatalogical sarcasm of Beckett's speaker in *Murphy,* and the 'caesura as
hard and fast as his own divine flatus'.

Like Yeats before him, Clarke presents the prosody of the Irish poem
in English in two lights, either as the 'submerged Irish poem' or as an
invention or experiment of his own. If the process is impure, following
MacDonagh, Clarke is careful to limit exactly what has been taken from
Gaelic prosody, the 'intricate' traded in for a paradox, where the desire
to found discussion of the metre of the Irish poem in English on the
'submerged' metres of the indigenous traditions of Gaelic poetry is based
on a set of similar examples in other European poetries. The sound of
the poem is the product both of an unavoidably poetical Irishness and
a deliberate modern invention, at one and the same time authentic and
artificial. Writing on the prosody of Irish poems in English may no longer be the pressing issue that these poets felt it was, but it does enable us
to hear again a poetry and criticism caught between these two poles of
authentic and artificial, regional and modernist. Leaving aside Welch's
excellent overview, *A History of Verse Translation from the Irish,* and
Bernard O'Donoghue's essay previously mentioned, the most system-
atic account is an article published by Sean Lucy in the *Irish University
Review* in 1978. Lucy is keen to posit a continuity of Irish writing in
English from the eighteenth century to the 1970s, in which Irish syllabic metres are heard to persist. In particular, he finds that the ancient
amhrán form, an old irregular accentual metre, survives through folk and
song metre despite the attempts of 'professional' Irish-language bards to
replace it with a formal system of prosody. *Pace* Beckett, the amhrán
is not pentameter but usually tetrameter, a metre which allows freedoms in the final foot, and may indeed allow the extra-metricality that
Sainsbury's outlawed from English verse, five, six or seven stress lines.
The metre allows for many irregularities and may better be described
as accentual verse: Lucy allows a comparison with English prosody in
this regard, comparing it with Gerard Manley Hopkins's conception of
'Sprung Rhythm'.

This is Lucy on three main aspects of the amhrán metre, and in it he introduces the extra element of music:

> To the ear trained in Irish music and song, then, the following metrical effects are usual and natural:
> 1. A very flexible stressed line often tending towards trisyllabic patternings;
> 2. Very free substitution in more clearly metrical arrangements, including much trisyllabic substitution in essentially disyllabic lines;
> 3. The use of essentially trisyllabic metres not only for fast 'light' effects but also for slow deep 'serious' poetic effect.[50]

A note of scepticism from O'Donoghue might gloss this passage: 'It is hard to be certain what is being described are features of Irish originals or a translating practice that has developed its own conventions for its own purposes.'[51] Introducing 'song' into this practice suggests that something else is cloaking the seeming attempt to replicate Gaelic metres, the tradition of fitting words to the tune, whether that be in street ballad or for the drawing room. As we have seen, Moore's first contact with Irish music had resulted in him composing for songs and exploiting trisyllabic metres in the English lyric.

Considering writing for music is one way of approaching the question of whether a prosodic effect noticed in the poetry of one language and then reappearing in the poetry of another is genuinely a consequence of a deliberate or even unconscious attempt at replication. Edward Larminie knew of the need for creative solutions, writing at the end of the nineteenth century that 'assonance' would serve as a means of doing 'something similar' to old Irish metres in English poetry, but Irish and English are, of course, geographically, historically and culturally linked, and both languages borrow words from each other. The contact has been long, and the linguistic as much as historical issue highly complex. To take just one example, as Raymond Hickey says, features of Irish English (such as those used in the discussion of nineteenth-century Irish poetry here) may be as likely to be those of the first English or Scottish settlers as from the Irish language.[52] Unlike English and Latin, say, the etymological linking is not widespread. Whereas we might usefully describe an English speaker or writer employing a Latinate vocabulary, the lexical examples might be small if we were to describe a Gaelicised or Hiberno-English vocabulary. In the matter of syntax and word order stylistic opportunities do exist: witness the Ferguson lyric discussed in Chapter 1. If we take the prose speech of the characters in John Millington Synge's drama, that is perhaps indebted more to poetic and song experiments in conveying a synthetic Irish accent than the English language of his West of Ireland characters (who, we must remember, were first overheard by him as Irish speakers anyway). We might describe a Scottish person speaking a distinct language called Scots; the controversial example of Ulster Scots aside[53], it is hard to find a non-synthetic Irish-English equivalent. The difficulties arise further when speaking about the lexis, grammar and prosody of Irish-English poetry.

Even if the over-preponderance of triple feet as anapaestic or dactylic substitutions, common in much Irish poetry written in English from the 1790s onwards, results from actual linguistic contact with the metres of the Irish amhrán, we must nevertheless seek for less specific, more generally cultural, reasons for these correspondences. The widespread contemporary critical view might be that such forms are the inevitable consequence of a culture seeking to establish a national identity through literary style under historical conditions that might be termed postcolonial, or at least striving to be postcolonial. Such forms are, as with the terminology here, frequently hyphenated: Hiberno-English, Irish-English and, until recently, Anglo-Irish. Further, these hyphenations have in turn been described as 'hybrid', the result being an often unforeseen mix of languages, the product of the progress of history as much as individual artistic intervention. Without openly using the term, O'Donoghue, for instance, sees 'the gradual creation, almost by a natural linguistic process, of a poetic language in English that derived from the traditions of translating Irish'.[54] The key word here is 'natural', although O'Donoghue is right to approach it from a scholarly distance: '*almost* by a natural linguistic process'. But of course literary language and poetic form are not natural things, they are cultural things, and talk of natural process or the metaphor from nature implicit in the hybrid or hybridised brings with it a heavy cultural determinism.

The academic recourse to nature is founded in a looser set of imagined cultural oppositions. Lucy, for instance, seeks confirmation for his version of a distinct Irish-English poetry from a number of critics, and most notably from the Irish mode. But the confirmation Lucy seeks of the latter is from MacDonagh's account of Irish speech in English that demotes the example of Irish metre in favour of writing from and for Irish music, resulting in what MacDonagh calls 'Irish poems that sing to the same air'.[55] MacDonagh gives three well-known examples, one from Moore ('The Irish Peasant to his Mistress' of 1810) and one each from Jeremiah Joseph Callanan and Samuel Ferguson (albeit discussed in reverse order[56]). Many critics have been drawn to the latter two examples.

Callanan's 1829 'Outlaw of Loch Lene' is supposedly 'From the Irish', as its subtitle tells us. Robert Welch has shown that it is better thought of as a lyric improvised around its first line, a near literal translation of the first line of the third verse of the Irish song 'Muna b'é an t-ól' ('If only for the Drink'), which runs: 'Is fada mé féin ag deanamh leanna sa 'ghleann'.[57] Callanan renders this: 'O many a day have I made good ale in the glen.' The English line accentuates its own musical effects of assonance and internal off-rhyme: the slight syllabic modulations in 'many a day' or the guttural repetitions resolving towards the end of the line, 'good ale … glen.' From 'good ale', where the etymologies are Teutonic and Old English, according to the *Oxford English Dictionary* to 'glen', from the Gaelic 'gleann', English and Irish lexical histories contribute to the synthetic Irish Mode effect of the line. By the final stanza, however, the lyric sounds much like the sort of English lyric Moore had been writing a few years previously, alternating anapaests and packed stresses in an explicit connection of naturalism and lawlessness, a sort of free love in a state of nature:

> 'Tis down by the lake where the wild-tree fringes its sides,
> The maid of my heart, my fair one of Heaven resides –
> I think as at eve she wanders its mazes along,
> The birds go to sleep by the sweet wild twist of her song.[58]

For 'I think as at eve she wanders its mazes along', we can hear an echo of Moore, the sound of 'I think, oh my love! 'tis thy voice from the Kingdom of souls'. Behind the emotive packing of stress into the hyphenated 'wild-tree' or triple stress on 'sweet wild twist' there is the echo of Moore's 'wild song'. In 'as at eve', 'wanders its mazes along', 'go to sleep', 'of her song' the syllables lengthen into anapaestic substitutions and resolutions. MacDonagh glosses such effects with reference to the English-born Belfast musician Carl Hardbeck, who performed 'tunes sung wandering with the wavering words of the old poems'.[59]

So, one solution for presenting English versions of Irish poems as well as something such as Callanan's improvised synthetic Irish-English lyric is a sort of translation of genre as much as words, of Irish music into English verse as much as Irish into English. The wavering and wandering is an effect in musical style adapted for a new poetry founded in the imagined 'old poems'. MacDonagh's third example is Samuel Ferguson's justly celebrated 1834 translation of the lyric of the Irish folk song from the eighteenth century, 'Caiseal Mumhan' or the 'Clár bog déil', variously known as 'Cashel in Munster', 'The Bog-Deal Board' or the 'Bare Deal Board'. For all this supposed wavering, the song has a certain explicit solidity:

> Phósfainn thú gan bha gan punt gan áireamh spré,
> Agus phógfainn thú maidin drúchta le bánú an lae.

> 'S é mo ghalar dubhach gan mé is tú, a dhianghrá mo chléibh,
> i gCaiseal Mumhan is gan de leaba fúinn ach clár *bog* déil.

In Thomas Kinsella's spare modern translation this is rendered

> I would wed you without cattle, without money or a counted dowry.
> I would kiss you on a dewy morning in the lightening day.
> Sad sickness I am not beside you, dear love of my breast,
> In Caiseal in Munster – let our bed be but a bog-deal board.[60]

Bog-deal is timber preserved in a bog for a long time, and is consequently exceedingly hard, more suitable for carving than lovemaking. '*Bog* deil' in Irish is a synthetic compound of Irish and German-derived words, as it is in English (thus, in Ó Tuama's printing it is italicised as a foreign English word in the Irish poem). The word 'bog', of course, is also the Irish word for 'soft', so there may be some wordplay here: although the Edward Walsh version of these lines, which I will discuss more, describes it rather more comfortably as a soft deal board, he doesn't duck the dowry-less, perhaps forbidden union. The song imagines sexual love surmounting mere comfort, and is sung as a song of the torments of lust, imagining the physical and economic hardships that will be braved by the lovers.

But it is, rather more safely, as a song of unconditional marriage proposal that the lyric became known from the early nineteenth century. The first English metrical translation was provided by Thomas Furlong in James Hardiman's anthology of Irish-language poetry with English metrical translations *Irish Minstrelsy*, published in 1831. Hardiman not only collected a large number of lyrics, but also organised a team of translators to provide versions of the poems. This is the first stanza of Thomas Furlong's English metrical translation of the lyric:

> I would wed thee my dear girl without herds or land,
> Let me claim as a portion but thy own white hand;
> On each soft dewy morn shall I bless thy charms,
> And clasp thee all fondly in my anxious arms.[61]

It is not difficult to see that the chasteness of Furlong's 'my dear girl' or 'clasp thee all fondly' has all the passion of an uncle for a favourite niece – and the creepiness attendant on that (from where does he get his 'anxious arms'?). It contrasts poorly with the frank portrayal of sexual love in the original. The physical actualities of the marriage bed are omitted entirely by Furlong. Most significantly, Furlong makes no attempt to retain the frankly un-English prosodic effect of three stressed syllables from the Irish 'clár *bog* déil'.

LIBRARY, UNIVERSITY OF CHESTER

These stressed syllables are replicated in a subsequent version by Samuel Ferguson, published as a counter-translation in 1834 in a series of articles that review Hardiman's volume. If we could find a text that first contemplates the scholarly and aesthetic challenges of giving English-language versions of Irish-language poetry these articles, this version of the song might be it:

> I'd wed you without herds, without money, or rich array,
> And I'd wed you on a dewy morning at day-dawn grey;
> My bitter woe it is, love, that we are not far away
> In Cashel town, though the bare deal board were our marriage bed this day![62]

Ferguson's version is literally between that of Furlong and Kinsella. It lies between a rhythmically dull drawing room piece and a sparseness in English that allows itself the alliteration through which (according to Ó Tuama and Kinsella) 'the ghosts of metrical procedures, give a hint of the easeful elaborateness and linguistic elegance' of the original.[63]

The strictest view of this is held by Breandán Ó Buachalla, who works from Ferguson's lyric to state categorically: 'Because of their different phonological and prosodic systems it is well-nigh impossible to render Irish metres into English.' This allows Ó Buachalla to comment perceptively that Ferguson's most successful versions employed 'English metrical patterns … the result being the more effective the less rigorously they were applied'. Losing rigour in English metres or from the demands of 'literal' translation such as Moore before him, Ferguson chances on a new English metre. In terms reminiscent of Beckett's satire on Clarke, where the pentameter is described as 'free as a canary in the final foot', Ó Buachalla says that Ferguson 'let the metrical line run free except for the final foot … and its end rhyme'.[64] The insistent 'array … gray … away … day' rhymes of his stanza take liberties both with the 'polish' of English verse and the rhymes of the Irish. In doing so, Ferguson synthesises what he calls the 'savage sincerity'[65] of a poem of sexual desire and seduction, and the musicality of a language adapted for representing a culture from which it is not only linguistically other, but from which the translator marks cultural difference.

And difference there is. Compare Ferguson's with a later, more strict attempt to replicate the prosodic effects of the Irish song. This is Edward Walsh's version, published over a decade later, in 1847:

> I would wed you, dear, without gold or gear, or counted kine;
> My wealth you'll be, would your friends agree, and you be mine –
> My grief, my gloom! That you do not come, my heart's dear hoard!
> To Cashel fair, though our couch were there but a soft deal board.[66]

Walsh's version has its charm, but the effect of the incessant internal and cross-rhyming is that it never sounds like an English poem. This might be taken as a term of praise, but Walsh's intention in his translations was to replicate both the rhythm of the original and that of the air to which the lyric was set.

Nearly a century earlier, Walsh found effects that Austin Clarke claimed he had discovered. Speaking of the lyrics in his collection of Irish poems he says:

> I have admitted nothing among them calculated, in a moral or political point of view, to give offence. I have also been careful to avoid that error which I have already censured in others – namely, the fault of not writing the measure of the translation to the exact song-tune of the original. The Irish scholar will perceive that I have embodied the meaning and spirit of each Irish stanza within the compass of the same number of lines, each for each; and that I have also preserved, in many of the songs, the caesural and demi-caesural rhymes, the use of which produces such harmonious effect in Irish verse.[67]

This is neither an attempt to obliterate linguistic difference nor to replicate Irish metres. Rather, it is a game effort to move the translation into the 'tune' of the original, content to produce what MacDonagh would later call 'Irish poems that sing to the same air'. Whether he has 'preserved' harmonious effect or not, Walsh finds that exploiting 'caesural and demi-caesural rhymes' in English will certainly enable the musical effect to be sustained. He has censored things that might give moral or political offence – the soft deal board might be representative of prudishness in nineteenth-century versions of the lyric. But Walsh also dares to challenge the ear accustomed to English poetry with the aesthetic offence that yoking English into such overt musicality might provide. The result is not doggerel; but it is a synthetic attempt to get one culture to carry the aesthetic conventions of the poetry and music of another. Moore, Walsh and Ferguson set the formal terms that might enable the Irish poem in English eventually to emerge as its own thing.

CHAPTER 3

From Moore to Mahony: The Transmigration of Intellect

A Small Seminal Principle

Samuel Ferguson's early Tory connections with *Blackwood's Edinburgh Magazine* and The *Dublin University Magazine* might not suggest a fellow follower of the latter-day Whig and erstwhile United Irishman manqué, Thomas Moore. But in Moore, Ferguson heard 'a combination of the most delightful attributes of music and poetry, unattainable otherwise than by uniting the music of a rude age to the poetry of a refined one.'[1] Ferguson's double-edged praise was published in the *Dublin University Magazine* in August 1834, and in the same month the Cork Jesuit Francis Sylvester Mahony, who had moved over from *Blackwood's* to its London offshoot, *Fraser's Magazine for Town and Country*, also turned his attentions on Moore. Mahony spoke in the person of his alter ego Father Andrew Prout, whom he imagined as one of the last remnants of a tradition of Tory satire that stretched back through the last days of the ancien régime to his sire in fiction and spirit, Jonathan Swift. Mahony and Prout's scorn of the ages of revolution or reform turned itself on the friend of Robert Emmet and the biographer of Lords Byron and Edward Fitzgerald. Where Ferguson found rudeness and refinement in union, Mahony accused Moore of a double hoodwinking of his audience. An inadequately acknowledged dependence on his sources inevitably prompted accusations of plagiarism, but it was conveyed through a drawing-room sentimentality that Mahony found at best cant and at worst subversive.

Not just Moore's reputation, but that of nineteenth-century Irish poetry in English has veered ever since between these two positions, dependent as they were on both the seemingly rudimentary forms of the ballad or the translated Irish-language song for authenticity and the need not to offend a newly expanding readership addicted to the print that abounded in publishing projects of many political hues. Both used the same recognition of a synthetic form seeking to forge the new from the seemingly competing aesthetic positions of the sentimental and barbarous; both found ample space for the promulgation of political controversy on grounds of taste as much as conviction.

Prout's 'reliques' were presented by Mahony and *Fraser's* as gathered from papers left behind by the recently deceased parish priest of Watergrasshill, County Cork, who had lived through the eighteenth century to see both Catholic Emancipation and the Reform Act, democratising measures he abhorred. These were achieved in part by the mobilisation of the masses by Daniel O'Connell, viewed as a demagogue by the *Fraser's* set. Determined not to give due credit to that quarter, Prout says that it was Moore's *Melodies* that won emancipation for the Irish Catholics by preying on the susceptibilities of the great market in England for the synthetic Irish thing:

> [F]or glorious Dan might have exerted his leathern lungs during a century in haranguing the native *sans culottes* on this side of the Channel; but had not the 'Melodies' made *emancipation* palatable to the thinking and generous portion of Britain's free-born sons – had not his poetry spoken to the hearts of the great and the good, and enlisted the fair daughters of England, the spouters would have been but objects of scorn and contempt. The 'Melodies' won the cause silently, imperceptibly, effectually; and if there is a tribute due from that class of the native, it is to the child of song.[2]

The target is first the 'effeminacy' of Moore's songs and then the secret society of their ur-nationalist background music. If the 'fair daughters of England' responded to the newly palatable refinements of the *Melodies*, the Irish sans-culottes owed more to the symbolist stealth of the songs than the explicit politics of their ostensible 'Liberator', Daniel O'Connell. To vary the Tory tone, Prout bags three birds with the same shot.

Mahony had no taste for the newness of the *Melodies* either: where Ferguson found a 'combination' or 'uniting' of the disparate materials of Irish music and English lyric, Mahony directed scurrilous satire at late-Romantic and early Victorian debates about ideas of such unions and their attendant metaphors of what we would now call hybridity or heteroglossia or intertextuality. For Mahony this was an Irish stew, and he watched appalled as it simmered away in the powerful synthetic forms of a new cultural nationalism, where the populism of O'Connellite Irish Catholicism met Moore's recycled Gaelic airs, all brought together in the alternate shaping of rhetoric and symbolism in a resurgent, possibly insurgent, Irish literature beginning to be written in English.

Ferguson's praise of Moore was conveyed in his great four-part review of James Hardiman's 1831 collection, *Irish Minstrelsy: Or Bardic Remains of Ireland*, and between Hardiman and his reviewer we have one of the founding critical controversies of Irish poetry in English – which I discuss further in Chapter 4. But hidden in its savagery and frequent obscenity, Mahony's 'The Rogueries of Tom Moore' essay, published in the same year as Ferguson's review, is an equal glory of Irish criticism. The May 1834 edition of *Fraser's* had presented two fictional characters: the magazine's editor, Oliver Yorke; and a young barrister from County Cork, Frank Cresswell, collaborating on a sort of patchwork edition of a conversation found in the Prout reliques between Father Prout and Sir Walter Scott on the occasion of the latter's 'pilgrimage' to Blarney Castle.[3] The piece capped its fantastic account of the origins of the Blarney Stone with Prout's establishment not only of the Greek 'original' of Richard Milliken's ballad 'The Groves of Blarney', but three other translations, as well: a Latin version; a French-Norman version from the 'Livre de Doomsdaye, A.D. 1069', extra stanzas written by Mahony; and a spoof 'Fragment of a Celtic MS., from the King's Library Copenhagen'. This latter presented a version of the most risqué of Milliken's stanzas in a print pastiche of the so-called Hardiman font, the type cast for the Gaelic poems in the *Irish Minstrelsy*.[4]

The invention of this 'Polyglot edition' of 'The Groves of Blarney' needed a sequel, and Yorke, Cresswell and Prout were combined again in the June 1834 number to give an account of 'Father Prout's Carousel', again with Scott, Oliver Knapp, the mayor of Cork and other characters. These included Terry Callaghan, a piper, whose contribution to the anthology of songs and their translations sung that night was the delivery of a wonderful blast of doggerel on the subject of the storming of Blarney Castle by a satanic Oliver Cromwell in 1628 (*sic*: Cromwell did not arrive in Ireland until 1649). Cromwell wins the day by walking on the water:

> Och! 'twas Crommill then gave the dark token –
>   For in the black art he was deep;
> And tho' the eyes of the Irish stood open,
>   They found themselves all fast asleep!
> With his jack-boots he stepped on the water,
>   And he walked clane right over the lake;
> While his sodgers they all followed after.
>   As dry as a duck or a drake.
>   O Blarney castle, etc.[5]

There was 'lots of fun at Prout's table at all times', the narrator tells us.[6] That word 'fun', according to the *Oxford English Dictionary* a 'low, cant word' for Samuel Johnson in the eighteenth century but newly embraceable by

Fraser's in the early nineteenth, mixes with Mahony's carousal, a Dionysian event that nevertheless looks very Irish:

> That banquet was in sooth no ordinary jollification, no mere bout of sensuality; but a philosophical and rational commingling of mind, with a pleasant and succulent addition of matter – a blending of soul and substance, typified by the union of Cupid and Psyche – a compound of strange ingredients, in which a large infusion of what are called (in a very Irish-looking phrase) 'animal spirits' coalesced with an abundance of distilled ambrosia; not without much erudite observation, and the interlude of jovial song; wit contending for supremacy with learning and folly asserting her occasional predominance like the tints of the rainbow in their *tout ensemble*, or like the smile and the tear in Erin's left eye, when that fascinating creature has taken 'a drop' of her own mountain dew.[7]

Prout's Carousal is filled full of such fun, equal parts satirical stereotype and anti-nationalist mischief. Why, for instance, Erin's *left* eye, in that reductio-by-allusion to a drunken performance of Tom Moore's 1808 lyric about the mixture of sentimental and humorous modes in Irish song, 'Erin! The Tear and the Smile in Thine Eyes'?[8] Does the other eye remain clear enough to size up further opportunities for mischief?

Introducing his description of this feast, Cresswell openly admits that he is doing so to congratulate *Fraser's* on their generous printing of 'that wonderful and more than *Siamese* bantling your "Polyglot edition" of the "Groves of Blarney"'. He repeats gossip that Prout is not the sole author of the various translations, and that 'your incomparable lyric must be referred to a joint-stock sort of parentage'. In an address to the magazine, he dismisses this with a plea for compendious authorship and textual completeness:

> How little do such simpletons suspect or know of the real source from which hath emanated that rare combination of the Teïan lyre and the Tipperary bagpipe – of the Ionian dialect blending harmoniously with the Cork brogue; an Irish potato seasoned with Attic salt, and the humours of Donnybrook wed to the glories of Marathon! Verily since the days of the great Complutensian Polyglot (by compilation of which the illustrious Cardinal Ximenes so endeared himself to the bibliomaniacal world), since the appearance of that even grander effort of the 'Clarendon' at Oxford, the 'Tetrapla,' originally compiled by the most laborious and eccentric father of the Church, Origen of Alexandria, nothing has issued from the press in a completer form than your improved quadruple version of the 'Groves of Blarney'.[9]

There is a nod to Prout's guest Walter Scott here, and before that to one of the great satires on the follies of the learned: the *Oxford English Dictionary* traces the first instance of the words 'bibliomaniac' and 'bibliomaniacal' to Scott's *Antiquary* of 1816, where mention is made of 'the most determined as well as the most earnest bibliomaniac upon record, Don Quixote de la Mancha'. The second *Oxford English Dictionary* instance of bibliomaniac is from *Fraser's* from February 1834, two months before the first appearance of Prout, casting aspersions on the self- (and implicitly vanity-) published 'bibliomaniac and genealogical enquiry' of the English poet, novelist and bibliographer Egerton Bridges. Prout's own crazed bibliomania ranges from Ximenes's first printed polyglot Bible back to Origen's *Tetrapla* (the first text to compile differing translations of the Bible) and up to Prout's quadruple 'Groves of Blarney'.

This is the 'compound of strange ingredients' of the Prout papers that has drawn a number of readers to their extraordinary comic juxtapositions of the classical and provincial, the high and low, and the sacred and blasphemous, so much so that Terry Eagleton invokes the Bakhtinian 'carnivalesque'.[10] The Siamese, the joint-stock parentage, the 'Irish potato seasoned with Attic Salt', are also all comic prefigurings of late twentieth-century debate about the original, authentic and hybrid, a mixture in which the shaky grasp on reality of the bibliomaniac is continually upended. *The Reliques of Fr Prout* were later to be rescued from the obscurity that its author might take to be the appointed fate of their subject. At the time, however, the articles derived their 'fun' from a picture of the synthetic Irish thing at the very moment of its emergence into form as a misshapen and polyglot object, better suited to satire than sentiment. But that fun was also tempered with a hint at the historical and political dangers that might follow if it were to succeed.

Prout is presented as an embodiment of one sort of conservative rhetoric, where the best way to combat change is to suggest that the new thing is simply the old thing in new clothes. To make the point we are taken back to the point of Prout's origin. The imagined 'editor' Oliver Yorke says that the obscurity of a true original attends the fictional priest, as Prout's 'celebrity (to use an expression of Edmund Burke) is as yet but "a speck on the horizon – *a small seminal principle, rather than a formed body*"' (Mahony's emphasis)[11]. From alerting us to a Burkean ancestry for the word 'celebrity' to the obscenities of the Swiftian mode (Prout was the supposed product of a secret marriage of Swift and Stella), Yorke encourages us to infer that Prout is sperm rather than completed conception, essence yet to find substance. Mahony was thirty years old when he began to write the articles for his friend William Maginn, although his fictional Prout persona would have been at least in his nineties in the year of writing. Indeed Prout's recent death had been announced on his first appearance in the April issue of the magazine, and given as the reason for publishing his 'Papers'.

Whatever the deliberate elasticity of Prout's age and origins, his *Reliques* share the politics and appetites of the migrant Mahony himself, who was trained across Catholic Europe from Clongowes Wood College to Rome and back to Clongowes, from whence he was dismissed in his first term as a master after a carousel with his students.[12] Prout, his editor tells us, was one of that order of Irish Catholic priests 'who were educated abroad, before the French revolution, and had imbibed, from associating with the polished and high-born clergy of the old Gallican church, a loftier range of thought, and a superior delicacy of sentiment'[13]. Mahony brought to *Fraser's* the increasing intemperance that put paid to his career as a priest. But he also brought a combination of the conservativism of European, as much as Irish Catholicism along with contemporary British Tory, fear of the sans-culottes who had been mobilised by O'Connell in Ireland. They were about to be seen and heard in a Chartist movement in England, as well, led by O'Connell's erstwhile friend – and (briefly) Member of Parliament for Cork – Fergus O'Connor. Prout, as with other contributors to Maginn's magazine, was placed in reactionary opposition to an 1830s United Kingdom in the business of gradual reform but soon to face calls for its rapid extension – not just the emancipation of Catholics in 1829, Act of 1832, but a mass political movement led by O'Connor and modelled in part on O'Connell's success, which later in the decade was to press for universal suffrage.[14]

In 'The Rogueries of Tom Moore', first published in *Fraser's* in August 1834, we can grasp the finesse of Mahony's factionalism, as he writes in the persona of a Cork Catholic Tory lambasting the Dublin Catholic Whig Thomas Moore. Its objects are both the old – antiquarian research – and the new: at the end of the article, Mahony offers us one of the earliest and best achievements of the Irish mode, in his part-comic, part-sentimental 'The Shandon Bells', which I discuss more later. The 'Rogueries' essay initially begins in the wake of the controversy over the Royal Irish Academy's 'Origin and Use of the Round Towers' essay prize of 1830, in which one of the two competitors, Henry O'Brien, propounded a theory that the Round Towers were pre-Christian fertility symbols. Of the tower at Clondalkin, for instance, O'Brien writes that it 'actually constructed its architecture after the model of the *membrum virile*, which, obscenity apart, is the divinely-formed and indispensible medium selected by God himself for human propagation and sexual profligacy.' The accompanying illustration requires little more from the imagination.[15] Joep Leerssen's classic account of this controversy gives it near-equal importance in the renaissance of Irish antiquarianism just before the Famine with the work of the Irish Ordinance Survey. He has some sympathy for O'Brien, but still refers to him as 'a pathological obsessive, suffering from paranoid delusion'.[16] Moore's biographer Ronan Kelly has less patience, describing O'Brien's essay as 'a farrago of lunacies'. Among Moore's views of O'Brien in a long attack of April 1834 in the *Edinburgh Review*, was that he had plagiarised various antiquarians seeking the origins of the towers and Celtic remains in North Africa.[17] Whatever the quality of O'Brien's work, his health was not up to the controversy, and he died a year later. With taste questionable even for its Fraserian contributors, the first 1836 collection of the *Reliques* reprinted Mahony's *Fraser's* obituary for O'Brien after the 'Rogueries' essay, along with an etching by Cork artist Daniel Maclise of O'Brien lying on his deathbed, a distinctly phallic round tower visible through an open window.[18]

From the point at which it joins this controversy, the 'Rogueries of Tom Moore' turns its radical conservative satire on matters of antiquity, origins and sincerity, all played out against the inauthentic, bogus and hybrid. Carlyle's *Sartor Resartus* was running in *Fraser's* at the same time as Prout, whose first appearance was in the April 1834 issue in which Carlyle proclaimed Teufelsdrockh's 'Everlasting Yea!': 'Our Life is compassed round with Necessity; yet is the meaning of Life itself no other than Freedom, than voluntary Force'[19]. Carlyle's antagonistic vitalism also came with its own editorial apparatus, its invented German philosopher and its cod-idealist philosophy of clothes. William Maginn's/Oliver Yorke's *Fraser's* played havoc with the authentic, preaching a doctrine of Carlylean sincerity through the deliberate counter-spirit of an array of impersonations, either ventriloquised through spoof-German philosopher Teufelsdröckh (literally, 'devil's dung') or the small seminal principle of the vast and useless learning of Father Andrew Prout. A brilliant Trinity-educated Unionist, a failed Cork Catholic priest, the Scottish nonconformist populariser of German idealism: the pages of *Fraser's* presented a mix of conservative talents gathered from across the United Kingdom to London to parody what they saw as the inauthentic liberalism of the age.

For all of the assumed old fogeyism of his persona, Mahony's satire edges him close to a sceptical approach to the possibility of the authentic or the sincere, in arguments that can sound like a parody of those surrounding the quality used to define hybridity:

> I am an old man, and have read a great deal in my time – being of a
> quiet disposition, and having always had a taste for books, which I consider

a great blessing [...] all I read now strikes me as but a new version of what I had read somewhere before. Plagiarism is so barefaced and so universal, that I can't stand it no longer: I have shut up shop, and won't be taken no more. [...] I'm sick of hashed-up works, and loathe the *baked meats* of antiquity served in a fricassee. Give me a solid joint, in which no knife has ever been fleshed, and I will share your intellectual banquet most willingly, were it but a mountain kid, or a limb of Welsh mutton.

I declare that the whole mass of contemporary scribblement might be bound up in one tremendous volume, and entitled 'Elegant Extracts;' for, if you except the form and style, the varnish and colour, all the rest is what I have known in a different shape forty years ago; and there is more philosophy than meets the vulgar eye in that excellent song on the transmutation of things here below, which perpetually offer the same intrinsic substance, albeit under a different name:

'Dear Tom, this brown jug, which now foams with mild ale,
Was once Toby Philpot, a merry old soul,' &c. &c.

This transmigration of intellect, this metempsychosis of literature, goes on silently reproducing what had been, and reconstructing what had gone to pieces; but those, whose memory, like mine, is unfortunately over-tenacious of its young impressions, cannot enjoy the zest of a twice-told tale, and consequently are greatly to be pitied.[20]

Mahony indulges in much theologico-critical high jinks. Vicesimus Knox's *Elegant Extracts* in prose, poetry and letters, which had been bestsellers since the 1780s, were anthologies of sayings or passages taken from their original contexts in essay, prose or longer poems. Rather than distilling essence, they effected the transmigration of what the Catholic cleric Prout calls, with Thomist propriety, the 'intrinsic substance' of originary texts into 'hashed-up works', the solid joint re-emerging in a stew. The creation of the Toby jug and its frothy pint is another result of such hybrid anthologizing. The song of Toby Philpot is sung by the character Dermot in *The Poor Soldier* (1784), by Irish playwright John O'Keefe. The 'jolly toper' Toby expires when drunk, and the jug, reconstituted from the 'dissolv'd' clay that is all that remains of his body, becomes 'sacred to friendship, and mirth, and mild ale'[21]. If we 'except the form and style, the varnish and colour' then of course many products will have existed 'in a different shape forty years ago'. But Mahony's joke knows that form, style, varnish and colour are the distinguishing marks of difference between things in the world as well as works of art, whatever the 'essence' of thing or text returning to dust only to be reconstituted again.

Mahony's irony places Prout's irony in metaphors of plainness and dietary wholesomeness set against the stewed, the tampered, the impure and the inauthentic. It then shows how such arguments may disappear into the dust of the grave or the froth of the pint. The separation of 'form' and 'content' by late-Georgian conservative scepticism does sound like a contemporary radical critical scepticism, where the originary product, 'the authentic', the 'solid joint' can be neither tasted nor achieved. In Mahony's reductio or transmutation of the argument, all talk of essentialism ends up in a blasphemous parody of the liturgy of the burial service, the remembering of the human whose dust doesn't so much return to dust as emerge reincarnated as a pint pot. Recovering the small seminal principle is an impossibility. It is already the object of ridicule here, although treated with rather more earnestness in the bibliomania of that contemporary literary criticism that seeks to link both the hybrid and postcolonial with accounts of emergent moments in English-language Irish literature among which Mahony's essays might be counted as one.

The mode is distinctly different, but working in a similar track of argument and counterargument, from an essay by Homi Bhabha (which in its turn had adapted Roland Barthes to write about Frantz Fanon). Richard Kirkland describes a process that 'erases any essentialist claims for the inherent authenticity or purity of cultures':

> This awareness enables the hybrid to become, not simply a point of interaction, but a point of transformation: a state of being *inbetween* that can never develop a unitary identity: it exists only as '*something else besides*'. It is within this construction that the full resonances of the subaltern formation within post-colonial criticism are properly revealed. Rather than classification, the subaltern becomes, as Spivak suggests, 'truly situational': at once both Gramsci's censored utterance utilizing the methodology of his six point plan in 'Notes on Italian History', that which does not conform to class analyses, and the unutterable counter to the totalizing agendas of teleological epistemes that locate themselves within a notionally centred logic of knowledge.[22]

For Kirkland's (and Bhabha's) essential and hybrid we can substitute Mahony/Prout's solid joint and fricasee. For 'inherent authenticity or purity of cultures' and these points of interaction, transformation and '*something else besides*', the priest gives us his 'intrinsic substance' giving way to 'transmigration of intellect' or 'metempsychosis of literature'. If Prout cannot find anything original in the present, he thus may suggest that hybrid forms say they are new while recycling the already used. As I understand it, Kirkland's adaptation of Bhabha points us away from the consolations of hybridity as sought by Irish critics such as Declan Kiberd or Luke Gibbons, and suggests that we must look at postcolonial subjects as always in process and never achieved, such as Prout's heretical metempyschosis. As Gibbons allows, 'It is precisely the absence of a sense of an ending which has characterised the national narratives of Irish history.'[23]

If such an ostensibly hybrid process cannot achieve closure, it does have issue, the textual product, work of art, or – as in this book – the Irish poem in English. The poem is the work of culture and not of nature. Indeed, no matter how it might appear to be grounded in 'difference', the 'intrinsic substance' of the poem – its content – and its form and style, colour and varnish are more closely linked than sceptical readings from the contemporary left or the post-Romantic right might suggest. Style in itself may be the content; the surfaces of the poem may be indistinguishable from its supposed depths or metaphysical, cultural, and 'essential' grounding. In seeking for such grounding, the organic metaphor of hybridity implies that postcolonial poems, or at least the colonial circumstances from which they might seek to emerge, are the result of a sort of marriage of the 'depths' (content, essence or identity) of the contrastingly dominant empire or pre-existent, indigenous authenticity. For the conservative Mahony as much as the contemporary radical critic, such depth is of course an illusion, part of an endlessly deferred, doubling or supplemental presence that neither colonised nor coloniser, self nor other can actually possess.

Hybridity itself may also be an illusion. Certainly it can be misleading if we attribute it as a quality of works of art, where the suggestion seems to be that the poem becomes a work of achieved miscegenation, as if poems cross over species rather than just families, and we mistake the false classifications of the empirical scientist for 'essence'. This, I think, is what Kirkland means when he suggests it is 'unutterably counter to totalizing agendas of teleological epistemes'; or indeed what Mahony refers to as 'the transmigration of intellect, the metempsychosis of literature silently reproducing what had been, and reconstructing what had gone to pieces'. The Jesuit in Mahony might counsel further that we do not make an ontological confusion between substance and accident. The danger, as Robert Young's contribution to earlier postcolonial debates about the ethics of the metaphor of hybridity suggests, is to give in to a metaphor for culture based in biological necessity, as if cultures interbreed, inevitably governed by sex in matters of historical and political destiny.[24] In the process, the analogy of the hybrid thrives when it elides not only matters of form (the inevitable results of convention, tradition and genre and the limits and paradigms of language, style and production), but also historical matters of context, ideology and economics, as well as factors about which more recent literary criticism has ceased to be embarrassed – the intention, choice and context of an empirically describable historical writing agent: the author.

It can also miss the fun. For the literary critic, there is the danger of finding an overdetermination of the achievement of the artist and the individual work of art by a combination of perceived historical process and discourses of ethnicity and gender derived from anthropology or linguistics. The biological metaphor of hybridity shades into the necessary or the inevitable, and the small parts that poems and poets play can get overwhelmed by the vast mechanisms of a history seeking narrative closure, as formal properties are swallowed up by an inherently contradictory, ever-disappearing, 'content' irrevocably sundered from its 'form'. 'I'm sick of hashed-up works, and loathe the *baked meats* of antiquity served in a fricassee', Prout says. 'Give me a solid joint, in which no knife has ever been fleshed, and I will share your intellectual banquet most willingly.' As the bibliomaniacal evidence of the Prout papers attests, Mahony, for one, must have known that such a joint would be dull fare. In his own way he is prefiguring in parody Bhabha's repudiated 'essentialist claims for the inherent authenticity or purity of cultures'. The riposte is in terms of form and style, and the invention, after Moore, of a new literary style in the English language adapted to carry an already extant Irish subject matter. If the 'intrinsic substance' exists at all, it can only be perceived through its new form, style, colour and varnish. But it reveals itself as in process, in specific historical and artistic circumstances that reveal nothing but cultural change. The intrinsic cultural forms meet a new set of political circumstances, and a new synthetic form comes to be written.

The Shandon Bells

Mahony was not the only critic to accuse Thomas Moore of being bogus, particularly given the great wealth and fame Moore accrued on the back of setting lyrics to the ancient Irish tunes that were collected by Edward Bunting and others. Prout's sarcasm provides a gloss, as he comments on the quality of Moore's 'translations' of the spoof French and Latin lyrics Mahony provides as the supposed 'originals' of the *Irish Melodies*:

> It will be seen [...] that Tom Moore can eke out a tolerably fair translation of any given ballad; and indeed, to translate properly, retaining all the fire and spirit of the original, is a merit not to be sneezed at – it is the next best thing to having a genius of one's own; for he who can execute a clever forgery, and make it pass current, is almost as well off as the capitalist who can

> draw a substantial check on the bank of sterling genius; so, to give the devil
> his due, I must acknowledge that in terseness, point, pathos, and elegance,
> Moore's translations of these French and Latin trifles are very near as good
> as the primary compositions themselves.[25]

With the back of his hand, Mahony admits that form, style, varnish and
colour, or 'terseness, point, pathos, and elegance', those things that make
up the work of art, belong to Moore, as translator or plagiarist.

From 'substantial check' through to 'sterling genius', Mahony lets on
more than might at first appear, at just how the counterfeit might play out.
Thus, the strongest accusations against Moore are not those of plagiarism,
but rather quite contradictory accusations, of cashing in on forgeries. His
Melodies are a synthetic union of Irish airs with English lyrics, containing
sentiments and images taken from European, classical or Romantic convention. To accusations of Moore desecrating Irish music through forcing
his *Melodies* into pianoforte arrangements, Mahony adds the sin of com-
modification, as the songs made their way into the repertoire of the English
and Irish middle classes. As seen already, Prout is wonderful on their success in making Catholic Emancipation palatable in the drawing rooms of
England. The charge of forgery has been made against others who worked
in the revival of the Celtic throughout Prout's supposed lifetime in the
eighteenth and nineteenth centuries, most notably Macpherson's Ossianic
fragments. These are described by Joep Leerssen in terms we might apply
to Moore, and indeed Mahony's attack on Moore's transmigrations of
intellect. Leerssen pictures a space of 'Ossianic liminality', 'a blurred grey
zone between the authentic and the counterfeit, a sliding scale from literal translation to free translation to adaptation to reconstitution to recreation to manipulation to imitation to falsification'[26].

How do we understand similar synthetic forms, unfamiliar and stale as
the fresh and the stirred may now have become, without heading either
into the 'blurred grey zone' of the liminal or the giddy global range of the
discourse of hybridity? The poetry discussed in this book traverses questions of the loss of the authentic, the source and the original, and the
best poets are fully aware that these are philological red herrings, waiting
for the eager nets of the unsuspecting critic. To take the example of the
mode that Mahony uses throughout the Prout article, parody is in many
ways an unconstrained textual and critical illocutionary act, dependent on
previous texts and criticism for effect. It is always aware that it is effect: it
contrives comedy no matter how its origins might lie in cynicism, anger
or a sort of wilful courting of colonial or provincial obscurity. So, how can
we leave all these literary-theoretical red herrings aside and return, if need

be, to a literary-critical point where we can begin to read again the links of style and content in actual works of art, written for effect at certain times in a describable historical context? If 'formalism' is maybe too Platonic a concept to describe what Romantic and post-Romantic Irish poems were doing, as seen here in Chapter 2, one option is to describe a sort of 'mannerism', and according to James Clarence Mangan, 'Mannerism is a grand thing'.[27], always on the verge of the doggerel with which the ballad continuously flirts. If we view the exaggerated sense of form that many of the synthetic English-language productions of Irish poets show us, then what might appear to be mere surface phenomena need attention: 'I am nothing if not striking,' Mangan's mannerist narrator Clarence says. 'It is imperative on me, therefore, to strike.'[28]

Such great transmutations of cultural history suggest a method to describe the form and style, varnish and colour of individual songs or poems in which the understanding may be in the very process of intellectual transmigration itself. Mahoney ends 'The Rogueries of Tom Moore' with his own 'The Shandon Bells', itself pushing the sentimental ballad as far as it will go in the direction of the synthetic poetic effects of doggerel. Take the third stanza:

> I've heard bells tolling
> Old 'Adrian Mole' in,
> Their thunder rolling
> From the Vatican,
> And cymbals glorious
> Swinging uproarious
> In the gorgeous turrets
> Of Nôtre Dame;
> But thy sounds were sweeter
> Than the dome of Peter
> Flings o'er the Tiber,
> Pealing solemnly; –
> O! The bells of Shandon
> Sound far more grand on
> The pleasant waters
> Of the river Lee.[29]

Mahony knows that doggerel – whether intentional or not – draws attention to the distortions of metre, diction and rhyme. Its effects need an exaggerated vocal performance in order to share the joke. Such a performance is generically expected by balladeer, singer and audience combined, who will share in smiles of recognition at extravagant rhymes and fantastic conceits, which may not necessarily impair the 'sincerity' of the performance or the performed. In its way, doggerel is merely a sort of mannerism. But even doggerel requires some skill, no matter how cynically deployed that might be. The rhymes on falling disyllabic feet, 'Peter/sweeter', 'grand on/ Shandon', and the outrageous mispronunciation required in advance to hear 'Mole in' with 'Vatican' or 'solemnly' with 'River Lee' wreak havoc on English metre.

But the effect is not entirely comic. One legend that accompanies the poem is that the homesick Mahony wrote it first on the walls of his room in the seminary in Rome.[30] To get the joke as conveyed from the pages of *Fraser's Magazine*, we must at least connive in the fiction that Prout is homesick for Cork. The foreign and exotic must pale before the homely and familiar, just as the seemingly slight can easily be puffed up into comic phantasmagoria. Mahony pretended to be appalled at Morgan D'Arcy's subsequent polite Victorian piano setting for the ballad. He suggested that its performance should be to the accompaniment of,

> half a dozen grand ones [pianos] at least, giving the glorious pealing of the bells together; but I prefer a mighty Gregorian voice, of half a hundred of such that would rouse the hearts and elevate the souls of the hearers. I meant to produce, as Victor Hugo did when he clapped the Hunchback athwart the bells of Notre Dame in rapid succession, a musical roar, some-thing more gladdening, more tumultuous; a storm of bells, a furnace of campanology, something that would even distantly imitate, in the language of the great romance itself, ten thousand brazen tones breathed all at once, from flute of stone three hundred feet high.

The performance is 'not as a ditty, but a dithyramb',[31] at once fantasti-cally absurd and, with the reference to Hugo, minutely aware of the limits of its own mock-Romance inflation. Similarly, the diction of the English poem is leavened in the refrain with a Cork colloquialism that makes for a supposedly unforeseen comic juxtaposition. The Vatican and Notre Dame may be 'grand' – magnificent, vast – but the bells of Shandon are 'more grand', as in the Cork dialect sense of the conversational 'fine, splendid.'[32] This is not just to explain away the joke: as Terry Eagleton asks, 'Is the homesickness' of the poem 'straight, tongue-in cheek, or poised on more likely some undecidable in-between?'[33]

The doggerel of 'The Shandon Bells' knows its place within an ongoing pedigree. Prout accuses Moore of stealing the image and sentiment for his popular 'Those Evening Bells', set to a 'Petersburg Air',[34] from 'The Shandon Bells'. Moore's is a much more conventional lyric of nostalgia than Mahony's lampoon. But Mahony himself admits he had borrowed the 'tune' of his ballad from the poem on which he perpetrated such a fantastic pedigree two months before in *Fraser's*, 'The Groves of Blarney'. Supposedly improvised by Richard Milliken in the late 1790s, that ballad possesses even more outrageous rhymes than those of his Cork successor, shading from the wryly historical into the obscene. Referring to the history of Lady Jeffers' Blarney Castle, Milliken moves the pastiche of the country house poem rather too close to the body of its present incumbent:

> 'Tis Lady Jeffers
> Owns this plantation:
> Like Alexander,
> Or like Helen fair,
> There's no commander
> In all the nation,
> For regulation
> Can with her compare.
> Such walls surround her,
> That no nine-pounder
> Could ever plunder
> Her place of strength;
> But Oliver Cromwell
> Her he did pommell,
> And made a breach
> In her battlement.[35]

Mahony provided his mock 'Celtic MS' version of this stanza in the 'Plea for Pilgrimages' Prout paper, recounting Scott's visit to the Blarney stone. Over a century later, Brendan Behan was to express surprise that 'The Groves' remained a frequently anthologised school poem, given the play it has with Lady Jeffers' chastity.[36] As noted previously with reference to Terry Callaghan's account of Cromwell's (non)siege of Blarney Castle, the grasp of Irish history would also be irresponsible in the classroom: the Jeffreys family didn't receive the castle until after the accession of William of Orange, in 1689.

Mahony also added his own piece of apocrypha to the 'Polyglot edition' of 1834:

> There is a stone there,
> That whoever kisses,
> Oh! He never misses
> To grow eloquent.
> 'Tis he may clamber
> To a lady's chamber,
> Or become a member
> Of parliament:
> A clever spouter
> He'll sure turn out, or

An out-and outer,
"To be let alone,"
Don't hope to hinder him,
Or to bewilder him:
Sure he's a pilgrim
From the Blarney stone![37]

A Cork accent might be required to rhyme 'clamber' and 'chamber', or maybe just the ballad reciter's mangled pronunciation. The Irish colloquial 'Sure he's a pilgrim' mixes accents with the Fraserian political satire at a parliamentarian 'out-and-outer': that is, a fanatic, possibly a repealer, who wants 'To be let alone' (sinn féin amhainn?), but also one who tells out and out lies, given that he has been gifted with the blarney. The *Oxford English Dictionary* locates a cluster of uses of the now obsolete 'out-and-outer' from 1819 to 1852, both in *Fraser's* and from Fraserians, including Hogg and Thackeray, meaning both 'one who goes beyond the norm' and 'a liar'.

If there is a wilful mangling of linguistic and other proprieties along with a cavalier attitude to history in these texts, there is nevertheless a fairly careful trail of influence and debt to be discovered in their relations to one another. The backwards transmigration of metre, sentiment and song doesn't end with Milliken. In his classic 1951 anthology of *Irish Poets of the Nineteenth Century*, Geoffrey Taylor says that Milliken places Blarney Castle in competition with nearby Castle Hyde, and puts his poem in 'the same metre' as that chosen by the anonymous author of the ballad of the same name.[38] This is not strictly true, because Milliken (followed by Mahony) over-eggs the metre by introducing strong comic rhymes that mimic the frequent but by no means ever-present internal and cross-rhyming effects of the ballad. Nevertheless, the sense of competition between places and poems is great, as in the final stanza of 'Castle Hyde', which travels across the British Isles from Blarney to Glasgow, failing to find comparison for the place it praises:

I rode from Blarney to Castlebarnet,
To Thomastown and sweet Doneraile,
To Kilshannick that joins Rathcormack,
Besides Killarney and Abbeyfeale;
The river Shannon and pleasant Clyde;
In all my ranging and serenading
I met no equal to Castle Hyde.[39]

The balladeer claims the authority of the well travelled as he scans Irish and Scottish place names within an English-language lyric, granting the contrast of at-homeness and strangeness that the poem's simple conceit of comparison demands. There is no need to invoke the Vatican or Notre Dame, or indeed Milliken's extravagant antecedents: 'But were I Homer/ Or Nebuchadnezzar/'Tis in every feature/I would make it shine'. Indeed, the skill of this stanza of 'Castle Hyde' resides in its ability to rhyme across languages, as the author provides half-rhymes for translated Irish place names within English, and full rhymes of Irish-English and Scots Gaelic or Scots: 'Doneraile/Abbeyfeale', 'Clyde/Hyde'.

These are simple ballad effects, and in their shifts of register can suggest the bathos that is ripe for the parodist's plunder. However, such a tonal shuttling between high and low, of the rhymes sounding comparisons across cultures as well as the boundaries of metaphoric decorum, occur in what may be one of the two 'sources' of this whole train of allusion and parody. Taylor states that the metre of 'The Groves of Blarney' is 'derived from the Gaelic', and from 'The Deserter' or 'The Deserter's Lamentation', by Irish lawyer and parliamentarian John Philpot Curran (also father to Robert Emmett's paramour, Sarah Curran, who was immortalized in Moore's 'She Is Far from the Land'). Philpot Curran's poem was a metrical version of the eighteenth-century Gaelic poet Riocard Bairéid's celebrated drinking song, 'Preab san Ól' ('Start Drinking' or 'Jump in the Drink'). Curran's version looks like a more-or-less conventional English language anacreontic, cast into ballad metres:

> If sadly thinking, and spirits sinking,
> Could more than drinking our griefs compose,
> A cure for sorrow from care I'd borrow
> And hope tomorrow might end my woes.
> But as in wailing there's nought availing,
> And Death unfailing will strike the blow,
> Then for that reason, and for a season,
> Let us be merry before we go![40]

This employs a trick we shall see later in this book used by poets such as Tennyson or Yeats to extend the metrical line to tetrameter or even hexameter by joining two-stress lines together, thus echoing a silent ballad tune through internal rhyme.[41] As with his successors, Curran achieves a pentameter line that retains such effects: 'thinking/sinking', 'sorrow/borrow', and so on.

If 'The Deserter' catches a recognisable sense of mutability in the midst of its uncertainty over the future, its original, 'Preab san Ól', has a lyric that is more attuned to a comic mix of place and language:

> An long ar sáile níl cuan ná cearda
>   I nach gcaithfeadh cáirde ar feadh an domhain mhóir,

Ó ríocht na Spáinne suas Gibráltar,
    Agus ansan áit a mbíonn an Grand Seigneur,
Le gach *cargo* ag líonfadh málaí
    Ní choinneódh an bás uaidh uair ná ló,
Mar sin, a cháirde, níl beart níos fearr dhúinn
    Ná bheith mar tá sin, 'cur preab san ól.[42]

[The sailing ship will not be denied a harbour anywhere in the wide world, from Spain to Gibraltar or the home of the Grand Senor. Each cargo full of riches will not keep death at bay, because, friends, it is better for every man not to be timid, but start drinking.]

Curran's version may be more attentive to metre than sense, but the poems by Milliken and Mahony, which along with 'Castle Hyde' borrow metre and mode from the Irish ballad, also borrow Bairéid's synthetic mix of place and language. This stanza mixes Irish, Spanish, French and English and provides internal half-rhymes as it traverses a world of trade, empires and aristocracy all joined together in a fondness for a drink. The Irish lyric scans the words 'Spáinne' and 'Gibraltar', and half-rhymes Irish and French ('an domhain mhóir'/'an Grand Seigneur') and English and Irish (the internal assonance, 'cairde/*cargo*/chairde'). Needless to say, the 'source' of the trail of allusion that ends up in Mahony's parody is itself a conspicuously allusive and parodic text.

The red herrings of translation and authenticity that have bedevilled discussion of the invention of Irish poetry in English by Moore may be, in Prout's words, the 'next best thing' to denying him and others like him 'a genius of his own'. Much Irish lyric from the nineteenth century claims authenticity when it is at worst 'invention' or at best 'original'. This trail of rewriting, allusion, translation, bragging and wistful half-comic mutability has one more conspicuous text emerging from it. Whereas 'The Shandon Bells' and 'The Groves of Blarney' share a metre with 'Castle Hyde', 'The Deserter's Lamentation' or 'Preab san Ól', in popular performance they do not share tunes. The first two do, although, share a tune with another Irish song of a distinctly less parodic hue, Thomas Moore's 'The Last Rose of Summer'.

The melody for 'The Groves of Blarney' was discovered by Moore in Irish collector Smollet Holden's 1805 *Collection of Quick and Slow Marches*. But its first appearance in print may have been in a book of Scottish tunes, as 'Saint Martin's Church Yard', in James Oswald's *Caledonian Pocket Companion* of 1750. In his compendious *Sources in Irish Traditional Music,* Aloys Fleischmann does suggest comparisons between these melodies and an original for 'Preab San Ól', collected in the second volume of James Johnson's (and Robert Burns's) great *Scots Musical Museum* (1787–1803). It also bears similarities to the eighteenth-century Limerick air 'Slán le Máigh'. Following one echo of melody through Fleischmann's work, the tune for 'Castle Hyde' is cited as that of 'Aisling an Oigfhir' or the 'Young Man's Dream' taken from Bunting's 1796 collection by Moore for his 1808 *Melody*, 'As a beam o'er the face of the waters may glow'.[43] That lyric is transmuted from one of the more explicitly erotic *aislingí* to a lyric of sourceless melancholy. Fleischmann and others link 'Castle Hyde' and 'Aisling an Oighfhir' fairly securely into the so-called Londonderry Air given to George Petrie by Jane Ross for his 1855 *Ancient Music of Ireland*,[44] although it may be a transmutation too far if it is suggested as working behind the melody of 'The Groves of Blarney' or 'The Last Rose of Summer'. The link with 'Castle Hyde' is in the metre of the spoken ballad, no matter how, as Prout would say, 'this transmigration of intellect, this metempsychosis of literature, goes on silently reproducing what had been, and reconstructing what had gone to pieces'.

The disputed authenticity of the 'Derry Air' and its 1910 lyric, 'Danny Boy' (written by the English Edwardian ballad composer Frederick Weatherly), vexes some who are wary of the synthetic Irish thing. Moore, of course, had no compunction about attaching English lyrics to melodies of some antiquity, as he did with 'The Groves of Blarney', for the fifth number of his *Irish Melodies* in 1813:

> 'Tis the last rose of summer
>   Left blooming alone;
> All her lovely companions
>   Are faded and gone;
> No flower of her kindred,
>   No rose-bud is nigh,
> To reflect back her blushes,
>   To give sigh for sigh.
>
> I'll not leave thee, thou lone one!
>   To pine on the stem;
> Since the lovely are sleeping,
>   Go, sleep thou with them.
> Thus kindly I scatter,
>   Thy leaves o'er the bed,
> Where thy mates of the garden
>   Lie scentless and dead.
>
> So soon may I follow,
>   When friendships decay,
> From Love's shining circle
>   The gems drop away.

When true hearts lie withered
    And fond ones are flown,
Oh! who would inhabit,
    This bleak world alone?[45]

In one sense, the extraordinary popularity of the song for which this is the lyric is completely understandable. To a generically 'Celtic' melody of joint Irish and Scottish parentage, suitable for the humorous as much as the pathetic, tone and feeling might be imparted simply by the tempo in which it is performed. This is a melody usually taken slow, in 'the drawling dead, doleful and die-way manner' abhorred by Edward Bunting, who saw this and other antique melodies turned to the synthetic. Reading Bunting's admonition, Moore defended his impatience in clearing away the 'authentic dross'[46] that lay about the antiquarian's work.

And 'The Last Rose of Summer' is in its way about authenticity and dross, about a final remnant giving way to a symbol of mortality and loneliness. Its symbolism is of the simplest variety, of rose and petal and seasonal transience. But its mystery ever-so imperceptibly suggests an allegory of nature and time ghosted by culture and history. In one sense, it is about its own fragile melody, recovered only to be lost again – never mind that contemporaries and successors quickened that same melody as they strove for comic effect. In another it sounds the theme of many of Moore's earliest *Melodies*, of being the last man standing, bereft of companions and love. Both Moore's best lyric, 'At the Mid Hour of Night', a song of bereavement and immortality discussed in Chapter 2, and the more histrionic 'The Minstrel Boy' accompanied this song on first publication in the 1813 *Irish Melodies*. The destruction of the rose in the second verse is reflected in the defeated and dying minstrel boy's last act: 'The harp he lov'd ne'er spoke again/For he tore its chords asunder.'

Such striving for effect in 'The Minstrel Boy' exchanges the delicacy of 'The Last Rose of Summer' for bathos, no more so given the implicit analogy it offers of its author Moore with its soldier-poet. Moore had no compunction in working as a British colonial administrator, or performing his songs to polite English Whig society. 'The Minstrel Boy' goes to a phoney war for the 'Land of song', sword and harp over-egging a double cultural and political symbolism. It is important not to over-read Moore's symbolism when more successful, as in 'The Last Rose of Summer', but through his 'kindly' scattering of living leaves Moore marks death, and thus a point of finality in all of the various hybridisations and transubstantiations that are endlessly shape changing through this song tune and its various texts.

He creates a figure for loss unutterably in excess of the seemingly slight subject matter and diction, the simple folk tune, the stock Romantic symbolism. The song's unanswerable final question – 'Oh! who would inhabit/ This bleak world alone?' – does figure an ending that forestalls consolation. There is no elegiac patterning here. But of course, the very fact of melody and lyric working together has effected a double act of renovation and the new.

Needless to say, the transmutation doesn't stop there. Byron's 1812 'The Kiss, Dear Maid, Thy Lip Has Left' was adapted by Beethoven for a version of the melody of 'The Groves' in Robert Burns's erstwhile publisher George Thompson's *Select Collection of Irish Airs* of 1814–1816. William Maginn couldn't resist a shot at it in his song of the end of the night's drinking, or even of the end of the drink, ''Tis the Last Glass of Claret' in 1820.[47] Perhaps it is fitting that Thomas Davis's best lyric, 'The Lament for Eoghan Roe O'Neill' appeared in 1845 in *The Spirit of the Nation* with 'The Last Rose of Summer' (not 'The Groves of Blarney') as the suggested tune. In whatever form it takes, this Irish poetry written within the time of the Union needs to be read as a form of longing, seeking even in its parodic moments by the Shandon bells or groves of Blarney to recuperate a lost past. Its claims of unity are with a sense of unity lost, passed away. Even writing for a Unionist or antiquarian audience, the forensic, historicist or parodic often defines its attempts at translation or original composition. At the same time, it is conscious of challenging and reinventing the forms of the content of the past for the purposes of poetry in English. Either in parody – Mahony – or in self-consciously sentimental lyric – Thomas Moore – in English the poetry finds a process for formal unions and disunions that bear a mimetic relation with the contexts of its composition. To write a synthetic poetic history of this poetry, we need to acknowledge that Mahony's 'form, style, colour and varnish' are given an outing as the fresh clothes of the new. Whether these together succeed in encapsulating *The Spirit of the Nation* is a moot point, especially given that a significant minority of the poets discussed here would not grant the legitimacy of that nation's desire for a new cultural form for its own 'spirit', its own 'intrinsic substance'.

CHAPTER 4

Samuel Ferguson's Maudlin Jumble

> One thing more before I cease; if I were asked to characterize, as
> shortly as may be, these poems, I should do so by applying to them
> the words of Spenser, 'barbarous truth'.[1]

'Barbarous Truth'

The new Irish lyric in English after Tom Moore gave as many opportunities for Tory fun as it did radical censure, combining the rude and refined
or the authentic and counterfeit in a strange synthetic stew. If Erin had a
tear and a smile in its eye, the mixing of the modes might also be difficult
to pin down: the tear was allied to a subject matter grounded in political as much as amorous defeat, and the smile suggested that amorous or
political mischief was never far away. The author of the *Irish Melodies* was
not just the friend of Byron, but his biographer and co-conspirator in the
destruction of the supposedly scandalous journals. He was also the thinly
veiled ventriloquist behind the *Memoirs of Captain Rock*, a text rather
closer to Irish mischief than its author's London Whig connections might
suggest.[2] Francis Sylvester Mahony's 1830s contemporary, the young barrister and Unionist antiquarian Samuel Ferguson, writing for an Irish Tory
audience, was more willing to accept that the tear was the true expression
of Gaelic poetry and music. He would, however, not shirk translating the
strangeness of writing from a Catholic culture that retained more than
just a memory of its Gaelic past. Not only was it not wholly vanquished,
but after the Emancipation of 1829, it was turning its attentions to the
Union of 1801 itself.

The successes of Daniel O'Connell's popular politics in the late-1820s
and early 1930s were not so much antipathetic background to Ferguson's
work as spur. Along with the Unionist intellectuals involved in the establishment of the *Dublin University Magazine* in 1833, Ferguson sought to
understand the persistence of the culture of a once-pauperised Gaelic

Ireland now turning into a mass English-speaking and increasingly English-reading constituency that was enjoying a first partial enfranchisement. By the 1840s, its first experiments in democracy were to find in the nationalism of the Young Irelanders an ideology developed from the French-inspired republicanism of the United Irishmen of forty years previously. According to Joep Leerssen, one difference between the 1790s and the 1840s was that 'a massive cultural transference took place in Ireland between the Gaelic tradition and the urban English-speaking educated classes' and resulted in 'a complete Gaelic re-orientation of Ireland's public space and public sphere, particularly after Catholic Emancipation'.[3] Leerssen's 'massive cultural transference' or 'complete Gaelic re-orientation' may look slightly counter-intuitive, given the great shift to the English language along with the move to the cities that occurred in these decades. But to take one small example, among the first students enrolled to learn Irish in the newly formed Ulster Gaelic Society in Belfast in 1830 were the Protestant Trinity Unionist Samuel Ferguson and his school friend – later Britain's first Catholic Lord Chancellor under William Gladstone – Thomas O'Hagan.[4] If Leerssen's 'complete Gaelic re-orientation' was given impetus by the participation in the project of the recovery of Gaelic by men concerned to make establishment careers such as Ferguson and O'Hagan, the literary and linguistic interest of that establishment in Gaelic culture was accompanied by a fear that a political transformation might follow the renewed cultural confidence of newly urban English-speaking and English-reading Catholics. Up to the middle of the 1840s, when famine was to disperse cultural revival along with a large part of the population of Catholic Ireland, the Unionist fear, as expressed a few years previously in Ferguson's 1833 *Dublin University Magazine* article, 'A Dialogue Between the Head and Heart of an Irish Protestant', was that this combination of political enfranchisement and cultural resurgence might result not just in repeal of the Union, but 'a violent separation'.[5]

Ferguson's early work served a post-Emancipation Unionist readership that needed to understand the new challenge to its supposed ascendancy. He found the grounds for this understanding in the matter of the poetry and song that had been revealed to English-speaking Ireland by antiquarian research. He also found the matter of that poetry to be inextricably bound up in aesthetic questions, and in particular the question of finding adequate forms for the new English versions of this source material. As noted at the beginning of Chapter 3, in the same month as Mahony's Prout broadside in *Fraser's Magazine*, Ferguson wrote in the *Dublin University Magazine* that no matter how modern, and thus inauthentic, the polite measures or prosodic proprieties of Tom Moore appeared to be, his lyrics still shared something with sources that appeared to come not just from a different aesthetic but a different society. Nevertheless, they offered common ground, if not community:

> The contrast between the native songs and the lyrics of Moore, is indeed strangely striking – as strange as uncouthness can present in juxta position [sic] with politeness, but still no more than that which may be admitted to have distinguished the *Merus Hibernicus*, from the modern Irish gentleman. We will look in vain for the chasteness, the appositeness, the antithetical and epigrammatic point, and the measured propriety of prosody, which delight the ear and the judgement, in a song by Thomas Moore, among the rude rhymes which accompanied the same notes two centuries ago; but the stamen and essence of each is interwoven and transfused through the whole texture and complexion of the other – for sentiment is the soul of song, and sentiment is the one imprescriptible property of the common blood of all Irishmen.[6]

Elsewhere, Ferguson was as wary as Mahony of the organicism implicit in bringing the 'juxta position' of the uncouth and polite forward into union, but here he does dally with metaphors of grafting that are allowed one further mix, into the troubled matter of 'common blood'.

To go from stamen to essence looks like a simple rhetorical shift in synonym, but going from texture to complexion seems inevitably here to lead to blood. It is stirred by sentiment: the 'one imprescriptible property of the common blood of all Irishmen' is the tear rather than the smile. Ferguson later asked that his readers 'no longer imagine that humour is the characteristic of the Irish. Their sentiment is pathetic. Desire is the essence of that pathos'.[7] At the beginning of his literary career, the young Ferguson's purpose was thus to release the sentiment that emerged in pathos from a 'desire' that was seemingly hidden as much in the ribaldry of a Mahony and Maginn as in the chasteness and measure of their bête noire, Moore. Claiming this 'imprescriptible property' for his Protestant readership would enable them to claim the post-Union Protestant patriotism for which Ferguson argued with much anguish. In one of its most telling passages, the 1833 'Dialogue' feared that the rewards of loyalism might be no more than the loss of identity within both Ireland and the larger United Kingdom, because the Irish Protestants might end up, 'neither English nor Irish, fish nor flesh, but a peddling colony, a forlorn advanced guard that must conform to every mutinous movement of the praetorian rabble'.[8]

To suggest a share in the 'common blood' that has as its property the sentiment expressed in Irish song is thus not quite a prefiguring of an

Arnoldian annexation of the imagined Celt into the British racial mix. As the 'Heart' side had earlier averred in the 'Dialogue', 'I know not whence my blood may have been drawn, but it circulates with a swifter liveliness at the name of this country, and I feel and know that I am the heart of an Irishman.'[9] This is more an early Victorian physiology of blood-stirring patriotism than the racial categories of mid-Victorian anthropology. Eve Patten suggests that Ferguson's part of the *Dublin University Magazine* project from the early 1830s through to the great disruption of intellectual revival by the Famine in the latter half of the 1840s was that of 'the young critic playing to a hard-line Unionist gallery',[10] and this might ultimately have been the case. But Ferguson's translating practice and its aesthetic strictures – in particular the terms under which he suggests an English-language culture might thrive in Ireland – were placed in negotiation with the recovery and translation of an Irish–language culture and respect for its corresponding aesthetic strictures. If the end result was to be an argument for the Union, then its considerable sophistication was that it was founded in a literary negotiation prefigured as a sort of poetic power sharing, in which an intuition of a commonality of culture might be allowed to follow the metaphors of a commonality of the blood of the patriot, whether Irish or British, Catholic or Protestant. Ferguson aspired to forge an imagined community that might mature enough in the United Kingdom to allow a peaceful admission of class, sectarian and linguistic differences.

Finding that the first translating efforts to render anew in English the older Irish poetry were unsatisfactory, he sought recompense in translation of a feudal bardic tradition and its successor in Jacobite lyric, both of which he saw as inherently pious (albeit Catholic) and thus recoverably conservative. But he was also prepared to do service in a late flowering of the sentimental expressiveness of a broadly conceived British Romanticism. The Irish contribution would be to find, after the example of Robert Burns or William Wordsworth, its own musical museum or lyrical ballads. As Patten has pointed out, this was a matter of civic idealism as much as scholarly conscience or poetic opportunity, a recasting of Irish Unionist patriotism in the interests of a new intelligentsia in a post-Union Dublin beginning to re-establish its cultural if not political independence within the United Kingdom. Patten rightly emphasises the example of eighteenth-century Scotland for Ferguson and his contemporaries as one British example of a public sphere created in the conditions of vibrant print culture.[11] Colin Graham goes further, stating that 'Scotland is the site in which Ferguson frequently tests out how to configure Irish difference, and, most importantly, how tactically to place Ireland over against England in order to further his goal of bringing Ireland to the centre of the Union, giving it, to twist a phrase, "parity of esteem" within the United Kingdom.'[12] Ferguson began his publishing career in *Blackwood's Edinburgh Magazine*, and it was to provide one model for the *Dublin University Magazine* as a deliberately Irish-centred Unionist forum, if perhaps also a journal concerned to effect the 'goal of bringing Ireland to the centre of the union'. After Ossian, and as one of the great corrective voices of poetic authenticity, Burns in particular provided a connection between something working in a register that was not only lower class but in a supposedly lower aesthetic register – namely folk song. But as we have seen, the lyrics of British folk song provided extraordinary imaginative impetus for the development of British Romantic art, song and poetry, both from the simplicity of diction and sentiment in lyric (the Wordsworthian 'real language of men') and the strong narrative drive of the ballad.

Ferguson nursed a fancy that Burns was 'in all probability of Irish blood', if only on the grounds that 'Had he been a foundling, his face alone would have been considered Irish enough for similar surmise.'[13] But it was the songs that Burns collected, edited and composed that suggested to Irish poets a successful class encounter between the civilised and the barbarous, enabling them to effect the creative linguistic combination of the synthetic in the institutions of the Scottish public realm. This was a combination now in need of creation in Ireland. In the mid-1840s, he saw that Burns's acceptance by 'civilizing institutions' could be of benefit for the programme of a strong Irish literary culture. He also wondered why it had not yet happened:

> Perhaps the main distinction will be found in the use of a language of civilisation, and in the presence of civilizing institutions to which the people were attached. The accident of using a barbarous, or a polished language undoubtedly makes the greatest difference.... Yet for a long time we have had the language and institutions under which these tastes grew up in Scotland among us here; and the question may reasonably be urged – why have they not here been attended with the like results?[14]

This is one of a number of statements of the question in the 1840s, made by Ferguson's nationalist contemporaries grouped around *The Nation* newspaper, which look very much like the statements later to be made again in the 1880s and 1890s at the beginning of an Irish revival that had separatist aims.[15] Ferguson's hope in 1845, given the promotion of original Irish writing in an organ of a different political bent from the *Dublin University Magazine, The Nation*, was that Irish literary culture was beginning to develop 'like results'. His 1847 'Lament for Thomas Davis' (a discussion of which will conclude this chapter), gains much of its power from the great sense of the loss of one exemplar for incipient 1840s literary revival. The other fact of loss, suggested throughout the 'Lament' in its metaphors of harvest and its failure, as well as its mode of indigenous Irish pastoral elegy, was that of Famine and the turning of revival to economic catastrophe and political upheaval as the 1840s progressed.

Even in the Spring of 1845, writing just before the first failures of the potato crop, Ferguson saw that Ireland had yet to establish the social and political conditions for the encouragement of a figure such as Burns. This was not just the security of recent Scottish history and its 'ten thousand modes of peaceful prosperity, and of respect at home and abroad'. It was also,

> that the middle and upper classes of that country were then, as they still are, proudly national, interested in every thing that concerns the interests or reputation of their native land; familiar with its local peculiarities of manners and dialect, and piquing themselves on the perfect sympathy that subsisted between them and the peasantry. If a young Irish farmer of the present day displayed ability, or wrote humorous, pathetic or philosophic verses, he might perhaps look for the worthless laudation of a local newspaper, provided there was a local newspaper of his party within reach; but that he should expect to be taken by the hand and caressed by the gentry of his neighbourhood, that he should hope, even, if he expressed himself with the independence becoming a man of genius, to avoid suspicion and repulse from his neighbours of condition, would be a thing unheard of – a mere suggestion of romance.[16]

If Ferguson's terms are unduly predicated on the imagined persistence of feudalism in Scotland, then those might be framing the issue for the class politics of a journal that hoped to emulate the successes of contemporary journals elsewhere in the United Kingdom. If they were to show a willingness to seek out the writing of another class, then that might be a little more surprising. To ally this with a reiteration of the claim for an Irish sense of nationality to equal that of Scotland, as made in the 1833 'Dialogue' by one who might be thought to be loyal to the Union, then the combination across categories makes Ferguson's contribution not so much an analysis of a culture in need of new matter and new forms, but as one prescription for its remedy. To return to the Hardiman articles of the previous decade, Ferguson had already suggested that the remedy lay in the supposed barbarity of the Gaelic folk song tradition, and the seemingly reckless abandon of its fugitive authors. After all, 'Burns's loose way of living', Ferguson admitted in 1845, 'excluded him from permanently enjoying the society of his best friends and admirers.'[17]

'Páistín Fionn'

Ferguson's various versions of the lyric 'Páistín Fionn' ('little fair child' or 'fair girl') are exemplary of his celebration of the mixture of desire and pathos of Irish song, allied to a sense of the thrill of the loose living of those of another epoch, another class. He called that mixture a 'maudlin jumble'. The publishing afterlife of the song meant republication in Ferguson's 1865 *Lays of the Western Gael*, a markedly different narrative version by Douglas Hyde in his 1893 *Love Songs of Connacht* and a place in Thomas MacDonagh's select anthology of poems of the Irish Mode in *Literature in Ireland*.[18] It is still in the repertoire of the traditional singer, often in macaronic versions. Yeats also published a number of versions of the lyric based on Ferguson's translation. It was first inserted into the 1911 revision of the one-act play *A Pot of Broth* along with the Tramp character's imagined memory of its performance by the lovesick boys of the parish: 'such of them that had any voice at all and not choked with crying, or senseless with the drop of drink they took to comfort them and to keep their wits from going, with the loss of you'. The Tramp relates its composition by a lovesick artisan poet:

> I was standing by the man that made the song, and he writing it with the old bit of a carpenter's pencil, and the tears running down –
>
>> My Paistin Finn is my sole desire,
>> And I am shrunken to skin and bone,
>> For all my heart has had for its hire
>> Is what I can whistle alone and alone.
>> *Oro, oro!*
>> *To-morrow night I will break down the door.*[19]

The lyric eventually came fully into the Yeats canon in 1935, as one of 'Two Songs Rewritten for the Tune's Sake'.[20]

In 1834, Ferguson's initial introduction of the song didn't promise much, but the terms are the same as those offered by Yeats's Tramp. Ferguson ventured an unmetrical translation of the final stanza and glossed it thus:

> Now, this is the conclusion of as maudlin a jumble of incongruous parts as ever came staggering into the imagination of a man half-drunk, half-desperate; yet it is arranged with a perfect minuteness of verbal propriety. When we call it a maudlin jumble, we do not mean to say that it makes the worse song. We are sure Pastheen Finn thought it all the better for evincing, as it does, the bothered state to which she had reduced her sweetheart; and only wondered, as we do, how, under the united influences of such a quantity of love and drink, he could attend so clearly to the minor details

of a subject, the general arrangement of which appears to have so much perplexed him.[21]

The stanza that provokes this praise of an aesthetic of incongruity alternating with 'perfect minuteness of verbal propriety' had been translated at first literally from the Irish text given by Hardiman:

> Tréigfead mo chápáid 's mo cháirde gaoil
> U'r tréigfid mé á mhaireann de mhnáibh a' t-saoíghil;
> Ní thréigfead le'm mharthainn tú, ghrádh mo chróidhe!
> Go sínfear á g-cómhra faoí chlár mé.[22]

> I shall forsake my friends and my friendly relations,
> And I shall forsake all the other girls in the world;
> But I shall not forsake, during my existence, you, love of my heart,
> Till I be laid in the coffin under the clay![23]

In its way, this looks like a stock declaration of undying love. But Ferguson has drawn our attention to 'the minor details', and these appeared in the eventual metrical version of the song published as one of the twenty 'Versions from the Original Irish' appended to the fourth and final article in the series.

These are the last three stanzas as printed in the fourth Hardiman article in November 1834:

> Were I in the town where's mirth and glee,
> Or twixt two barrels of barley bree,
> With my fair Pastheen upon my knee,
> 'Tis I would drink to her pleasantly!
> > Then Oro, come with me, come with me, come with me,
> > Oro, come with me, brown girl sweet!
> > And, oh, I would go through snow and sleet,
> > If you would come with me, my brown girl sweet!

> Nine nights I lay in longing and pain,
> Betwixt two bushes, beneath the rain,
> Thinking to see you, love, once again;
> But whistle and call were all in vain –
> > Then, Oro, come with me, etc.

> I'll leave my people, both friend and foe,
> From all the girls in the world I'll go,
> But from you sweetheart, oh, never, oh, no,
> 'Till I in the coffin, stretched cold and low!
> > Then Oro, come with me, etc.[24]

Ferguson's gloss is in keeping with the precocity of his performance in the Hardiman articles as a whole, and, as he had shown in his 1833 'Dialogue', what he describes as an instinctive desire to 'declare ourselves one of the

number of those who can feel for, and sympathise with, the poor Papist'.[25]
If Ferguson at one stage suggests he might feel one with the papist, he
eventually holds back from such union, and a romantic feeling for the
oppressed meets its successor, Victorian sympathy. In his understanding
of a lyric such as 'Páistín Fionn', Ferguson aspires in his Hardiman articles
to serve what will become both a romantic and an antiquarian ideal, of
the understanding and toleration of difference not unity within the whole
culture of Ireland. With remarkable prescience, Ferguson's early *Dublin
University Magazine* essays work out in the 1830s a formula for the ces-
sation of antagonism and hostility through tolerance within the United
Kingdom.

A 'maudlin jumble' is not a continuous, sympathetic, unified, aesthetic
artefact. Whatever the mimetic achievement of the drunken desperation
of the lover speaking through a drunkenly desperate lyric, Ferguson can
admit that the jumble of incongruous parts is matched by perfect minuteness of verbal propriety. He wonders at the art of the translated balladeer
while worrying over his state of mind. Little is hidden or sentimentalised
in Ferguson's version: the girl's lover veers from the fantasy of two full barrels of beer and easy sex to the desperation of his nine nights sleeping out
alone in the rain, and the eventual imagining of his own ageing and love-
struck death. Those two barrels, two bushes and nine nights are retained
in Yeats's version, which in its eventual revision and publication becomes
a lyric attached to an aged libertine, a song from an old man, perhaps a
dirty old man. The two barrels, two bushes and nine nights suggest either
some blaspheming on Catholic liturgical numerology (the novena, for
instance) or naturalistic particularity: the indigent lyricist really did sleep
out for nine nights. The lyric is barely constrained in sentiment, while
precise and economical in expression: the pleading of the refrain conveys
simple unornamented desire for its peasant object, who despite her fair
hair has the sunburnt skin of the worker in the fields – she is a brown girl
sweet. Ferguson allows in the characteristic prosodic decorations of direct
repetition ('brown girl sweet' rhymes with 'itself'), and the lyric extravagance of obsessive internal rhyme: 'And oh, I would go, through snow and
sleet.'

And he makes certain decisions about translating the Gaelic, both
literally and in terms of the considerations of finding adequate English
verse form. Take the last stanza with the two barrels of beer. This was
Hardiman's 1831 Gaelic 'original':

> Dá mbeinnse insa mbaile i mbí súgra is greann.
> Nó idir dhá bharaille lán de leann;

Mo shiúirín im aice 's mo lámh faoina ceann,
Is súgach do ólfainn a sláint.
    Is óró bog liomsa! Bog liomsa! Bog liomsa!
    Is óró bog liomsa! A chailín dheas dhonn!
    Is óró bhogfainn, dá mbogfása lion
    I dtús an phluide go sásta.[26]

Here is Ferguson's literal translation in the April Hardiman reviews:

If I were in the town where's mirth and glee,
Or between two barrels full of ale,
My little darling near me, and my hand under her head,
It is pleasantly I'd drink her health.
    Then vourneen come with me – come with me – come with me,
    And vourneen come with me – damsel beautiful, brown;
    And vourneen I would go, if you would go with me![27]

If we compare these versions with the eventual English poetic version printed the following November, we can say with Breandán Ó Buachalla that 'the basis of Ferguson's success was his strict adherence to the line as the basic metrical and semantic unit ... [in his translating] whatever difference there is being due mainly to metrical exigencies'. As we have seen in Chapter 2, Ó Buachalla is clear that 'the 'different phonological and prosodic systems' of Irish and English mean that it is 'well-nigh impossible to render Irish metres into English', but he does allow the success of an effect in another of Ferguson's translations where he 'let the metrical line run free except for the final foot'.[28]

That is, in deciding on an eventual English-language poetic version in 1834, Ferguson brings it all back into rhyme. There, the triple feet that introduce four full rhymes – mirth and glee, barley bree, upon my knee, pleasantly – sound strange, even primitive, in English. And the odd word there, 'bree', is another sort of translation, of beer into whiskey, and Scotch whiskey at that. Burns's 'Scotch Drink', first published in the Kilmarnock edition of his *Poems* in 1786, counsels, 'How easy can the *barley-bree* / cement the quarrel'. Keats picked up the phrasing in his sonnet written in Burns's cottage in Ayr in 1818, finding, 'My pulse is warm with thine own barley-bree'.[29] Whether Scots-derived or not, the first line of Ferguson's version of 'Páistín Fionn', to follow Ó Buachalla, is hardly even English, syntactically or prosodically: 'Were I in the town where's mirth and glee': 'were' and 'where' link together a line trying not to break up into English common measure at 'town'. Although 'town' does pick up its assonantal music at midpoint later in the stanza with 'Pastheen' and 'drink', and then in the refrain, 'brown', 'snow' and 'brown' again. English is carrying an approximation of both the Irish song and its tune, in assonantal, slant and even sight rhymes.

To grasp just how fresh Ferguson's achievement was in his translation of this little lyric, it must be remembered that he had another English version of the song in mind when he made his. It is one to which he was aware his would act as a corrective, or a sort of counter-translation. It is John D'Alton's English version supplied by Hardiman in the *Irish Minstrelsy*:

> With what rapture I'd quaff it, were I in the hall
> Where feasting – and pledging – and music recall
> Proud days of my country! While she on my breast
> Would recline, my heart's twin one! And hallow the feast.
>> Then Vourneen! fly with me – fly with me – fly with me
>> With thy nut-brown ringlets so artlessly curled;
>> Here is the one that will live and will die with thee,
>> Thy guard and thy guide through the wilds of the world.[30]

Starting with the word 'quaff', D'Alton never gives us more than an insipid drawing-room version of the stanzas. The whiskey barrels are translated into a civic banquet and the desire until death of Ferguson's version is written as drawing-room pastiche, a series of stock sentiments of regret, memory and immortality, stray angels and all. One particularly unfortunate solecism exchanges the brown skin of the blonde country girl (páistin fionn/fair-haired girl) for a dye job and perm: 'nut-brown ringlets so artlessly curled'.

Nothing could be further from the Romantic characteristics of Irish song, as they appeared to Ferguson: 'Desire, despair, and the horrible reality of actual famine – these are the three dread prompters of song', he says. Together they make 'nothing impure, nothing licentious' but rather the 'savage sincerity' that is characteristic of Irish poetry 'in its association with the despondency of conscious degradation, and the recklessness of desperate content, is partly to be found the origin of that wild, mournful, incondite yet not uncouth sentiment which distinguishes the national songs of Ireland from those of perhaps any other nation of the world'. On the one hand this is an assertion of the utter singularity of Irish song. On the other, it represents the challenge to the English poem, or the poet writing in English who might hazard a translation or version of this savage sincerity given the inherent differences of the English and Irish: 'We believe that no dissipating continuance of defeat, danger, famine, or misgovernment, could ever, without the infusion of Milesian blood, Hibernicize the English Peasant; and that no stultifying operation of mere security, plenty or laborious regularity could ever, without actual physical transubstantiation, reduce the native Irishman to the stolid standard of the sober Saxon.'[31] If we hear an irony directed at hybridity here in Ferguson's 'infusion' and 'transubstantiation', in terms which are reminiscent of a similar Tory attack on the synthetic Irish poem published by Mahony in *Fraser's* in London in the same month, Ferguson still moves the argument on.

In the third article his own savagery is reserved for the long footnote in which the severe strictures he places upon D'Alton's versions in Hardiman are even more marked towards other contributors:

> Mr D'Alton's perversions are, however, mere petty-larceny travesties compared with the epic grandeur of Mr Curran's heroic declaration of war against the original. This fierce invader of the barrenness of Irish Literature, gives no quarter to the absence of whatever tropes, sentiments or episodes he may conceive best suited to its creditable Saxonisation. War to the knife against all deficiencies is his slogan, and with pruning-hook in one hand and grafting-knife in the other, he hacks, he hews, he notches, buds, mortises, and mangles; sticks in a ramification of metaphors here, claps on a mistletoe-bough of parasite flowers there, and, in a word, so metamorphoses the original, that it (the Roman Vision for instance,) comes out of his hands as unlike itself as an espalier stock that has been once a crab-tree.[32]

Ferguson particularly savours the irony of the English-language half of Hardiman's ur-nationalist project aspiring for full 'Saxonisation'. But with this emphasis on incongruous parts and maudlin jumble as opposed to Hibernicising the English peasant or Saxonising the Irish poem, what does the Unionist Ferguson think he is doing in his contribution to this debate? Although he seems to be both courting and parodying a discourse of impurity and adulteration, there is also a suggestion that his is an altogether more earnest attempt to revert back to some unadulterated, unadulterable, pre-hybrid feudal state, in which the Irish character existed before or beyond its language, culture, religion and class. A new variety must result from the grafting of a maudlin jumble in the process of Saxonisation.

The extra complication, of course, is that the aesthetic limits placed on the new hybrid form as it crosses over in the process of translation may be at odds with the political aspirations of the critic who describes them. Ferguson, after all, was writing in an organ associated with the landed, Protestant class in Ireland. In the self-same articles he defended property and the Union as the honourable result of a victory won by the class from which he came and for which he wrote. He himself was of Ulster-Scottish 'stock', certainly not willing to be grafted onto the aboriginal Irish

Catholic masses. But through the ironies of his criticism of the nationalist Hardiman he seems to hold out against the aesthetic and antiquarian dangers that Hardiman's practice had unwittingly courted. That is the grafting of the savagely sincere feudal Irish ballad with the polite Whig British lyric, or the intermingling and eventual blending of cultures and classes that might have resulted in the new hybrid poetry of the now thirty or so years of the United Kingdom of Great Britain and Ireland. He certainly did not ascribe to the hopes of one originator of English versions of Irish poems, Charlotte Brooke, who as we have seen in Chapter 1 wrote well before revolution or the Union of the 'nearer acquaintance' between Britain and Ireland that would be achieved by poetry, an acquaintance bearing family resemblances: 'Let them tell her, that the portion of her blood which flows in our veins is rather ennobled than disgraced by the mingling tides that descended from our heroic ancestors.'³³ Brooke envisages her act of translation of Irish poems as creating the circumstances for seduction, teasing the Irish muse out of her embowered state. Not that this teasing need then result in the marriage of Ireland and Britain: that is a fact already for Brooke, given the ennobling of British blood through its mingling with the greater antiquity of Irish heroic tradition.

Samuel Ferguson's version of this is perhaps the best remembered part of his Hardiman articles. He doesn't envisage that his antiquarian project seeks only the high ground of culture, transcending sectarian, class or political conflict. Rather, at the end of the third article, the *Dublin University Magazine* Unionist envisages the 'perfect society' of the 'nation' (his terminology) as shown through the conservative principles the Irish poetry before him shows. But this won't result in a bland union. Before presenting the reader with his version of 'The Fair Hills of Holy Ireland'/'Uileacan dubh O!', Ferguson swaps the high ground for love of country:

> Alas, that a nation glowing with the most enthusiastic courage, moved by the tenderest sympathies and penetrated by a constitutional piety as devoted as profound should so long have misapplied these noblest attributes of a high-destined people! What material for an almost perfect society does the national genius not represent? Instinctive piety, to lay the only sure foundation of human morals and immortal hopes; constitutional loyalty, to preserve the civil compact inviolate; legitimate affection, to ensure public virtue and private happiness; endless humour, to quicken social intercourse; and last – and save one attribute, best – indomitable love of country to consolidate the whole. This sacred loyalty we have reserved for our conclusion, as a green spot of neutral ground, where all parties may meet in kindness, and part in peace.³⁴

This is not union nor consensus nor agreement. Nor is it the forgiving and forgetting that English poems on Irish subjects suggest might be an eminently reasonable solution. Ferguson sees that the parties of Ireland must agree to differ, or in the terms of his later praise of his friend – if political opponent – Thomas Davis: 'Wherever he went, he was surrounded by an atmosphere of good will, which hostile politicians could not enter without mutually conceding "the right to differ", and arguing to do something for the common good'.[35] Nevertheless, as here, for all their kindness given the land over which they claim sovereignty, the parties will part.

As I have argued, Ferguson found in Jacobite and Reformation-era Irish poetry a feudal culture well suited to the Tory readers of the *Dublin University Magazine*: he opens his articles viewing a divided contemporary Ireland, in which his religion had just suffered the trauma of Catholic Emancipation, and his party and class that of the Great Reform Act. Irish poetry presents a simpler, feudal, we might say more Romantic, age. We could easily imagine Walter Scott condoning such sentiments as Ferguson makes, introducing the ancien régime of Irish poetry to his Tory readers: 'We will look nearer to the time when those who had high treason in their hearts had arms in their hands ... when victors and vanquished could afford to seem what they really were, and genuine feeling found utterance undisguised, in the passionate sincerity of exultation or despair.'[36] This passionate sincerity attaches to peasant and aristocrat alike and is manifest in the aesthetic forms of both the heroic and the lyric. Attending to such shifts in category and keen to seek out 'allegories of union', the contemporary critic may still try to run them together rather too quickly. David Lloyd, for instance, is very good on the way in which the plainness of diction or 'uncouthness' of Ferguson's literal translations finds its way in to the eventual verse translations to become 'an essential part of the verse in rhythm and idiom, reflecting exactly Ferguson's idea of the primitive but powerful sentiments of the Irish race'.[37] This may be, like so many of the inventions of Irish poetry in the early nineteenth century, a happy accident as much as conscious artistic design. But primitivism is not entirely the object, given the pressure of epic and heroic models that Ferguson found in the medieval material with which he was to work later in his career, not to mention his more immediately post-Romantic interest in ballad and song.

For Lloyd, Ferguson's sectarian and class politics run easily into the aesthetic theory behind his translations:

> Ferguson's aim was to present a theory of the gradual development of the native Irish loyalties from the immediate clan to the idea of a constitutional

monarchy, obliging a transition from investment in the sensuous to investment in the supersensuous. Knowledge thus becomes unifying rather
than – as with Hardiman – divisive and sectarian. The ideal of transparent
translation repeats this theory [...] it ensures a continuous transition into
which no arbitrariness enters ... [and it] allows for the undisturbed reproduction in English of the essential quality of the Gael, which, for Ferguson,
as for Arnold thirty years later, is 'sentimentality'.[38]

This might well describe Brooke's enlightenment project and Arnold's
liberal call for the renewed study of Celtic literature. But Ferguson's
Romanticism is at odds with such transparently Unionist conceptions of
translation. The notion of an 'ideal of transparent translation' is borrowed
from Robert Welch's praise of Ferguson's English versions, 'remaining
absolutely true in as many particulars as possible, to the spirit, tone and
rhythm of the originals, and to their curious, if at times chaotic image
sequences'.[39] Welch's 'absolutely true' is too strong, and may be answered
by Lloyd's rather bland dismissal of it as naïve; 'a continuous transition
into which no arbitrariness enters'. But most talk of arbitrary signs forestalls much discussion of poetry, and Welch does attend to something
of much more interest in the 'originals' themselves. This is their 'chaotic
image sequences', or indeed, Ferguson's own phrasing: 'as maudlin a jumble of incongruous parts as ever came staggering into the imagination of a
man half-drunk, half-desperate'.

What is this romantic aesthetic of the chaotic, incongruous and jum-
bled? In its way it is an aesthetic of taking your mind off the matter in
hand, distractedness, anomaly and anachronism rather than, to borrow an
apt musical term, the unison envisaged by Charlotte Brooke's 1789 vision
of the British and Gaelic muses walking hand in hand. The year 1789 is
also a date remembered in European history for reasons other than the first
translations of Irish poetry. In Ireland's case it was to be nine years before
revolution of a sort was to come, and one unintended effect of the 1798 rising in Ireland was the Union. Returning to poetry, 1798 was also the year
of Wordsworth and Coleridge's *Lyrical Ballads*, and the preface later fixed
to that production in the year in which the Union took effect – 1801 –
would lay down rules of plain and simple diction that Ferguson could not
ignore thirty years later. It is facile, perhaps, to elevate such coincidences
into the conditions of writing, but writing in 'the real language of men'
became an aim for any number of nineteenth-century poets, a liberating
aim in particular for those keen to sound regional accents. Wordsworth's
preface also offers a description of the metre of poems as a kind of incongruity, a challenge to the sonic mimesis of a poetry in which the sound
must seem an echo to the sense. Wordsworth rewrites Pope when he says

he hears 'something regular' in metre, and that serves a sort of therapeutic function, as it 'cannot but have great efficacy in tempering and restraining the passion by an intertexture of ordinary feeling, and of feeling not strictly and necessarily connected with the passion'. Wordsworth heard this most strongly in the 'artless' metre of 'the old ballads'.[40] The challenge is not only an aesthetics of decorum and appropriateness, but when applied to the Irish poem (or indeed novel), a challenge to the desire that literary form will effect the necessary connections of hybridisation, Hibernicisation, Saxonisation or indeed union.

For Wordsworth's intertexture of feeling not strictly and necessarily connected with the passion, compare Ferguson introducing his English metrical versions of Irish poems in the last of the Hardiman articles:

> Nothing, however, will perplex him [the translator] more than the reconcilement of measure and sentiment. We do not here allude to the compressed character of Irish versification before noticed; but to the marked difference between the characters of the prosody and the sentiment, rendered still more striking where the original is associated with any of the more ancient melodies. Here, while the rhythm and music breathe the most plaintive and pathetic sentiment, the accompanying words, in whatever English dress they may be invested, present a contrast of low and ludicrous images as well as of an incondite simplicity of construction the most striking and apparently absurd. In the original this want of adaptation is by no means apparent; but to preserve in English those almost evanescent touches which there counteract the otherwise inevitable absurdity of the piece is next to impossible. True, the words of such songs are invariably less ancient than their music; and from being confined to the peasantry, may well be supposed to have acquired a corresponding uncouthness by frequent interpolations and corruptions of the original text. Poetical art is the greatest desideratum in all; in none, even the most grotesque, is there any lack of poetical feeling.[41]

Ferguson is talking about much more than the conundrum of translating the sounds of poems here. It is a highly sophisticated poetic argument borrowing in equal parts from a Romantic aesthetic of expressiveness or 'sentiment' and an antiquarian concern for textual history or the 'incondite simplicity' of the authentic. The rhythm of the Irish lyrics owes much to the melodies for which the lyrics were composed, melodies often much older than the lyrics themselves. By a sort of double archaeological process the translator must both convey the Irish-language lyric excavated from the past and hint at the quite separate history of its melody.

As we have seen in Chapter 2, Ferguson's contemporary Edward Walsh insisted on 'writing the measure of the translation to the exact song-tune of the original', and his inheritor Thomas MacDonagh recognised the textual differences of 'Irish poems that sing to the same air'.⁴² Both suggest that considerations of melody allow both effective translation and an acknowledgement of the histories of textual difference when song and melody may have allied themselves in a number of differing partnerships without fear of accusations of promiscuity. If histories of lyric and melody, like prosody and sentiment, may allow marked differences, as Ferguson puts it, then the low and ludicrous in the sentiment can only hint at the plaintive and pathetic mode they borrow. A Wordsworthian 'intertexture of ordinary feeling' must be conveyed in the English poem. And for all the difficulty of doing that in translation, Ferguson seeks to suggest 'those almost evanescent touches which there counteract the otherwise inevitable absurdity'. The perplexity at 'the reconcilement of measure and sentiment', the 'marked difference' of prosody and sentiment, the counteracting of verbal propriety and peasant feeling: nothing could be further than an 'ideal of transparent translation'. Sect, class and imagined ethnic difference all agree to differ. Whereas the English version seeks to convey the jumble of the peasant original, to mark its difference albeit in English, the hope is that when English and Irish part, as they must, it will be in peace.

'this *Random Clink*': 'The Fairy Thorn'

Using acts of translation as political acts is of course explicit in Brooke and Ferguson, and implicit in Wordsworth. One romantic aesthetic, however, promotes disjunction and difference where the political circumstances might have led us to expect the outcome that Brooke felt translation could deliver, the union of Britain and Ireland. Both Ferguson and Wordsworth had another model for their related poetics of jumble or 'feeling not strictly connected with the passion'. As hinted previously, this was in the example of the languages of Scotland and the matter of Scottish song. Hardiman's *Irish Minstrelsy* gave rise to many Victorian publishing projects from Ferguson's reviews and counter-translations and his later *Lays of the Western Gael*, through the anthologies of Young Ireland in the 1840s and the vital collaborations of James Clarence Mangan with James Duffy. Behind them lay four great 'United Kingdom'/'British' publishing projects of the late eighteenth and early nineteenth centuries. In Dublin and London, these were the Power brothers' publication of Thomas Moore and John Stevenson's blockbusting *Irish Melodies*. In Edinburgh, the other three were James Johnson's *Scots Musical Museum* (1787–1803), George

Thomson's *Select Collection of Scottish Airs* (1794–1818) and Walter Scott's 1802 *Minstrelsy of the Scottish Border* (to which Hardiman's title paid tribute). The first two involved the great examplar for all this new poetry of the vernacular, Robert Burns.

Johnson and Thomson's projects are quite different. The earlier was concerned, as stated on Johnson's title page, to retain 'the original simplicity of our Ancient National Airs ... unincumbered with useless Accompaniments & graces depriving the heavens of the meet simplicity of their native melodies'.[43] Compared with this claim for authenticity, Thomson's project seems to add airs and graces aplenty, offering the symphonic accompaniments to Scottish melodies that, when, as with those accompaniments later composed by Sir John Stevenson, would bring such antiquarian calumny on Moore's melodies. Thomson was as much entrepreneurial editor as publisher, and Burns's early correspondence with him is full of defences of the language of contributions that might not play so well among Thomson's polite subscribers. Burns knew that he was taking many liberties with the Scots originals that he remembered or collected for these publishing projects. But the concern is more with renovation than translation or composition anew. He was keen to keep authentic elements within them. To this end he took extraordinary pains with the rhythm of the lyrics to be attached to the airs chosen. More than this, he insisted on maintaining Scots:

> If it were possible to procure songs of merit, I think it would be proper to have one set of Scots words to every air – & that the set of words to which the notes ought to be pricked. – There is a naïveté, a pastoral simplicity, in a slight intermixture of Scots words and phraseology, which is more in unison (at least to my taste, & I will add, to every genuine Caledonian taste,) with the simple pathos, or rustic sprightliness, of our native music, than any English verses whatever.[44]

This is just one example of Burns's defence of Scots: elsewhere it is 'a sprinkling of our native tongue' or 'a dash of our native tongue'. It is all in the interests of 'Simplicity', the simplicity of the 'native features' of the 'National Music': 'frequently wild, & unreduceable to the modern rules; but on that very eccentricity, perhaps, depends a great part of their effect.'[45] In the extract here, the musical term 'unison' is achieved, somewhat paradoxically, by a 'slight intermixture', which tells strongly against 'English verses'. Thomson, too, printed 'English' lyrics to the melodies as well as Burns's synthetic Scots, Scots-English or 'British' versions, with their sprinkling, dash or 'slight intermixture of Scots words and phrases'.

These are matters of composition and taste, but as with Ferguson later, they amount to a deliberate courting of elements of dissonance, stirring the smooth waters of late Augustan song by rocking the decorous boat of unison:

> There is a peculiar rhythmus in many of our airs, and a necessity for adapting syllables to the emphasis, or what I would call the *feature notes*, of the tune, that cramps the poet, & lays him under insuperable difficulties. – For instance, in the air My wife's a wanton wee thing, if a few lines, *smooth & pretty*, can be adapted to it, it is all you can expect. – [...] on farther study I might give you something more profound, yet it might not suit the lightsome gallop of the air so well as this *random clink*.[46]

From maudlin jumble back to random clink: Ferguson claimed Irishness for Burns, his features, his name, his sentimentality. Ferguson's difficulties with Irish prosody are matched by Burns's confession of difficulty with the folk tune.

Burns, like Ferguson, attended not just to the setting of English and Scots words to tunes, the adaptation, renovation or translation of words and music. In one sense, Robert Crawford is quite right when he says, 'Burns often writes as if the political Union of 1707 has effected a linguistic union, giving him an enlarged territory in which to operate. Linguistically, he is the most brilliantly distinguished eighteenth-century example of a British poet.'[47] Looking at other poets who worked within an even more enlarged Union, the implicit metaphor of union as marriage can inhibit those who might hear the immense subtlety of prosodic difference, jumble and deliberate randomness in the linguistic and literary aspects of these projects of archaeology and renovation. For all his efforts at claiming 'Britishness' for a writer such as Burns, Crawford cannot but admit the mixed nature of the project as English, Scots, Scots-English or whatever. Ferguson joins Burns – in the terms of G. Gregory Smith's classic study of Scottish literature, published from his Chair of English in Queen's University Belfast in the middle of the Irish War of Independence in 1919 – as a sort of ventriloquising editor, writing 'alternate layers or a mosaic of styles', employing 'the delicate colouring of standard English with Northern tints'.[48] Smith remembers Tom Moore's rather more satiric comments on the experiments of Scottish novelist John Galt's language, 'Scotch, English, and slang, in promiscuous alliance',[49] a rather risqué linguistic union, as there seem to be at least three in the bed.

It was when Ferguson carried this contact of English poetry with the random clink or maudlin jumble of the languages of his sort of Northern

Britishness into the first attempts at original poems that a desire for translation or renovation began to shade into an originating moment for the Irish-English, or perhaps even 'Ulster-Scots', poem. At the risk of courting anachronism, this phrase might be applied to Ferguson's celebrated 'Fairy Thorn', and its companion piece, 'The Fairy Well of Lagnanay'. In the terms used about Burns previously in this chapter, it was composed through the 'accident of using a barbarous, or a polished language', and the poems shuttle with some aplomb between both registers. As such they might be compared to a poem such as Burns's 'Tam O'Shanter', which was written in both Scots and standard English, and conveys both the recklessness of a night on the tiles and an effective supernatural chill. In the poems by Burns and Ferguson a twilit voyeurism plays through the inherent eroticism of the supernatural. Where Burns is bawdy, Ferguson's poem edges into a pre-Victorian version of the eroticised fairy abduction poem, in which predominantly female adolescent characters are led into melancholy and withdrawal, or worse, death and disappearance. It would not be until Yeats's 'The Stolen Child', first published in the year of Ferguson's death in 1886, that the fairy poem could celebrate a surrender of this world for a mingling dance with its mystical alternative. Before then it was composed by Ferguson as wild speechless terror, and variously by Christina Rossetti in 'Goblin Market' (1862) as a rite of passage from which only a sisterly love might serve to salve the trauma, or in Robert Browning's 'Pied Piper of Hamelin' (1842) and William Allingham's 'The Fairies' (1850) on a sliding scale of mischief, from the 'fear of little men' to the abduction of an entire generation of children in revenge for magic not adequately repaid.

Ferguson's two fairy poems seem to mingle in two linguistic worlds, both that of the late Romantic art-poem, suitable for publication in *Blackwoods* or the *Dublin University Magazine*, and that suggested by the subtitle of 'The Fairy Thorn: An Ulster Ballad'. To begin with 'The Fairy Well', the first published of the poems (although mistakenly so, according to Peter Denman who recounts Ferguson's insistence that the poems were a pair and should have been published as such).[50] The poem begins with a refrain, 'Mournfully, sing mournfully', borrowed from the refrain of Wordsworth's faux-Scottish ballad of 1807, 'The Seven Sisters': 'Sing, mournfully Oh! mournfully/The solitude of Binnorie'. It is also the opening line of Felicia Hemans's 1829 'Nightingale's Death-Song'. Hemans's poem turns from its theme of a mournful mutability to one of joy in a sort of common-measure casting of Keats's 'Ode to a Nightingale' in reverse.[51] Wordsworth's ballad had relocated a German tale to Scotland, with the seven beautiful daughters

of Archibald Campbell fleeing from Irish marauders and plunging together
into a lake, as they prefer the consolations of suicide and supernatural
remembrance to the loss of their virtue:

> The stream that flows out of the lake,
> As through the glen it rambles,
> Repeats a moan o'er moss and stone,
> For those seven lovely Campbells.
> Seven little islands, green and bare,
> Have risen from out the deep;
> The fishers say, those sisters fair
> By faeries all are buried there,
> And there together sleep.
> Sing, mournfully, Oh! Mournfully,
> The solitude of Binnorie.[52]

In a simple synthetic recreation of ballad forms and diction, Wordsworth
blends the sounds of Scottish-English – 'glen', 'the 'rambles'/'Campbells'
rhyme, 'Binnorie' – with a Romantic refrain and the lore of place.

In 'The Fairy Well', Ferguson's refrain serves other purposes, constructed
as it is in four complex twenty-line stanzas. A different refrain opens and
closes every stanza, rhyming parenthetically twice more within the stanzas,
striking a strong determinant of rhyme. When the refrain is not rhyming
with itself – that is, in full repetition – it needs six more rhymes in the
stanza, thus ten lines together contributing to a sort of mournful ballad
monotone against which the tale of a girl actively seeking fairy enchantment is told. Take the example of the third stanza, where the repeated
refrain comments in differing ways on the behaviour of the peasant heroine of the poem, Una Bawn, behaving with less than modest virtue:

> All alas! and wellaway!
>   'Oh, sister Ellen, sister sweet,
> Come with me to the hill I pray,
>   And I will prove that blessed freet!'
>   They rose with soft and silent feet,
> They left their mother where she lay,
>   Their mother and her care discreet,
> (All alas! And wellaway!)
>   And soon she reached the Fairy Well,
> The mountain's eye, clear, cold and gray,
>   Wide open in the dreary fell;
>   How long they stood 'twere vain to tell,
> At last upon the point of day,
>   Bawn Una bares her bosom's swell,

(All alas! And wellaway!)
>   Thrice o'er her shrinking breasts she laves
The gliding glance that will not stay
>   Of subtly-streaming fairy waves; –
And now the charm three brackens craves,
She plucks them in her fring'd array; –
>   Now round the well her fate she braves.
All alas! and wellaway![53]

From the stock 'wellaway' ballad refrain onwards, this mixes the archaic and Romantic and forbidden in quite unsettling ways. It also mixes etymologies and antiquities of English, while also hinting at Irish. Una Bawn, or 'fair Una', is maybe only a small Gaelicism, although Gaelic had appeared earlier in place names: the mountain of Sleamish and the townland of Lagnanay, and later in the name Jurlath Daune. But the precision of the Old Norse 'freet' (anything to which superstition attaches, a charm) rhyming with the odd description of the girls' mother as 'discreet' (judicious, prudent, cautious) sets up a strand of English archaisms of various derivations through the stanza. A 'fell' comes from the Old Norse for 'mountain' and remains a Northern British word for 'wild moorland'. 'Laves' is Latin and possibly German, meaning 'to wash', although the figurative use of 'gliding glance', of appearing to wash her breasts in light, might have come to Ferguson through a piece of Walter Scott's supernaturalism: *Oxford English Dictionary* gives an example from *The Lady of the Lake*: 'And, when the midnight moon did lave/Her forehead in the silver wave.'

'The Fairy Well of Lagnanay' certainly deserves to be rescued from the unfortunate obscurity that followed its odd publishing history, but it is best read as a less-successful iteration of the poem that Ferguson intended to precede it. 'The Fairy Thorn', published in the *Dublin University Magazine* a year later, in the month before Ferguson's Hardiman articles, is a masterpiece of narrative and linguistic dissolution, at once ending in a dissolve of human into inhuman while still suspending itself in a mixture of the languages of the United Kingdom and the prosodic form of Ferguson's Irish-English ballad metre. Its tale is not so much of the lore of place, such as Wordsworth's 'Seven Sisters', as a deliberately vague tale of enchantment and the supernatural that might have slipped into the more obvious enchantments of Celticism if it wasn't for its deliberations over the specifics of its linguistic and prosodic form. Its influence on much of the Irish poetry that followed it in the nineteenth century was as much to do with its diction and melodic form as it was to do with its subject matter. Take three-quarters of Hugh Kenner's extraordinarily high praise of the first stanza:

> 'Get up, our Anna dear, from the weary spinning-wheel;
> For your father's on the hill, and your mother is asleep:
> Come up above the crags, and we'll dance a highland-reel
> Around the fairy thorn on the steep.'

> This haunts with its density of consonance and assonance – *hill* for instance is part of the *wheel-reel* cluster, and *dear* and *weary* echo one another from the second and fourth strong beats in their line, so do, less obviously, *crags* and *dance*. Later *Fairy* remembers *dear* and *weary*. And that hypnotic, elusive rhythm with its arrested fourth line – has anything like it been heard in English before? Only music can explain such seeming invention on the part of a minor though industrious poet. Ferguson had, as the Celts say, 'a chune in his head', not anything counted by syllables.[54]

Leaving aside the gratuitous dig at the innumerate musicality of the 'Celts' at the end of this passage, to say that 'The Fairy Thorn' conceives of its prosody as gained from 'not anything counted by syllables' remembers the example of Moore most strongly, and was in turn picked up by such as Yeats and MacDonagh in the retrospective construction of 'Irish Mode' verse. Yet it is also a form of Romantic lyrical ballad, in one sense aware of its status as art object, and in another concerned to speak the real language of men – or, in this case, women.

That language is the English of the Northern counties of Ireland, both Gaelicised and telling of the histories of the waves of English that had settled into that place. The word 'Ulster' in the title might be derived from the Irish *Uladh Tír*, 'land of the men of Ulster'. The word 'crag' appears in the first stanza, a word possibly derived from the Gaelic *carraig*, or 'rock'.[55] But the diction of what follows mixes the archaic, seemingly obsolete and dialect with extraordinary density of effect. The girls in the poem set off to 'dance a highland-reel.' They are 'merry maidens fair in kirtles of the green' ('kirtles' is an old English or Old Norse word for a petticoat; *Oxford English Dictionary* doesn't record it after 1825). There are rowan trees beside the Fairy Hawthorn, Norse rowan against Old English haw and Saxon thorn. The rowan trees gave the hawthorn 'ruddy kisses' (Old English), as the girls 'caroll'd' (Middle English from Old French) around them. We go on to encounter 'haunted braes' (Old Norse, but *brae* is also a Scots ballad poeticism) and 'the gloaming' of the light effects of the Celtic twilight ('gloaming' is actually a word with Old

English etymology, but the *Oxford English Dictionary* is full of examples from Burns and Walter Scott):

> But solemn is the silence of the silvery haze
> That drinks away their voices in echoless repose,
> And dreamily the evening has still'd the haunted braes,
> And dreamier the gloaming grows.
>
> And sinking one by one, like lark-notes from the sky
> When the falcon's shadow saileth across the open shaw,
> Are hush'd the maiden's voices, as cowering down they lie
> In the flutter of their sudden awe.[56]

A 'shaw' is a small wood, already an archaic or dialect word by the beginning of the nineteenth century. Ferguson incorporates the word into the mouth music of the poem, in that cluster of sounds from 'shadow saileth' through 'shaw' into 'hushed' and the rhythm of enchantment of the final line, which is allowed to resolve into rhyme: 'In the flutter of their sudden awe' where 'flutter' is allowed to presage four unstressed syllables, thus shoring up the emphasis on 'sudden awe'.

If this is an effect not achieved by counting syllables, then once the girls in the poem stop dancing and the fairies appear, the diction of the poem changes and becomes a more conventional late-Romantic English-language narrative: 'And they sink down together on the green', where green is both grass and village green, English common land. The poeticisms of 'faint enchantment ... anguish and perilous amaze ... quivering eyes' are followed by the beautiful archaism reserved for the waking of the remaining girls to the fact of the loss of their friend:

> Till out of night the earth has roll'd her dewy side,
> With every haunted mountain and streamy vale below;
> When, as the mist dissolves in the yellow morning tide,
> The maidens' trance dissolveth so.

'Dissolveth' seems to dissolve itself into the concluding voiced dental fricative of its archaic ending, consonants submerged in the lengthening of syllable as if holding out a last hope of solid form in the face of poetic as much as moral dissolution.

Colin Graham only slightly overstates the case when he says that Ferguson's praise of Robert Burns is replicated in his 'Lament for Thomas Davis':

> As Burns seeps into Davis so Ferguson is able to give substance to the vision he has of an Irish poetics which proclaim place but not politics, which are replete with manliness but not excess, and which will, through the force of

nature and its transcendent embodiment of a national culture, ensure the future under, or just maybe outside, the union.[57]

That seeping of a Scottish poet held up as an examplar of union into the short-lived liberal intellectual leader of the Young Irelanders is maybe not quite the dissolve at the end of 'The Fairy Thorn'. But to turn from what Yeats could readily adopt as a fairy and folk tale of the Irish peasantry to the pastoral elegy that is 'The Lament for Thomas Davis' is to conceive of a generic breadth, if not quite a maudlin jumble. Ferguson was to collect his lyrics in the 1860s and devote his considerable literary and antiquarian energies in ways perhaps to be expected from a Royal Irish Academician. His versions of Irish epic had their adherents, Yeats among them, for whom they exemplified Spenserian 'Barbarous truth'.[58]

'The Lament', however, does mark one sort of ending for the first flush of Irish lyric written in English before the Famine. Another sort of ending, even if it is an aesthetic of perpetuating an end in 'ever-mourning memory', might be seen in the example of the career of James Clarence Mangan, subject of Chapter 5. In both cases, strong personal matter is pushed up against the limits of Irish-English poetry at this phase of its union with Great Britain. 'The Lament' was written at a time of personal illness and on the day of Davis's death, according to Charles Gavan Duffy.[59] The poem is also from the first year of a famine that was to change the fortunes of more than Irish poetry, but in its geographical reach, from Ballinderry (Shannon) to Ballyshannon (Ulster) and Derrybawn (Wicklow), it traverses a fecund country, scattering seed, watching salmon leap and listening to the eagle's cry. As Ferguson was to announce (anonymously) in his *Dublin University Magazine* obituary for Davis, which concludes with the poem, it is also written in a consolidated Irish style, 'in the language as expressed at the time, of one of his friends, who has adopted the peculiar Irish taste in his composition, which it was poor Davis's delight to inculcate, and which though it invites to a composition that may seem rugged to English eyes, possesses a regular melody for Irish ears, and comes home to Irish hearts'.[60] The 'Lament' ends with the Carlylean and manly virtues of self-help and progress familiar to many students of Victorian literature:

> Oh, brave young men, my love, my pride, my promise,
>   'Tis on you my hopes are set,
> In manliness, in kindliness, in justice,
>   To make Erin a nation yet;
> Self-respecting, self-relying, self-advancing –
>   In union or in severance, free and strong –

> And if God grant this, then, under God, to Thomas Davis
> Let the greater praise belong.

The poem adds in what looks like a note of unconcern for the future, which might perhaps be unexpected in the pages of the *Dublin University Magazine*: 'In union or in severance', as if both were up for grabs in 1845. It might be said that it agrees to differ, if not to indifference, before the loss of his friend. But it manages to celebrate the life of one who strove 'To make Erin a Nation yet', echoing Davis's most famous song lyric, 'A Nation Once Again'. It is a task to which this poem contributes, moving the maudlin jumble of the rugged but regular into national melody.

CHAPTER 5

Mangan's Golden Years

The Contemporeity of the Past

Writing in 1983, during one of the darker periods of recent Irish history, the historian Oliver MacDonagh sought to provide context for two centuries of Anglo-Irish conflict by distinguishing between English and Irish conceptions of time. Tracing conflicting historiographies back to the eighteenth and nineteenth centuries, he found Irish histories to be 'ahistorical' when compared with the British story of social development and beneficial change:

> But if change is the 'objective' historian's point of concern, time is the coinage in which he deals; and if this early phase of history-writing is remarkable for its imperception of change, it is no less remarkable for its conception of time. This is relevant to us today because the early history-writing both shaped and solidified what was to prove an enduring characteristic in Irish political attitudes. Negatively, it may be described as an absence of a developmental or sequential view of past events. Positively, it implies a mode or habit of judgement and apprehension outside a chronologically-calibrated, or indeed any, time scale.

MacDonagh goes on to view this as one consequence of a 'deeply Christian' worldview, by which he means Catholic: 'at any rate, by those Christians who sheer off from the idea of predestination', those who 'view God as standing outside time entirely, without yesterdays or tomorrows, omnipresent in an ever-present'.[1]

A distinctive Catholic Irish historiography, founded on a notion of what MacDonagh calls the 'contemporeity of the past',[2] has become less sectarian in recent accounts of nineteenth-century writing, from a variety of critical and historical positions. Even if mid-century Catholic Ireland couldn't quite believe in predestination, Chris Morash suggests the famine-stoked populist fears of millenarian catastrophe.[3] This apocalyptic strain is just one symptom of what Clare O'Halloran describes as a popular Irish Victorian history writing attracted to a semi-mythical 'Golden Age', arrested by colonisation but still promising an epochal return: 'All shared the same sense of the past as ever-present, its intransigent problems only to be solved by the future-to-come.'[4] As we will see in Chapter 6, Colin Graham describes this as a turning to a future that could be utopian or Atlantean (or even American), but critics such as David Lloyd and Michael Cronin find the writing of this period caught in a temporal and historiographical paradox. For Lloyd, 'A tension can be seen to subsist' in a text such as James Clarence Mangan's poem 'The Warning Voice', between an imperative for 'the nationalist projection of unification into the future' and, in Lloyd's wordplay, 'the situation that provokes that *imminence*, that is of the realisation of the *immanent* idea of the nation'.[5] For the historiographer as well as the literary critic, this sense of the contemporary past is played through the contrary urges of the empirical and imaginative, between the collecting of the antiquarian and imaginative appropriations of the translator. Cronin tells us that William Hamilton Drummond pointed out in 1852 that the performance of the Irish-language songs and lyrics he was collecting and translating for posterity 'is not yet altogether obsolete'. So although the Gaelic lyric tradition was by no means past, it suited one sort of historiographical practice to treat it as such. Cronin invokes the anthropologist Johannes Fabian to call this the 'denial of co-evalness',[6] but such an antiquarian need to deny the coeval was often in paradoxical relation with a Romanticism drawn to ruins while at the same time compelled to conceive their imaginative repopulation.

MacDonagh is clear that this need not be an exclusively Irish debate over what is a cyclical view of history, suggesting that it was shared by Machiavelli and Vico, for instance. They were later to be much plundered and parodied by James Joyce along with the Catholic Irish historiography he also lampooned. One predecessor who so influenced the young Joyce also viewed contemporary Irish history as doomed to repeat the defeats of the past, and quite frequently with similar alternations between the confessional and the parodic. That predecessor was James Clarence Mangan, and he provides MacDonagh with a closing illustration of 'the national sense of the illusoriness of apparent achievement and the suddenness with which fair prospects might dissolve'.[7] MacDonagh's example is the last stanza of Mangan's 1846 'Vision of Connaught in the Thirteenth Century'. It ends with a sudden 'change/From light to darkness, from joy to woe!' where a vision of the repopulated Golden Age is interrupted by an apocalyptic mid-century landscape peopled only by the remains of the human:

> But lo! the sky
> Showed flekt with blood, and an alien sun
> Glared from the north
> And there stood on high
> Amid his short beams, A SKELETON![8]

An interruption such as this might be one of what Seamus Deane calls 'the intricate negotiations of cultural nationalism with its version of a discontinuous history'.[9] Certainly such a wilful narrative discontinuity is not so much the contemporary forcing itself into a recreation of the past, as the pulling up short in the catastrophic circumstances of famine a desire for the eternalising visionary moment. It is despairing both of redemption and aesthetic completion: that capitalised, exclamatory, 'A SKELETON!' is both gothic upset and prosodic ruin. The voice will eventually be held up by the demands of the metre in the ghastly rhyme of 'alien sun' and the paradoxically quietening iambs of the Irish-accented 'a skele*tun*'. Expecting the gothic, the effect is eventually only one of the dis-ease of returning metrical regularity.

Gothic upset and prosodic ruin such effects might be, but they are also distinctive features of Mangan's style that we have to learn to read again. On occasions such as this, Mangan gives to poetry in English a new aesthetic form pressed into a set of historical conditions and historiographical and theological diagnoses from which there seemed no political, let alone aesthetic, opportunity for escape. 'History encloses him so straitly that even his fiery moments do not set him free from it,'[10] Joyce said of Mangan, and that 'History' is both context for the writing and oppressive determinant of its form. Form and content, style and sense, tempo and change, predestination and hindsight: Mangan's aesthetic is bound up with his contrary subject matter throughout his writing. The difficulty is that although the content views both the seeming impossibility of change and the endurance of suffering in time, form may similarly mark only endurance or, as is more likely, incessant return to the dilemmas of a sense of the 'contemporeity' of the defeats of centuries before. As Ian McBride put it, writing twenty years after MacDonagh, 'The time-warped character of Irish mindsets has become a cliché of scholarly and unscholarly Irish writing.'[11] A poetry thus enclosed straitly in Irish history may also be doomed only to cliché, endlessly to repeat itself as it is tugged into the predestinations of its characteristically mannered rhymes.

It would be insular, however, to suggest this was entirely an Irish pre-occupation in the nineteenth century. Mangan is not the only English-language poet of the time who was drawn to repetition and its attendant aesthetic claustrophobia. In 1854, Matthew Arnold could accuse himself and other Victorian poets of writing a poetry that lacked the Goethean, and before that Aristotelian, '*Architectonicè* in the highest sense; that power of execution, which creates, forms, and constitutes'. Instead, there can be no 'poetical enjoyment' from situations 'in which a continuous state of mental distress is prolonged, unrelieved by incident, hope, or resistance; in which there is everything to be endured, nothing to be done'.[12] Arnold may very well have had the foremost English poet of the day in his sights, Alfred Tennyson, a poet drawn to the drawn-out. When not writing seem-ingly endless elegy governed by incessant refrain and repetitive structures, Tennyson appeared compelled to the imaginative impersonation of a long-gone classical, and then British Arthurian, past. *In Memoriam* (1850, but written over seventeen years from 1833), invokes Goethe at its beginning, only to mark Tennyson's difference from a Goethean view of a progressive 'evolutionary' sense of self and human history:

> I held it truth, with one who sings
>   To one clear harp in divers tones,
>   That men may rise on stepping-stones
> Of their dead selves to higher things.[13]

'I *held* it truth' and can no longer. Mangan shared Arnold's interest in a German-influenced alternative, but that was not the preferred classicism or epic Arnold admired in Goethe. Mangan did translate Goethe, but it was, as Robert Welch and David Lloyd have pointed out, German poems of *Sehnsucht*, or those that lingered in an aesthetic of unachievable long-ing, to which he was attracted.[14]

For Welch this resulted in the achievement of a translation such as the 1840 'An Elegy on the Tyronian and Tyrconnellian Princes, Buried at Rome', which is

> a static poem … a *caoineadh*, a lament, and its structure is the simplest structure of all, a catalogue of things which were, of how things might be had the lamented lived, the deeds of the dead. This structure which is hardly structure at all in the Aristotelian sense suits Mangan's poetic temperament. He, like many an Irish poet, does not like structures that develop, because that involves traffic with the movement of time, and so, ineluctably, the self.[15]

Welch's fine observation reminds us that although Mangan is translating poetry and not writing history, both the historical retrieval implicit in the act of translation and the translated text itself result in a lack of *archi-tectonicè*. The poetry looks like history – and Irish history at that – not poetry.

The Aristotlean specification is that 'in the form of narrative verse, clearly its plots should be dramatically constructed, like those of tragedies; they should centre upon a single action, whole and complete; and having a beginning, a middle, and an end.'[16] But these conflicting classical and Romantic conceptions, of shaping artistic power and imaginative recreation of actions in the past, as well as their peculiar mid-Victorian accommodations in the work of a critic such as Arnold, lead us to the paradox, or perhaps better, ambiguity, which confronts the reader of Mangan. His best poetry is at one and the same time structured around a sense of being coeval with various past historical moments (German and Oriental as much as Irish) and an aesthetic that consistently recreates those past moments through an awareness of the difference of his own position as a mid-nineteenth-century poet.

Mangan writes an English poetry that sounds differences of time (through etymology and translation) and place (the disparate locations of his translations and imaginative recreations). It courts the 'ahistorical', in MacDonagh's terms, but even if his structures are merely suspended and repetitious, and thus hardly structures at all, Mangan knows that they are new. His poetry asks us to seek out not only the coeval – in particular, the simultaneity of seemingly inconsolable loss – but also a divided sense of the present of the modern, a present that seems to be working (terrifyingly for the Catholic Mangan) without an obvious redemptive end. One fictional or mythic recompense for the structure that Arnold found missing from mid-nineteenth-century poetry was the strong Victorian sense of originary beginnings and utopian ends. Certainly, Mangan's Young Ireland contemporaries in 1840s Dublin saw the attractions of such origins in the European models for nationalism now available. Mangan's, though, is a special case, either as Victorian poet or Young Ireland polemicist. At best undecided between beginning and end, Mangan writes a poetry of the perpetual middle, caught between the temporal and structural ambiguities of the original in both of its senses, as the originary and as the new. His is like a repetitive originality, a remaking of the past in an unrepeatable style.

The One Mystery

Writing as the anonymous editor and translator of the second number of 'Literae Orientales' in the March 1838 number of the *Dublin*

University Magazine, Mangan promised that this would be his last piece on Ottoman Poetry. He went on to say that he was not much inclined to continue into Persian or Arabic poetry: 'To acknowledge the truth, at the end of our paper, *we dislike Eastern Poetry*. Its great pervading character is mysticism – and mysticism and stupidity are synonymous terms in our vocabulary'. It is a typically Manganesque self-destructive moment, both facetiously throwaway and genuinely weary. However, Mangan then says something less typical, derived both from the effort of translation and interpretation that he and his readers have just given to the 'Literae Orientales' and the impossibility of writing anything 'original' in its stead:

> Ideas resemble all other things; there is but a certain useable number of them in the world; and though that number may be vast, it is not infinite. The very phrase 'march of mind,' indicates the existence of a goal, or it follows that we are all in the monstrous condition of travelling without a purpose of terminating our journey. The stock in trade of the mind – an embargo being first laid on all commodities, the sale of which were a fraud on the purchaser – (and really a poet should have as much conscience as a pedler [sic]) is soon catalogued. 'The thing that has been is that which shall be,' only into another shape transmuted. To repudiate all that is antiquated, merely because it is antiquated, as the Hindoos drive the aged of their kindred into the Hoogly, is fashionable, but wrong. Poets do not stand the higher in the estimation of the rational for writing insufferable nonsense about embalmed reminiscences, and sunny tresses, and spirit-voices. Instead of creating nondescript forms out of new materials they should rather endeavour to mould existing materials into new and more beautiful forms.[17]

As with Mahony's Prout papers in *Fraser's Magazine*, this passage ventriloquises a reactionary periodical voice, in this instance for the Tory readers of the *Dublin University Magazine*. Mangan was attracted to the anonymity that came with such conventions, but his journalism often takes this as a cue not to mean what it says. Thus, while the tone requires a *Dublin University Magazine* reader attuned to disentangling the self-deprecating from the earnest and the stock from the fresh, it is at the same time in a parodic relationship with a readership that expects levity, humour and even pastiche.

Mangan ends the passage both mischievously reaffirming the practice of translation as a plagiarist's charter and knowingly rehearsing the conservative arguments of Prout about the impossibility of originality. While doing so, however, it also smuggles realism into a debate about the insubstantiality of the idealism and sensuousness of Oriental art that has up until now preoccupied the translator. It places that realism alongside the modern, at the chilling heart of the passage where one outcome of 'the march of mind' is envisaged as 'the monstrous condition of travelling without a purpose of terminating our journey'. Its fears are held up in this odd Irish-Oriental vision of mid-Victorian progress, where terrifying change can be halted only by a twin recourse to the authority of the antique and its sudden transformation into 'commodities, the sale of which were a fraud on the purchaser'.[18] 'The thing that has been is that which shall be' the riddle goes, and Mangan holds past and future artistic form against each other, fearing the perpetual present of modernity and the market. The transmutations are not of matter, but those of the replication of shape or form. Whereas the content seems doomed to repetition, the style admits innovation.

Throughout his writing career, Mangan's poetry was frequently caught in a stalled perpetuity between the original and the rehashed and between the temptations of mysticism and the reminders of the real. As such it shared in a recognisably post-Romantic anxiety about change, the future and the originality of self. His best poetry, however, was written through the specific circumstances of Ireland's brush with the modern in the 1840s, and its catastrophic failure in the circumstances of famine. It is tempting to read the concerns of Mangan's poetry as those of that decade, where after the ideological optimism of the temperance movement, the campaign for Repeal of the Union, and the rise of Young Ireland, Irish nationalism suffered the deaths of O'Connell and Davis, the horrors of the Famine, and the eventual debacle of incompetent rebellion and the transportation and exile of a generation of intellectuals. As the young James Joyce recognised, Mangan thus became one type of the Irish artist, imprisoned within circumstances too powerful to admit imaginative freedom.

Mangan himself knew this, and even in the visionary mode, his poetry of the 1840s replays the lyrical and narrative stasis he sought in the German, Oriental and eventually Irish poems that were to provide so much of the material he refashioned in his own odd English style. In 1850, a year after his death, the short-lived Young Ireland newspaper, *The Irishman*, introduced a piece on Mangan written in the person of 'E.W.', 'a medical man', in their series of 'Sketches and Reminiscences of Irish Writers'. It was Mangan himself who was the author of this series. The trail of authorship, impersonation, recycling, recontextualisation and third-person autobiography doesn't quite amount to moulding 'existing materials into new and more beautiful forms'. Rather, it enables him to accuse his subject – himself – of 'a great number of literary sins, which, taken together, as a quaint and sententious friend remarks, would appear to be "the antithesis of plagiarism"'.[19] In his biography of Mangan, D.J. O'Donoghue exasperatedly quotes this as an example of the way in which Mangan regularly belittled his own considerable talents, and recounts a conversation on the topic: 'I once asked Mangan why he did not pre-fix his own name to his anti-plagiaristic productions, and his reply was characteristic of the man—"that would be no go [...] I must write in a variety of styles!"'[20] For Joyce, following John Mitchel's earlier celebrated portraits of Mangan as a type of the unfulfilled and abject Irish artist, the failure of Mangan to write out of 'a narrow and hysterical nationality'[21] is paradoxically marked in his mastery of style, a mastery that is won at its own expense.

As Mangan parodies and impersonates style, he tells us that he writes without his own style. Yet at the same time, doomed to obscurity and oblivion, this very obliviousness of self is marked in the writing. If we can't say that Mangan has no style, it could be said he has too much: as his narrator says in his 'Extraordinary Adventure in the Shades', 'Mannerism is a grand thing.'[22] The most sustained criticism of Mangan the manner-ist, as a kind of postmodernist *avant la lettre*, is by David Lloyd, who writes of this mannerism as the riposte of the colonised to classicism in the uncontainable paradox of a deliberate elaboration of style that is at the same time inherently conventional. Its purpose, as a literal reading of the passage from the 'Literae Orientales' might bear out, is to react, in Lloyd's words, against 'that striving for authenticity and autonomy through originality that his contemporaries demand as the means to rec-oncile the individual with the universal'.[23] The mannerist style is either insufferably artificial or suffering in its artificiality, the poetry of joke, pun and doggerel that O'Donoghue disparaged or Joyce found typical: 'There is a likeness between the desperate writer, himself the victim of too dex-trous torture, and the contorted writing.'[24] Joyce's insight aside, the style appears to be estranged from the content. At the same time, both content and style are doomed to repetition: 'The thing that has been is that which shall be.'

Repetition, however, is not necessarily unified or monologic in the broadest sense. It is often a symptom of the inability to resolve either style or argument, leading to formal and conceptual endings that wilfully seek to maintain a division of poetry and purpose. To take an early example, the young William Butler Yeats viewed Mangan's mannerism as a style that lacked the clarity of Thomas Davis, thus offering not originality but exoticism and difference. Yeats was writing when he himself was fashioning his own distinctive style in the late 1880s, and he gives a clue with his choice of text to illustrate this facet of Mangan:

> He can never be popular like Davis, for he did not embody in clear verse the thoughts of normal mankind. He never startles us by saying beautifully things we have long felt. He does not say look at yourself in this mirror; but, rather, 'Look at me – I am so strange, so exotic, so different.'
> But this man, Mangan, born in torpid days in a torpid city, could only write in diverse fashions, 'I am Miserable.' No hopes! No philosophy! No illusions! A brute cry from the gutters of the earth! and for solace or rather for a drug – this –

> No more, no more; – With aching brow,
>   And restless heart, and burning brain,
> We ask the When, the Where, the How,
>   And ask in vain.
> And all philosophy, all faith,
> All earthly, all celestial lore,
> Have but ONE voice, which only saith –
>   Endure, – adore![25]

This ends with the last stanza of 'The One Mystery', an original early poem, published in the *Dublin Penny Journal* in 1833, a year before Mangan made his first foray into translation. The phrase 'No more' is a deliberate avoiding of the answers to the questions that run through the previous four stanzas of the poem and culminate in typical intellectual vacillations. These questions are both a post-Romantic, or even a post-Romance, questioning of the vigour of a departed heroism ('Shall the sacred pulse that thrilled/Thrill once again to Glory's name?') and a Catholic questioning after the second coming of Christ ('Reborn, revived, renewed, immortal.') Deliverance in the future will not be allowed into the poem, which ends, in Yeats's words, either as solace or drug, or both. The ONE voice only saith not one but two words, 'Endure – adore!'

So, how do we read this double ending? 'Endure' could be forced into a half-rhyme with 'lore', but 'adore' sounds like a willed correction, echoing on from both words. The moment is like that of the rhythm of will evident in other Victorian dramatic poems of the period, correcting the verse into a full rhyme and at the same time correcting his heterodox conscience. One reading could be that the correction is also like the reminder of the Christian redemption the penultimate stanza had asked for. Another possibility is that the 'ONE voice' has simply been misheard, or is being guessed at: what did she say? 'Endure?' Surely not – 'Adore!'

The prophetic note is of little use if life is merely endurance; better to turn
it to another related, if equally static, state – adoration, willingly abject
before revelation, if not entirely sure what it is that has been revealed.
'The One Mystery' remains just that – untranscended – and barely heard,
let alone understood.

Through the final decade and a half of his career, Mangan sought
form for these moments, filtered through his deliberately synthetic,
often bogus, translations and impersonations of German, Oriental and
Irish poetry, particularly where those poems and genres were drawn to
states of immovability, repetition and the possibilities or impossibilities
of some liberating apocalyptic moment. Following the young Joyce's
imaginative association of himself with Mangan as a fellow Irish artist
suffering under the betrayals of a philistine country, much attention has
been given to the mythic aspects of the tragic minor poet, drunkard or
hack, doomed to accusations of plagiarism from those who seek authenticity of style. The texture of his writing, and its substantial formal and
stylistic achievements, resonate in the context of Mangan's immediate
antecedents or contemporaries who wrote Irish poetry in English. The
temporal wavering of Moore's rhythm is strong. Yeats joined Mangan
with Davis and Ferguson as one of the company of poets with which
he wished to be counted in revived Irish coming times. However, as
Jacques Chuto, general editor of the *Collected Writings* has discovered,
much of Mangan's writing was derived from English versions of German
and Oriental poetry, frequently translating the Oriental poetry through
Joseph von Hammer-Purgstall's eccentric German collections, which
were themselves often translations from a variety of occluded sources.[26]
This introduced Irish poetry to the odd forms and sonic – particularly
rhyming and repetitive – patterns of those Oriental poems. Importing
the sensualism and transcendentalism of German interest in Persian,
Ottoman or Coptic poetry into English, the eventual contact with Irish-
language poetry provided an odd synthetic encounter indeed. Mangan's
Irish poetry sounds not just the Celtic but also the Teutonic, the gothic
and the Oriental, and frequently his English poetry achieves utter stylistic
originality: 'It is not English poetry', Frank O'Connor said of Mangan's
1844 pseudo-Turkish translation, 'The Caramanian Exile'.[27] Add in those
moments of doubling as well as those of indirection and wilfully static
non-conclusion ('Endure, – adore!'), and we have the often infuriating
play with a poetry unable and unwilling to break free from its desire to
remain in 'the monstrous condition of travelling without a purpose of
terminating our journey'.

A Curious Anticlimax

The 1840 *Irish Penny Journal* article 'Stray Leaflets from the German Oak –
Second Drift' contained Mangan's first version of Friedrich Rückert's
poem 'Chidher', 'The World's Changes'. It was later to be rewritten as
the extraordinary experiment in highly irregular couplets, 'Khidder',
which appeared unattributed and unsigned in the *Dublin University
Magazine* in 1845.[28] Based on the same original, 'The World's Changes'
and 'Khidder' share plot and theme, in which a time traveller views the
same place at thousand-year intervals. The traveller notices great changes
between epochs; the occupants believe that their time is as it has always
been. Where the better-known 'Khidder' is written as monologue, 'The
World's Changes' narrates the allegorical figure of Time himself, 'The
Solemn Shadow that bears in his hands/The Conquering Scythe and the
Glass of Sands'. Both versions end where they had begun, with the vision
of a great city. Although it had at first been a proud imperial capital, after
4,000 years in which the place had also been lake, sea and forest, the final
vision is of the nineteenth century. The crowded city in 'The World's
Changes' is described thus:

> And what saw the Shadow? A city agen,
> But peopled by mechanical men,
> With workhouses filled, and prisons, and marts,
> And faces that spake exanimate hearts.[29]

Mangan toys with the notion that this vision represents a final phase in
the world's changes, a notion borne out by the archaism ('agen') and odd
adjective 'exanimate'. The word means to be deprived of life, a synonym
for 'inanimate'. *Oxford English Dictionary* records that although the word
would be pressed into service as a term for the fossilised in the 1840s, it
was itself soon to become extinct, its last example dating from 1858.

The poem ends ambiguously, contemplating a possible finality, an end
to history. The Solemn Shadow asks 'one of the Ghastly' about what is
now called 'ominous Change' and the man answers:

> 'Change? What was Life ever but Conflict and Change?
> From the ages of eld
> Hath affliction been widening its range.'

The Shadow vanishes and the youth of the earth passes away, 'to return
with no To-morrow'. These are inventions of Mangan, at odds with
Rückert's original, translating change as finality, and playing with typical Manganesque oxymoron and tautology. 'Ever' tells against and along

with 'Conflict and Change': ever change, the perpetual transitory. But the modern place seems to tell of a finality, in which history is merely the widening range of suffering.

As Seamus Deane, Chris Morash and Melissa Fegan have said, much Irish writing of the decade that ensued – the 1840s – was preoccupied in different ways with differing prospects of change. From mid-decade, it was also to suffer the apocalypse of famine. Not all poetic and political versions of change were dystopic, such as 'The World's Changes', and visions of political deliverance tended to veer between what Deane calls 'that powerful dialectic between a spurious Eden and an unattainable United Irish utopia'.[30] Working with Deane's observation, Morash points to a millenarianism in Irish Catholic and Protestant writing that is widespread in the famine poetry of Mangan and the other writers who published for the Young Ireland newspapers, *The Nation* and its more radical successors, *The Irishman* and *United Irishman*. In this writing, according to Morash, 'the idealized past is imagined as the promised land of the future', one articulation of 'the apocalyptic moment of the famine as written by the millenarian lyric'. Historical change is merely return, and thus nothing new. In its absence, then, a poem like Mangan's ambitious 'A Vision: AD 1848' ends only by waking its dreaming poet up, and returning him to a present from which there is to be no visionary deliverance. In Morash's words, the ending is 'a structural loop, entrapping the reader in an unending apocalyptic present'.[31]

In Mangan, the personal intrudes most strongly on these pressing matters of futurity. Indeed, Melissa Fegan has argued that his death from cholera makes him a victim of famine, the shame of which was hidden by his myth-making biographers.[32] Yet disturbing personal anecdotes did surface, and D.J. O'Donoghue retells the tale of a famine poem from 1846, 'The Warning Voice', a poem written in the style of the more strident productions of *The Nation*. The poem was exchanged at midnight for the advance the editor had forbidden, money needed to cure its desperately dyspeptic, if not also starving, poet.[33] The poem's second stanza addresses the present and future:

> To *this* generation
> The sore tribulation,
> The stormy commotion,
> And foam of the Popular Ocean,
>   The struggle of class against class;
> The Dearth and the Sadness,
>   The Sword and the War-vest;

> To the *next*, the Repose and the Gladness,
> 'The sea of clear glass,'
> And the rich Golden Harvest!

Deliverance seems to be promised, and the sea of clear glass, Mangan's note tells us, is that of Apocalypse, IV, 6, the sea that surrounds the throne of the Lamb. We can't forget, though, that the poem was written to cadge a drink, and more immediately, that the glass is one that is clear of the poet's personal debilitations. Appetite and addiction are entwined with the historical and economic arguments of the time, dramatised in a mode of tonal instability, as shown in a ballad double-syllable rhyming at odds with the seriousness of the subject matter: 'generation'/'tribulation', 'commotion'/'Ocean', 'Sadness/Gladness'. The effect eventually runs out of control, so that Mangan ends up inventing a word. Unfortunately, the spondee 'War-vest' doesn't quite rhyme with the falling trochee, 'Harvest'. Discussing Mangan's 1849 famine poem, 'The Funerals', Ellen Shannon-Mangan says, 'In the national disaster he found a representation of his personal dissolution [...] In the midst of Ireland's tragedy he is almost breathtakingly self-concerned.'[34] The solipsism of the alcoholic disturbs the consolation provided at the end of 'The Warning Voice', of a future that might be longer than personal and national craving might suggest. It ends with the Christian consolations of personal salvation: 'Until Destiny summon you hence/To the Better Abode!' (111–112).

The sufferings of the present, the deliverance after death, the redemption of a drink: although the reader is never quite left laughing, there is always the suspicion that there must be a black joke somewhere. The reader of Mangan is rarely allowed to settle with the poet into his poetry's structural loops and its prolonged or doubled apocalyptic moments ('Endure – adore!'). When the personal and historical matter is filtered either through translation or indeed through characters created by bogus translation, grasping the poems' unique tonal relation to their synthetic forms provides its main interpretative and aesthetic challenge. One way Mangan faced this challenge was in the matter of the history of the English language in which he wrote, a language used for poetry published in a Western place – Ireland – but frequently drawn eastwards to its Gothic origins and post-Romantic Oriental fascinations. When, rather late in his career, Mangan found new form for the English poem, his achievement was filtered through a translating and impersonating practice grounded in his earlier translating commissions. And when an 'original' text was not at hand for such commissions, he could invent one, anyway.

No Mangan criticism can avoid his translating practice and habits of impersonation. Robert Welch in particular has invoked Mangan's pen portrait of John Anster for an insight into Mangan's own views of translation.[35] The Dubliner Anster was the most widely read translator of *Faust* throughout the nineteenth century, much praised by George Henry Lewes, for instance. Mangan's praise of him in *The Irishman* of 1849 is a classic of his criticism, proclaiming what at first appears to be a more than common enthusiasm for Anster's work:

> Dr Anster has not merely translated 'Faust:' he has done much more – he has translated Goethe – or, rather, he has translated that part of the mind of Goethe which was unknown to Goethe himself. The great German, as I have already hinted, continually limped and staggered; but Anster furnishes him with a pair of crutches. He sheds light upon the dark places that he meets; he fills up every vacuum, and reduces to a common level all inequalities. He is a hundred times more Goethian that Goethe himself. He sees through his author, as through glass, but corrects all the distortions produced by the refraction of the substance through which he looks. In a few words, he has actually made of Goethe the man which his German worshippers proclaim him to be – he has created a soul under the ribs of that Death which they had revered as a Jupiter – he is, in short, *the real author of* 'Faust.'[36]

Welch reads this wonderful passage rather seriously, taking it literally that Mangan believed the translator must show 'a high degree of imaginative penetration and appropriation' and also that 'translation [...] becomes to all intents and purposes original poetry in its own right.'[37]

For Mangan, the move from translation to original poetry could be a matter of forgery as much as impersonation, but hyperbole hides a sarcastic barb aimed at Anster's pseudo-scholarly account of his own objective translating practice. In the long preface to his *Faust*, Anster worries that he might be translating too well. He conscientiously plots his way through his practice, attempting to prevent himself from giving an interpretation of the symbolism of the original: 'When I have seemed to myself to see the meaning lying before me on the surface, [I] have hesitated to break it up for the purpose of digging into some supposed mine beneath.'[38] The excavation of the allegorical structure is, Anster suggests, the great temptation to the translator, giving the meaning but also giving the game away. Tasso, he points out, did not know his allegory until he had half-finished *Orlando*. For Mangan to say that Anster had 'translated that part of the mind of Goethe which was unknown to Goethe himself' is to say that he has trespassed so far down into mines of meaning that he has destabilised the aesthetic structure. The mines may be those of etymology and the revealed and shared history of words themselves. Anster writes of,

> [...] the mistake, which it would appear to me has deceived some of our discoverers in metaphysics, of looking for the thought rather in the etymology of the words which the author employs, than in the meaning which they have acquired in their practical application: I may have fancied metaphors continuing to lurk, with a sort of sly meaning, in phrases originally metaphorical, but to which custom has affixed a certain application, and the low familiarity of the language of Mephistopheles is, of course, not unlikely to create mistakes of this sort. I am not aware of the existence of such mistakes, yet I cannot but apprehend the possibility of them.[39]

One concern of Anster was over Goethe's 'Prologue in Heaven', in which God and Mephistopheles are shown wagering over the soul of Faustus. This shocked the poem's first Christian English readers, and Anster's translation was notable in providing a previously suppressed scene.[40] But he needed to do this with a modicum of tact, a tact that can sound like priggishness: 'I am not aware of the existence of such mistakes, yet I cannot but apprehend the possibility of them.' In Mangan's joke, Anster does his translating job so well he transgresses his own scholarly conscience.

Nevertheless, Mangan also takes a lead from Anster's account of the dangers of playing with etymology, of revealing the metaphors implicit both in a low or coarse diction as well as the higher allegorical structure. Etymology itself can create an allegorical structure in Mangan's poetry, bringing as it does the past of words into their present. Given the broad European etymologies of English it also suggests not so much a mixing of geographical sources of the languages that have created it as a laying bare of those very source languages. In 1844, Mangan paired two poems by his German alter ego Selber ('Self'), 'Schnapps', a drinking poem, and 'The Coming Event', its temperance companion. The coming event was an expected apocalypse, when 'the souls of men shall be tried in the fire/Of the Final Probation.' As so often in Mangan, the pairing and the pseudonymous, fake German attribution places the poems in an ambivalent relationship with pressing contemporary contexts: the temperance movement, millennial apprehension and the author's own alcoholism. Above all, celebrating the pleasures of the present in true anacreontic fashion, or looking to the future judgement that might follow such pleasures, Mangan finds himself dragged back into the times and places from which the language of those present and future experiences might have come.

These later Selber poems reprise the subject-matter of 'Twenty Golden Years Ago,' published under the same pseudonym four years earlier. This was a poem on the dry, its speaker placed in the surrounds of a German coffee house recreated as a kitsch approximation of middle Europe. Its speaker remembers a youth not so much of debauchery as of domestic and companionable sociability. Selber's self-pity is now of one who is

> Wifeless, friendless, flaggonless, alone,
>> Not quite bookless, though, unless I chuse,
> Left with nought to do, except to groan,
>> Not a soul to woo, except the Muse –
> O! this is hard for *me* to bear,
>> Me, who whilome lived so much *en haut*,
> Me, who broke all hearts like chinaware
>> Twenty golden years ago!

This is, of course, written at a number of tonal removes from its ostensible 'content', like a pastiche of the cliché of Romantic ennui. As so often with Mangan, the personal sounds through what might appear to be at worst a literary, at best a merely intellectual and self-conscious play not just with words but with the words poems have used. The lexis is odd, even the spelling: 'chuse', rather than 'choose'. 'Whilome', of Anglo-Saxon etymology, would have been, if not archaic, deliberately old-fashioned in the 1840s. Its Germanic origins add appropriate gothic flavour. As the editors of the *Collected Works* tell us, '*en haut*' does not mean 'upstairs', but is a French transliterated from English, 'on high'. And although 'chinaware' provides a doggerel mosaic rhyme and metrical mimic of '*me* to bear', by a process of association it brings us back to the location: coffee house not tavern, china (Delft? Dresden?) not clear glass, coffee cup not flagon. 'Flagon' already has archaic and continental associations in mid-nineteenth-century English, according to *Oxford English Dictionary*.

This is all rather more than wordplay: a Germanic history of English displaces the English of the poem back into an imagined continental source. Origins, however, are not to be found there. A conceit is carried through the puns, a conceit of time lost and never to be redeemed. This is the punning representation of personal damnation, played as a conundrum to be worked out by a fellow scholar – possibly a former drinking companion – from the past of English itself. The conceit begins as Mangan invites the reader to follow his meaning, or even his feeling, from a series of puns that begin with an obvious play on the word 'dun':

> But my loneliness hath darker ills
>> Such dun duns as Conscience, Thought and Co.,
> Awful Gorgons! Worse than tailors' bills
>> Twenty golden years ago!

'To dun' is to importune for debts owed, and the etymology is Old Norse. 'Dun' is the colour of such dunning, but the etymology there is Gaelic, from *donn*, "brown". The sound of the word echoes as part of a strain of slight assonantal variations throughout the lines: '*lone*liness ... *dun duns* ... *Conscience* ... Gor*gons*!'

The strain of thought, the strained thought, continues on into mention of unpaid tailor's bills, and the theme of unpaid debt that emerges as a metaphysical conceit for the state of the now abstemious soul. Can such debts be redeemed? The lyric works up a stream of sounds echoing off each other, tempting a cacophony that at first appears deliberately meaningless. It begins by thinking about fellow poets, antecedents and the question of posterity:

> Yet may Deutschland's bardlings flourish long!
>   Me, I tweak no beak among them; – hawks
> Must not pounce on hawks; besides in song
>   I could once beat all of them by chalks.

It is as if those consonants are impersonating a Teutonic accent: 'tweak', 'beak', 'hawks' all resolve in 'chalks'. The word 'chalk' entered English from German, according to the *Oxford English Dictionary* (though previously derived from Latin, *calx*). The verb 'to chalk' brings us back to dunning and tailor's bills. Literally, 'by chalks' means by a long chalk, but the drinker's tally used to be chalked up, and this, we can see, has not been paid.

The final stanza is rather morose about the possibility that this debt will be redeemed:

> Tick-tick, tick-tick! – Not a sound save Time's,
>   And the windgust, as it drives the rain –
> Tortured torturer of reluctant rhymes,
>   Go to bed, and rest thine aching brain!
> Sleep! – no more the dupe of hopes or schemes;
>   Soon thou sleepest where the thistles blow –
> Curious anticlimax to thy dreams
>   Twenty golden years ago!

For all that this ends with the celebrated self-description of the speaker that is often applied to Mangan, 'tortured torturer of reluctant rhymes', a sort of resolution is achieved in the figure he uses for the impossibility of redemption. 'Tick-tick, tick-tick' is of course the clock, a clock which doesn't tock, and is thus the last joke on the theme of unpaid debt, of living on tick. *Oxford English Dictionary* tells us of the derivation of this expression, that the 'score' of the credit given in alehouses used to be ticked in chalk. Mangan's speaker, Selber, is caught in a rhythmic stasis by the rhythm of the clock. 'Not a sound save Time's', he says, in a rhythm of repetition, not the progressive rhythm of change. The resolution is only in the figure of damnation as unredeemable debt, and there does not seem any way out of this impasse. The Faustian theme is suggested, but that might suggest a heroic alternative, some attainment in the past: previously, 'I had a grand Byronian soul/Twenty golden years ago' (55–56). The sound of time leads only to death, but even that lacks its satisfactions: it is a 'Curious anticlimax'.

The achievement here, in June 1840, is of a sort of coterie poem, intended to be read by those bardlings who could follow the conceit, those who would get the jokes. In one way it is also an addict's poem, and its imagined readers are fellow takers of the pledge, doomed to an eternity without a drink. Even given his association with a variety of editors who promoted poetry and translations that obviously had an audience, it is still hard to say what exactly Mangan's coterie was. But one positive outcome was to follow, and a poem such as this laid the groundwork for what he achieved in the 1840s. Mangan's Gothic-Irish poem can't quite redeem the past of English, but it does begin to tally some of its etymological debts. The 'curious anticlimax' of the ending is a temporal stalling, which tells only of the past and is unable to follow through on the pledge it might have taken. The achievement is provisional, and the style remains addicted to the punning and parodic.

So, does Mangan's poetry ever get beyond its own sense of curious anticlimax, or must it remain suspended in its own middling, *mitteleuropäisch* formula? Two months after he published 'Twenty Golden Years Ago', in August 1840, George Petrie, editor of the *Irish Penny Journal*, commissioned a new series of translations from Mangan, 'Ancient Irish Literature'. This series contained Mangan's first versions of Irish poems, beginning with 'The Woman of Three Cows', a tour de force of peasant misogyny and mock-historical learning. The initial contact with Irish poetry became 'Jacobite Relics of Ireland' in 1841, but was then put aside as Mangan returned to Oriental, German and Italian translations. He did not pick up Irish translation again until James Montgomery's *Specimens of the Early Native Poetry of Ireland* in 1846. This hiatus after small beginnings discourages any impression that the contact with Irish poetry immediately provided an authentic delivery from the formal anticlimax that 'Twenty Golden Years Ago' had deliberately courted. And those few Irish poems are chosen from historical periods that tell of elegy, defeat and the desperation for a deliverance. The lapsed time between their original composition and translation into English has not been redeemed. In all of them, Mangan chose texts that have to reimagine outcomes which the realities of defeat and exile have rendered as personal and national humiliation.

'The Lamentation of Mac Liag for Kincora' is an elegy for Irish aristocratic culture after the defeat of Brian Boru. Mac Liag's focus is one that Mangan returns to throughout the 1840s, a ruin. 'An Elegy on the Tironian and Tirconnelian Princes Buried at Rome', after Owen Roe Mac an Bhaird, spends eight of its eighteen stanzas engaged in macabre counter-history, imagining the increasingly bloody ways in which those Ulster Earls who had taken flight in 1607 might have died in the glorious battles their exile had denied them. Formally, the elegy cannot be completed: with neither the funerals nor the remains of the lost nobles, the bard is denied ritual consolation. The poem ends only with a prayer to the now-defeated Catholic God who is asked to watch over 'our dreary state,/And through the ages that may still/Roll sadly on'(211–213). Those dreary ages had rolled on for nearly 250 years, a defeat not to be consoled by the freedom with which Mangan imagines the poet from the past. The lapse of time is reimagined as the bleakness of a mourning that the poet cannot get over. In the words of the irregular Petrarchan sonnet also published at this time, 'The Departure of Love', Mangan's relationship to history is one of perpetual loss. '[T]he world's chill breath' is countered only by 'ever-mourning Memory', which 'always, with a low despairful sound,/ Tolls the disastrous bell of all our years'.[41] In Oliver MacDonagh's terms, mentioned at the beginning of this chapter, this is the 'the contemporeity of the past', a past which has yet to be redeemed in any consolatory act or shift in feeling.

Given such subject matter – defeat, exile and death – and their ever-mourning memory, these poems provide neither consolation nor forgetting. In the circumstances, repetition is both rhetorical structure and subject matter. The following year – 1841 – Mangan's attention turned to the eighteenth century, and a proposed series of 'Jacobite Relics of Ireland' for the *Irish Penny Journal*. The author of the 'original' of 'Kathaleen Ny-Houlahan' was not given, but the poem is based on 'Is fada milte dhá gcartadh síos agus suas ar fan' by Uilliam Ó hAnnracháin, a lyric written for what Mangan calls 'the old melody' that predated it, 'Caitlín Ní Uallachain'. Ó hAnnracháin's lyric had called for deliverance through an Irish Moses: given that his version appeared just before his association with *The Nation* newspaper and the Young Irelanders, Mangan might have had Daniel O'Connell in mind. If the ageing O'Connell no longer fitted the part, a 'translation' that ends with Exodus, and first thinks about reawakening the sovereignty figure in Ó hAnnracháin's text, was an early sign of the mixture of apocalyptic portent and political point that was to feature throughout Mangan's tonally shifting 1840s Irish poetry:

> Long they pine in weary woe, the nobles of our land,
> Long they wander to and fro, proscribed, alas! and banned;
> Feastless, houseless, altarless, they bear the exile's brand,
>   But their hope is in the coming-to of Kathaleen Ny-Houlahan.

Mangan is above all a poet of repetition, where the wished-for end can appear stalled by a rhetoric that doesn't appear to be going anywhere: the figures here include anaphora ('Long they pine ... Long they wander'), homoioteleuton ('Feastless, houseless, altarless') and pleonasm or tautology ('proscribed, alas! and banned').

If these are figures of a certain sort of temporality, Mangan cannot resist anachronism, either. Any possible sublimity in the awakening of the sovereignty figure is thrown away by the modish phrasing, 'the coming-to of Kathaleen Ny-Houlahan'. To come to in the sense of recovering consciousness is recorded once in the sixteenth century by the *Oxford English Dictionary*, but not again until the nineteenth century: the examples include Dickens and Browning, in light-hearted mood.[42] Kathaleen must also come to in English and not in the Irish 'original', and the poem achieves this through a technique that James Joyce praises – 'musical echo'. Initially stating that Mangan's prosody is more 'cunning' even than the achievements of his contemporary Edgar Allan Poe, the young Joyce stated that Mangan's 'mastery [...] obeys' the untaught, originary 'interior command' of his style. He gives the example of the refrain of 'Kathaleen Ny-Houlahan', which 'changes the trochaic scheme abruptly for a line of firm, marching iambs'.[43] Joyce must have been thinking of the fourth and fifth stanzas: 'We wait the Young Deliverer of Kathaleen Ny-Houlahan' or 'To cast a look of pity upon Kathaleen Ny-Houlahan'. These lines shift away from Mangan's experimental metre, which interchanges lines of six- to eight-foot trochaic and stress rhythms, hard into the Irish name forced into English iambs. Joyce hears the iambs marching, I suppose, in that they carry the longing for the deliverance of Ireland as Israel had been delivered. Ó hAnnracháin's biblical typology is a repetition of sorts, matched by Mangan's version of it in its turn.

Such rhythms are a mannered performance to the English or American ear, even though other poets played with similar trochaic hexameters, fourteeners or octometers in poetry in English through the 1840s: Tennyson's 'Locksley Hall', published a year later in 1842, similarly pushes the syllable count of the English poetic line, as does Longfellow's *Evangeline* of 1847. But Mangan's mannerism is that of a poem striving to sound unusual triple rhymes while playing with a sonically related refrain. The word Houlahan repeats as refrain throughout, and also takes half- and assonantal rhymes with the triple rhymes, most subtly in the echo and repetition of the ls first suggested in the word 'mild' through this stanza:

> Sweet and mild would look her face, O none so sweet and mild,
> Could she crush the foes by whom her beauty is reviled;
> Woollen plaids would grace herself and robes of silk her child,
>   If the king's son were living here with Kathaleen Ny-Houlahan (9–12)!

The initial figure of repetition is epistrophe, 'sweet and mild' opening and closing the first line of the stanza. This opens up the sounds that follow, not just the distinctive triple rhymes 'reviled' and 'child', but also the echoing ls in 'look', 'Woollen plaids', 'silk' and then the name 'Kathaleen Ny-Houlahan', the refrain in itself becoming the figure of repetition that gathers together the structure of the whole poem.

In the final stanza this 'Houlahan' sound is allowed assonantal rhyme with the other three full rhyming syllables:

> He, who over sands and waves led Israël along –
> He, who fed, with heavenly bread, that chosen tribe and throng –
> He, who stood by Moses, when his foes were fierce and strong –
>   May he show forth His might in saving Kathaleen Ny-Houlahan (21–24)!

In his 1847 version of Uilliam Dall Ó hIfearnáin's poem on the same theme, 'Caitlin Ni Uallachain', the refrain rhymes the Gaelic name Caitlin Ni Uallachain with 'drawn' and 'bawn' and so on.[44] Thus, pronounced Hoola*haun*, the word rhymes assonantally with 'along', 'throng' and 'strong'. Writing with the examples of Ferguson and Walsh in earshot, Mangan's 'musical echo' imports the cross-rhymes and internal and assonantal rhymes in an approximation of the Irish amhrán: for instance, at other parts of the poem, 'woe/fro, seen/unseemly, Foes/face'. But in this last stanza the technique mounts to excess: 'He who fed, with heavenly bread'; or the string of sounds which run from 'chosen' into 'Moses, when his foes'. Add to this the anaphora of 'He, who' at the beginning of these lines and we have more than the sonic approximation of 'faithful' translation. It is simultaneously a sort of renovation, an attempt to redeem the time lost between the composition of the Jacobite relic and its translation a century later, and a marker of the fact Kathaleen didn't come to in the 1740s and it didn't look like she would in the 1840s either.

The poem's attempt at this formal simultaneity is through the excess of repetition of refrain and rhyme, and the triple rhymes that Mangan had learnt from his translations of German Romantic translations of Persian poetry. These also amount to repetitions of the visionary, if such a thing could be possible, which is in ironic relation with the deliverance of the Israelites in the Book of Exodus. Millenia may have lapsed, but Mangan's poem seems to think of itself in barely altered historical circumstances. As so often when reading Mangan, it is hard not to think that for all the seriousness of the material, given that so much remained at stake in the Jacobite material he is having a joke at various people's expense. Among them we might count his persecuted predecessor, the indigent bard Ó hAnnracháin, 'proscribed, alas! and banned'. On the other hand, he doesn't shirk the strangeness, the sense of foreignness to English that his translation conveys, an impersonation that approximates the experiments of the emerging Victorian dramatic monologue in its recreation of a voice from the past. Music gives way to a recreated speech, but a speech held together with a refrain strung along on that Irish name, Kathaleen Ny-Houlahan.

From East to West

Mangan had returned to Irish poetry in the first years of the Famine, in the pages of Henry Montgomery's 1846 *Specimens of the Early Native Poetry of Ireland*. There, he opened with 'Prince Aldrid's Itinerary Through Ireland', a 1,000-year-old vision of the idyllic unconquered Inisfail, an Ireland of fecundity, prosperousness, and saints and scholars. Those medieval scholars are not spared a Victorian joke. The fourth stanza:

> I also found in Armagh, the splendid,
> Meekness, wisdom, and prudence blended,
> Fasting, as Christ hath recommended,
> And noble councillors untranscended.

For all of his insistent returns and deliberate courting of historical stasis, Mangan does allow himself the odd anachronism, as if now and again updating old material. The fourth double-syllable rhyme allows the poet a poke at Germanic, and indeed Protestant, transcendentalism when he should be picturing the lost idyll of a pre-Reformation monastic world. But the parallels are often not to be redeemed by such scholastic doggerel.

Dislocating himself temporally in his treatment of Irish material, Mangan learnt much from the spatial dislocations required for his German and Oriental translating projects. In particular, techniques of repetition and refrain were matched by the metaphysical tug into the slothful, sensuous or transcendental.

Take, for instance, the ghazal or, in Mangan's spelling, ghazel. It is a Persian verse form, usually a love poem, in which a word must be repeated at end line throughout. Its most famous practitioner was the fourteenth-century poet Hafiz, from whom Mangan said he stole much even if he never actually translated him. In a headnote to Mangan's pseudonymous sketch of himself written just before his death, the editor of *The Irishman* recalls Mangan's quip to John Anster, who had complained that a poem ascribed to Hafiz 'certainly bore little or no resemblance to the original: "Ah!" said Mangan, "it is only *Half-his*."'[45] Recent Mangan editors feel that 'Ghazel' (1849), attributed to Mohir-Ibn-Khalakan, is probably original. Indeed, it takes quite some time to go nowhere: 'The worst abyss a/ Poet falleth down is tedious length'. In doing so, the poem manages to keep up steam by following the requirements of repetition in ghazel to use the word 'eternal' at the end of ten out of its forty lines, and to find thirteen rhymes and repetitions for the word 'remain'. A week earlier in *The Irishman*, Mangan had published the mock-exhortatory 'Bear Up!', another bit of grim cheer in the midst of unrelieved suffering, which had begun with the phrase, 'Time rolleth on.'

Mangan could deal with stasis and repetition in creative ways and not always as a series of jokes. The typical oxymoronic moment of 'No more, no more' in 'The One Mystery', which Yeats chose to illustrate the torpid Mangan, is just one of a number of instances of the phrase 'no more' in Mangan's work. The word 'more' was the last word of his 1837 translation of Goethe's 'The King of Thule'. As such, it is a 'Talismanic word!' in Mangan's gloss, 'the sound of which in England is Life, and in France is Death'. It is of course also the sound that Poe said gave rise to the single word refrain of 'The Raven' (1845), 'nevermore', as it is formed from 'the long o as the most sonorous vowel in connection with r as the most producible consonant'.[46] And as Seamus Perry tells us, it is a phrase with a Wordsworthian heritage ('That time is past/And all its aching joys are now no more', 'Tintern Abbey') that subsequently did duty for Tennyson. One of the teenage Tennyson's first poems began, 'Oh sad *No More*', and the phrase rounds out one of his best-known lines: 'Oh death in life, the days that are no more' ('Tears, idle tears')[47]. In Mangan's hands though, the word and phrase travel across languages, most notably from the German bardling to whom he was most drawn, Friedrich Rückert. Mangan translated Rückert's 'Und dann nicht mehr' as an English ghazel, 'And Then No More' in 1845. The title phrase is used to end sixteen of the poem's twenty-four lines, and the remaining eight lines are full rhymes.

In advance of the playing with refrain of his contemporaries Poe and Tennyson, the ghazel form provided Mangan an opportunity for full repetition beyond the mere similarities of rhyme. In 1842, he had translated Rückert's 'Hingegangan in den Wind' as 'Gone in the Wind'. Mangan's editors suggest that Rückert's poem was one of his imitations of Persian poetry, itself possibly an original poem. But it was written in a loose ghazel form, and Mangan provided an approximation of this, as if his translation were correcting Rückert's pastiche.[48] The poem repeats the word 'wind' at end line throughout the poem's nine stanzas, and elsewhere only rhymes a word slightly modulated out of wind – 'Blind' – as if for relief. 'Gone in the Wind' is a poem of the loss of the civilizations that are insistently repeated from its opening lines through five refrain stanzas, until in proper ghazel fashion, and for want of adequate denouement, the poet names himself and his fate in the final stanza:

> Solomon! Where is thy throne? It is gone in the wind.
> Babylon! Where is thy might? It is gone in the wind.
> I, Abul-Namez, must rest; for my fire hath declined,
> And I hear voices from Hades like bells on the wind.

Mangan's addition to Rückert is to name the poet, jokingly of course: in foreign-accented English, 'I, Abul-Namez' for 'I, Abul my name is'. (Mangan creates a whole poem around a similar joke in his celebrated 1846 'To the Ingleezee Khafir, Calling Himself Djaun Bool Djenkinzun'.) The effect here is merely of a split second of relief before the lyric's intimation of a future that will simply be an exchange of one passed culture for another loss of state in eternal damnation.

The trail of imitation, translation, retranslation and prosodic, accented recreation is Mangan not so much trying to be, like Anster with Goethe, more Rückert than Rückert himself, as more Persian than Rückert could be. It is a false trail seeking an authenticity that nevertheless has a pedantic flavour to it. Mangan insists on relief only in eternity, and not in human history. He plays this theme through two earlier Oriental poems, the 1837 translation of a text he found in Von Hammer-Purgstall, 'The Time of the Roses' and the 'original' poem of 1840, 'The Time of the Barmecides'. The former poem dwells at length in the expected sensuousness, but it is the sensuousness of the imperial 'Peace' of 'Soliman'. The latter is on the more familiar ground of defeat, a repetitious mourning for the past Barmecide culture quelled by Haroun Al-Rasheed.

The time of Haroun Al-Rasheed, David Lloyd reminds us, was the subject of an earlier English piece of Orientalism, Tennyson's 1830 'Recollections of the Arabian Nights'.[49] It is also the subject of Felicia Hemans's 'The Mourner for the Barmecides', published along with other historical recreations, including the Celtic, in her *Records of Woman* in 1828. Mangan's poem is more a shadow of Hemans's than a borrowing or allusion, even though her poem is initially a strong source. But, as with Rückert, Mangan eventually takes issue with his source. Both Mangan and Hemans construct a speaker grieving for a past heroic culture, and Mangan exchanges Hemans' Orientalist alexandrine couplets into a ten-line virtuoso stanza, with a refrain repeated twice throughout the six stanzas of the poem. After a blank-verse narrative frame, Hemans's speaker begins desiring death:

> And shall I not rejoice to go, when the noble and the brave,
> With the glory on their brows, are gone before me to the grave?
> What is there left to look on now, what brightness in the land? –
> I hold in scorn the faded world, that wants their princely band![50]

Mangan's poem is monologue:

> My eyes are filmed, my beard is grey,
>   I am bowed with the weight of years;
> I would I were stretched in my bed of clay,
>   With my long lost youth's compeers;
> For back to the Past, though the thought brings woe,
>   My memory ever glides –
> To the old, old time, long, long ago,
>   The time of the Barmecides.
> To the old, old time, long, long ago,
>   The time of the Barmecides.

From this point, the texts depart, and although Hemans finishes her mourner's speech with a reiterated desire for death, Mangan simply repeats the first stanza's death wish with minimal modulations, including even the anapaestic lengthened line. The line acts like a memory of Hemans's alexandrines, but also lengthens the line into the long memory of loss: 'For back to the Past, though the thought brings woe' is repeated as 'For with them and the Past, though the thought wakens woe'.

In one other respect, these texts differ significantly, and that is the frame that Hemans places around the mourner's speech. In the narrative of her poem, it is actually being listened to by Haroun himself, as the mourner's previous dissenting lament for the Barmecides is the cause of a death sentence. Haroun is so moved by his eloquence that he pardons him. Mangan is interested in neither narrative nor reprieve, and he leaves the poem becalmed and repetitious to death and possibly eternity. It would be interesting to know, too, what he felt about another poem in Hemans's *Records of Woman*, 'Carolan's Prophecy', where in true Thomas Moore fashion the 'bard' attempts to play a 'bridal melody' for a beautiful girl, but is compelled by 'some wailing spirit in the strings' of his harp to sing a song of grief. In the narrative frame, the tears of his listeners after the song give way to dawn and spring.[51]

In Mangan's corrective version of Orientalism, there can be no spring, and in his 'original' poems, he seems to seek to still even further the stasis and grieving he found in his German and English sources. He effects a further transformation of this Eastern material when he turns to the West, by turning his Western material eastwards, in a sort of widdershins direction against the movements of the sun. The best known of these geographical dislocations is 'Siberia' (1846), a masterpiece of silence, grief and the inertia of colonial exile where, in the second stanza, the diurnal course of time blurs: 'Night is interblent with day'. It has long been thought to be an original poem and a fairly clear-cut allegory of the Famine, but Jacques Chuto has discovered that the German poet Ernst Ortlepp's 'Sibirien', written about the 1830 Polish uprising, is its source. Jan Jędrzejewezki convincingly suggests 'Siberia' shares the concern of *The Nation* in the 1840s with the oft-cited similarity between Polish and Irish Catholic nationalism and insurrectionary movements in both of those countries against powers to their east.[52] Mangan's relation to Ortlepp seems to be like that between 'The Time of the Barmecides' and Hemans's 'original', working from suggestion as much as direct translation or even plagiarism. Indeed, 'Siberia' might just be about Poland and Russia and not Ireland at all.

The content is crucial, of course, to these issues of interpretation and influence in the mid-1840s. But what Mangan's poem adds primarily is a solution in technique, as in a number of these experiments with Oriental and other verse that sought to inhabit the enclosure of a straightened history. He offers an invented prosody of frozen numbness, a sort of zombie metre. In the regular toll of the clipped rhythm and syntax, rhythmical variation serves only the purposes of an irony turned against the sun: 'For the sands are in his heart,/And the killing snows.' 'Siberia' also enables the geographical dislocation in the metaphor to perform what many metaphors of insurrection find they have to do: secrete its message within the metaphors of a poem that appears to be located in a foreign place. Except there will be no Hemans-like pardon here in the Famine conditions of 1846, and any rebellious message appears to hold out little consolation:

> Therefore in those wastes
>   None curse the Czar.
> Each man's tongue is cloven by
> The North Blast, that heweth nigh
>   With sharp scymitar.

The diction of the poem is filled full of English archaisms and tongue-twisting challenges to the cloven tongue: in addition to 'heweth nigh' here, elsewhere in the poem, 'Woundeth,' 'toothèd,' 'doth' and the Scots 'drees'. Mangan seems to work against the metaphor's dislocation, reintegrating one history of English and thus effecting the obliteration of difference. 'Siberia' is tugged at first, away from and then widdershins into, the literary language from which it might be expected to show a profound exile. Almost despite the metaphoric translation of the poem itself, the languages of Britain (English, Hiberno-English, Scots) like night and day in the poem appear to be 'interblent' with a pastiche of the orient ('Siberia', 'Czar', 'scimitar'). If the syncretic linguistic form has been achieved, its results have been of a cloven tongue. 'Siberia' gives one idea of what might result from an achieved linguistic act of union.

This is played out as an exchange, something that is part blended union of East and West and part mere geographical and linguistic hinge, in another poem of 1846, 'A Vision of Connaught in the Thirteenth Century'. Mangan doesn't quite conceive a consoling frame for the poem, and at the end reveals a speaker viewing the scene from 'castled Maine ... the Teuton's land'. It begins and ends with the speaker watching the sun: ending, as we have seen already, under the 'alien sun' of the North, but beginning with 'wondrous excess of light' of a sun that outshines even that of a southern European space, Spain. So, although the sun doesn't appear to move throughout while Mangan maps a triangle across Europe (Connacht, Germany, Spain), the poem appears ready for the ripeness of the Golden Age. That is referred to four times as a 'clime', a repetition not strictly connected to the need to find a word for space to rhyme with 'time'. For instance,

> 'O, my Lord and Khan,
> What clime is this, and what golden time?'
>   When he – 'The clime
>   Is a clime to praise,

The clime is Erin's, the green and bland,
And it is the time,
These be the days,
Of Cáhal Mór of the Wine-red Hand!'

Those repetitions serve to fix both the space described and any urges the
verse might betray for the utopian or even paradisal. The 'green and bland'
'golden time' of Erin is only slightly offset against the foreign speaker
enquiring after the Khan of this place.

True to form, Mangan refers to an imagined etymology to justify the
speaker's mistranslation: a footnote tells the reader that Khan is 'Identical
with the Irish *Ceann*, Head or Chief; but I the rather gave him the
Oriental title, as really fancying myself in one of the regions of Araby
the Blest [*sic*]'.[53] In his brief treatment of Mangan's Orientalism, Joseph
Lennon takes such moments as a 'strategy of inversion' of Orientalism,
but Mangan is enjoying this play with the pseudo-ethnology of supposed
Celtic Oriental origins too much for mere inversion.[54] The allusiveness and
false linguistic history spins the text in two directions, just as it is trying
to suggest the blandness of a becalmed perpetual sun, like Tennyson's 'The
Lotos-Eaters' of 1832 and its 'land/In which it seemèd always afternoon'.[55]
Other English antecedents were involved in creating imaginary golden
ages, such as this one in Mangan:

Then saw I thrones,
And circling fires,
And a Dome rose near me, as by a spell,
Whence flowed the tones
Of silver lyres
And many voices in wreathèd swell;
And their thrilling chime
Fell on mine ears
As the heavenly hymn of an angel-band –
It is now the time,
These be the years
Of Cáhal Mór of the Wine-red Hand!

The thrones, fires, domes and lyres suggest a mixing of Wordsworth's dru-
idic imaginings at Stonehenge on Salisbury Plain (first published in 'Guilt
and Sorrow' in 1842) and Coleridge's 'Kubla Khan'. Both are visionary fictions of a past imagined through Celticism or Orientalism. In such pagan
circumstances, the Catholic Mangan adds in angels singing hymns, as if
offering saints and scholars as a corrective to Wordsworth's human sac-
rifice and Coleridge's luxuriousness. But of course at the back of these

recreations, and in the explicit Ceann/Khan wordplay, are Kubla Khan's 'ancestral voices prophesying war'. Nevertheless, the jolt into a present that only suggests the failed crop of the second Famine summer of its publication date, July 1846, cannot be contained by the poem's location of the vision back East to Germany or even to closer English Romantic antecedents. For all its supposed 'contemporeity', the Teutonic Maine is no more precise a *lieu de memoire* than Xanadu, pre-Christian Stonehenge, or thirteenth-century Connaught.

Redundance of Blood

The place that is revealed at the end of 'A Vision of Connaught in the Thirteenth Century' is a hostile, ahistorically static place, strung across at least three points of a compass that encloses the vision rather than opening it out across the vast spaces and millennia its geographical and temporal scheme at first seems to suggest. The cosmic gives way to famine. For all that the poem is 'original', like 'the Time of the Barmecides', it still seems concerned with correcting the recreations of the past of the poetry of the English language in which it is written. It might be consoling to think that Mangan paradoxically found his 'originality' or some sort of authenticating vision in his Irish translations, but that would be to betray the same sense of defeat, dispossession and desire that can amount to the frenzy that he saw in those Irish originals. His two most successful versions of Irish poems of the sixteenth and seventeenth centuries suggest such extraordinary imaginative recreations of place, voice and feeling that their vaguenesses about the future, when placed against the preciseness of their sense of loss in the past, make for themselves a new Irish poetry in the English language.

The speaker of Mangan's 1846 version of 'O Hussey's Ode to the Maguire' is the hereditary bard to the Maguire family, Eochaidh Ó hEódhasa, viewing a hostile landscape that somewhere hides his Chief and his followers. Imagining what it is to be a fugitive, the poet also imagines himself suffering all the hardships of the army and so celebrating his own poet's heroism as he celebrates the heroic integrity of the warlike. Given themes of clan loyalty, betrayal, chase, hardship and war, the poem finds its refuge, along with Mangan, in an unlikely place – an English poem:

> Where is my Chief, my Master, this bleak night, *mavrone?*
> O, cold, cold, miserably cold is this bleak night for Hugh,
> Its showery, arrowy, speary sleet pierceth one through and through,
> Pierceth one to the very bone.

The first three lines build in syllabic length, from twelve to fourteen to sixteen syllables, as if daring the reading voice to locate a recognisable metre in English within them. The final shortened line hastily picks up a rhyme with the end of the first line, not filling out to the challenge of the long stress-packed lines that have preceded it. The repeated word, 'pierceth' challenges the bounds of a containable and measurable English syllabic 'quantity'. It also challenges a satisfactory vocal performance of the poem: the English archaism in 'pierceth' rubs its 'th' sound close up against 'through and through' and 'the very bone', as if daring the reader to avoid a lisp. The speaker of the poem is imagined snuffling in Irish in the cold. Yet the lines are not written merely in stress or sprung rhythms, and certainly not as experiments with quantity. The lines don't so much rhyme as repeat sections of themselves, seemingly indiscriminately. The positioning of whole phrases – 'this bleak night', 'pierceth one' – as full-scale verbal repetition serves to mark up the rhythmical effects around which those phrases serve as sonic anchor. The 'showery, arrowy, speary sleet' is a packing of stresses against the long consonantally stopped 'sleet', so that the slur across the tongue-twister at 'pierceth one through and through' mimics, in the sound of the line, an effect of weather that is explicitly compared to an experience of battle.

The language of the poem must be adapted in order to carry the betrayals of a poem published in 1846, a poem that reflects, like 'Siberia' and 'A Vision of Connaught', a landscape being destroyed by the seeming betrayal of a natural catastrophe that destroys difference, and thus the economy of the land:

> The tempest-driven torrent deluges the mead,
> It overflows the low banks of the rivulets and ponds –
> The lawns and pasture-grounds lie locked in icy bonds,
> So that the cattle cannot feed.
>
> The pale bright margins of the streams are seen by none.
> Rushes and sweeps along the untameable flood on every side –
> It penetrates and fills the cottagers' dwelling far and wide –
> Water and land are blent in one.
>
> Through some dark woods, 'mid bones of monsters, Hugh now strays,
> As he confronts the storm with anguished heart, but manly brow –
> Oh! What a sword-wound to that tender heart of his were now
> A backward glance at peaceful days.

As 'Siberia' had imagined the obliteration of temporal difference – 'Night is interblent with Day' – these stanzas imagine the obliteration of geographical difference: water and land, lawn and pasture, field and cottage are 'blent in one'. Similarly, Mangan blends linguistic difference. The iambic or trochaic norms of verse in English are challenged in the packing of stresses around key phrases, forcing the voice away from the recognised partition of the foot as the basic, describable, metrical unit of an accentual-syllabic prosody. Elsewhere in the poem, Mangan achieves this through internal rhyme, as in the example of the repetitions above, or the distinctly mannered, 'Though he were a wild mountain eagle, he could scarce bear he' (15) or 'Oh woe is me, where is he?' (23). In these stanzas he achieves it through forced and seemingly unnecessary hyphenation ('tempest-driven ... pasture-grounds ... sword-wound') and a widespread prosodic effect of semantic units held together by two and sometimes three packed stresses, as in 'low banks', 'pasture-grounds lie locked', 'pale bright margins', 'some dark woods', 'Hugh now strays'.

Such stylistic effects speak beyond the mere consideration of style itself. Mangan places the speaking voice of a now-fictionalised Gaelic bard in a language that attempts to sound its contact with the language of those from whom it might proclaim a bitter difference. The poem tries to find refuge for its character in a language that desires to blend gradually with its imaginary Gaelic source, while at the same time mourning the destructive effects of the blending of difference into geographically indistinguishable, but politically and economically destructive, 'oneness'. The recognisable line of English verse, 'Water and land are blent in one', an initial trochaic inversion corrected into three perfect iambs, shows that the refuge to be found in oneness, union with another linguistic culture, will mark not only the end of difference, but the end of place.

Seeking recourse to such alien refuge – in his case emigrating to the English poetic tradition – is something that Mangan in 1846 would have seen as a temptation to many of his fellow countrymen and countrywomen. The editors of the *Collected* Mangan point out that a theme of betrayal has been invented for the dramatic purposes of this version of the poem,[56] so that whatever its source in the tradition of the hereditary bard, given the dramatic licence that Mangan introduces into his version, the poem is an achievement in English that seeks to mark refuge or escape from such betrayal. This is in a poetic tradition that will allow him, sonically as well as metaphorically, to translate his hardships into a substantial poetic form, to escape into articulation. The poem's prosodic inventions are indeed consonant with what Mangan might feel is the new synthetic form coming into English verse, what Thomas MacDonagh will later call 'the Irish Mode', as described in Chapters 1 and 2. But, quite self-consciously, the poem secures its form with recourse to traditions of verse in English, not Irish. The sleet 'Pierceth one to the very bone' just as the showers of April have 'perced to the very roote' the March drought in that originary English source, the Prologue to Chaucer's *Canterbury Tales*. Joyce borrows his characterisation of Mangan as straitly enclosed in history from John Mitchel, who had said of Mangan, 'Like Ireland's his gaze was ever backward.'[57] But the 'backward glance at peaceful days' in the Ó hEóchasa version is also in the third book of Keats' *Endymion*. What might be a sword wound to Maguire had for Keats been one that would dispel 1,000 years of storm, tempest, misery and captivity.[58] Yet the deliberation in this allusive contact with the English tradition is one that reflects only the poem's confidence, its sense of reproof.

Reading the poem seventy years after its publication, MacDonagh praised the poem as coming from 'one of the finest examples' of 'The Irish Mode' in poetry in English. The poetry and the Irish Mode come with their own elocutionary warnings: 'To read correctly Anglo-Irish poetry one must follow either Irish music or Anglo-Irish prose speech.' He adds, also in relation this poem: 'O'Hussey is not a modern man, yet though Mangan gives him words and phrases that were scarcely ever colloquial, he gives him a natural directness that goes with emphatic speech all the world over, at all times … Mangan's […] escape is from precipitate half-unmeasured music to a regular tolling.'[59] MacDonagh's final image is not so much of refuge in aesthetic form as escape, although the escape is not from Irish: the half-unmeasured music belongs to the late Victorian and Edwardian rhythms he heard gaining much benefit from the example of the new poetry in English then being written in Irish accents. The 'escape' of Mangan, and through him Ó hEóchasa, is achieved by a poetic language that is not colloquial, but has the 'natural directness' of speech itself. Although English poetry after *Lyrical Ballads*, particularly in the experiments with dramatic monologue of Mangan's English contemporaries Tennyson or Browning was at this period exploring the consequences of sounding the rhythms and movement of speech against metrical form, they did so in 'modern' Victorian speech. MacDonagh's worry over O'Hussey's lack of modernity would not have worried the medieval or Renaissance speakers of a similar Browning monologue, say, for whom 'natural directness' of 'emphatic speech' is often in prosodic conflict with a high degree of metrical mannerism. For 'Mavrone' in Mangan, think 'Grrr' or 'Zooks' in Browning.[60] Mangan's version of Ó hEóchasa's poem shares much with this mid-Victorian sense of voice and poetic form coming together in creative opposition as much as direct mimetic relation.

The reader is asked to follow an imaginary Irish accent while reading a poem. But Mangan finds something in the poem by Ó hEóchasa, which he realises in English – both refuge and escape from the natural directness of emphatic speech, and the imagining of situation and dramatic context.

Mangan's source for his version of the 'Ode to the Maguire' was not Ó hEóchasa himself but Samuel Ferguson, and his literal translation of the poem. This had been published in his *Dublin University Magazine* review articles based on James Hardiman's *Irish Minstrelsy* twelve years earlier. For both poems, literal translation and synthetic version, the speaker's sense of previous prosperity utterly changed by the material and cultural differences of a transforming historical situation dominates. Ferguson states explicitly in his gloss on the poem that it reminds him of accounts of Napoleon's retreat from Moscow, a retreat in the not-so-distant past, which for Mangan would have resonated with the crushing of Irish revolutionary hopes of delivery by France. Yet both versions end with the consoling memory of victory in war. In Ferguson:

> [...] his tresses softly curling are hung with ice –
> *Cause of warmth to the hero are the shouts of war,*
> *And the many mansions lime-white which he laid in ashes.*[61]

And in Mangan, introducing the theme of betrayal:

> [...] he wanders frozen, rain-drenched, sad, betrayed –
> *But the memory of the limewhite mansions his right hand hath laid*
> *In ashes warms the hero's heart!*

It is memory that holds both speaker and Chief together. And it is a dispute over the characteristics of that memory that both joins together and separates Mangan and Ferguson's different approaches to the matter of the poem. Both approach a backward glance to a lost history their recreative acts of translation and version attempt to bring back to the memory of their differing mid-nineteenth-century audiences.

Mangan's Ó hEóchasa might just commit the crime of Anster's Goethe, as more Ó hEóchasa than Ó hEóchasa himself; that is, a vocal recreation of the bard in the surrounds of a mid-Victorian dramatic monologue. In another great translation of 1846, Mangan goes even further, not shying away from uncovering the disputed allegory of the lyric of Gaelic dispossession and political desire. Thomas Furlong's version of the lyric of the song 'Róisín Dubh' had appeared in Hardiman's *Irish Minstrelsy* in 1831. Hardiman glossed the song as a seventeenth allegory of Irish history, in which the Ulster chieftain Red Hugh O'Donnell addresses the Ireland from which he was forced into exile in 1602, after the Battle of Kinsale.[62] The reading attracted the ire of Samuel Ferguson in his reviews, even if he couldn't resist telling O'Donnell's story at some length as a Waverley-style Romance for his *Dublin University Magazine* readers. For Ferguson, Furlong's translation and Hardiman's reading of it removed the erotic charge of the poem. Indeed, he read it as a love poem of transgressive desire between the speaker – an exiled priest – and his lover – figured as a little black rose. Closely following the Irish, Ferguson translated the speaker as saying that he would read the gospel in mass for her, take her 'youth' and 'make delights behind the fort'. Blasphemy shades into illicit desire, while pandering to one sectarian prejudice of Ferguson's Protestant readers, of the shortcomings of Roman Catholicism's celibate priesthood. Furlong's coy version had written the desire of the song's celebrated final verse with misty mountains and 'the crimson hue' of 'the wild waves of old ocean'. Merely through literal translation, Ferguson's speaker renders the sexual excitement of the geography of the entire country in an extraordinary surfeit of pathetic fallacy:

> The Erne shall be in its strong flood – the hills shall be uptorn;
> And the sea shall have its waves red, and blood shall be spilled;
> Every mountain-valley and every moor throughout Ireland shall be on high,
> Some day before (you) shall perish, my Roiseen Dubh.'[63]

Like his two versions of Kathleen Ni Houlahan, Mangan ran together these conflicting readings of the Irish song in two different Roisín Dubh poems.[64] The better-known 'Dark Rosaleen' appeared in *The Nation* in May 1846. Mangan's version of 'Roisín Dubh' thus lends the note of indignation that Joyce had seen in his poetry to its new contexts, where the Hardiman/Furlong Jacobite version of the poem in turn becomes a Young Ireland allegory. The eroticised politics of the aisling tradition, of the bereft girl pining for the exiled O'Donnell, emerge in the new conditions of Irish nationalism, which, given Young Ireland's rehabilitation of the United Irishmen, was now Republican and militant. Mangan is quite happy to follow Furlong, and keep the girl and her lover at a platonic distance in 'Dark Rosaleen'. The mounting sexual excitement, however, is kept as an index of feeling for the resurgence that would transform the speaker of the poem's complaint of abject 'pain and woe'. The speaker sees that a smile would give him 'A second life, a soul anew', and the poem then appears to shed both allegory and fidelity to the 'original' in its final stanza as it contemplates an insurgent national desire. 'Dark Rosaleen' ends with a contemporary, mid-1840s speaker, where the sexual excitement of Ferguson's lines have been transferred to the nation-as-woman trope, now contemplating a violent apocalypse:

> O! the Erne shall run red
>> With redundance of blood,
> The earth shall rock beneath our tread,
>> And flames wrap hill and wood,
> And gun-peal, and slogan cry,
>> Wake many a glen serene,
> Ere you shall fade, ere you shall die,
>> My Dark Rosaleen!
>> My own Rosaleen!
> The judgement hour must first be nigh,
> Ere you can fade, ere you can die,
>> My Dark Rosaleen!

Neither 'gun-peal, and slogan cry' nor 'judgement hour' appear in any previous versions, but they are adaptations for new contexts: *The Nation* newspaper, the growing crisis of famine, the falling apart of nationalist consensus after the death of Thomas Davis.

Mangan does more than just update the text, however. Like 'O'Hussey's Ode to the Maguire', the poem is ostensibly a translation, but it reads more like an impersonation or a dramatic monologue. He weaves together loose, Gaelic-approximated sound patterns along with the transforming powers of metaphor implicit in subversive uses of the aisling tradition. A modulated assonance sounds quietly within the indignation of the envisaged apocalypse: 'blood', for instance, takes only half-rhymes, with 'tread' and 'wood'. There is a delicate string of related sounds suggested from the anglicised name of the river Éirne onwards: the sounds in 'Erne', 'run' and 'red' are anagrammatically reordered in their very excess in 'redundance', and the sounds are accented on through the stanza, in 'gun', 'slogan', 'glen' and 'serene'. The latter modulation gains full rhyming association with the poem's title, the anglicised name 'Rosaleen', thus linking back with the English rhymes Rosaleen had taken throughout all seven stanzas of the poem. These patterns would not be out of place in a sound poem. Here, they serve to echo the transformations that have been worked in the metaphor through the possible 250 years of the poem's textual history, from the defeat and exile of the Gaelic aristocracy after Kinsale, the underground allegories of the aisling tradition and on through the coy bourgeois sexuality that had provoked the contempt of Ferguson. Yet throughout, the text also questions the powers of certain types of figuration in the national tradition, as it plays with the dangerous content of those figures. Although not exactly agitprop, the speaker of 'My Dark Rosaleen' certainly gets agitated, all in the insecure, inauthentic surrounds of what is now a synthetic English poem.

According to John Hollander,

> In general, lyrics from the Renaissance on – poems whose relation to song-text is itself figurative – have tended more and more to trope the scheme of refrain, to propound a parable out of its structural role [...] historically belated or locally troped refrains would seem to have the property of remembering: their own previous occurrence in the poem, their distant ancestry in song and dance and their more recent poetic parentage are recollected at each return.[65]

Certainly, although 'Dark Rosaleen' is concerned to make as immediate as possible its distant ancestry, not just in history but also in song, we could not imagine singing it to its well-known melody. It is a version from the Irish, not – as MacDonagh or Edward Walsh were to demand – 'an Irish poem that sings to the same air' or one measured against 'the exact song-tune of the original'.[66] It is a poem built around a refrain, repeating sounds not just within itself but across the history of the differing versions of its 'source' material. Its refrain is parabolic, in Hollander's terms, a sonic property that assumes the character of the translated memory it represents. Mangan's refrain thus renders its textual past contemporary while marking the loss and defeat that is all that past appears to bring before the present of its author.

James Clarence Mangan remained caught between the finality of a lost past and his own attempts at redemption within it. 'The Nameless One' was published after his death, aged just forty-six, in 1849. If the speaker is Mangan himself, he seems to have lied about his age – it is spoken by one who was 'Old and hoary/At thirty-nine' (49–50). 'The Nameless One' has tempted many readers into viewing it as an invocation of posterity, and indeed it has its own 'Ireland in the Coming Times' moment, describing a different poet in retrospect than the one whose swansong this might have been:

> Roll on, my song, and to after-ages
> Tell how, disdaining all earth can give,
> He would have taught Men, from Wisdom's pages,
> The way to live.

For all the autobiographical titbits the poem gives us,[67] we must remember that this is the production of a poet as much addicted to spurious autobiography as he was to the other substances that hastened his death:

X

And he fell through that pit abysmal
The gulf and grave of Maginn and Burns,
And pawned his soul for the Devil's dismal
Stock of returns –

XI

But yet redeemed it in days of darkness,
And shapes and signs of the Final Wrath,
When Death, in hideous and ghastly starkness,
Stood on his path.

XII

And tell how now, amid Wreck and Sorrow,
And Want, and Sickness, and houseless night,
He bides in calmness the Silent Morrow
That no ray lights.

These stanzas move through the tenses of the subject's own damnation, from pawning his soul to the redemption of the debt, only to face 'now'. In the Ireland of the late 1840s 'now' meant 'Wreck', 'Sorrow', 'Want' and 'Sickness', all seeming allegories for its obliteration: 'shapes and signs of the Final Wrath'. The poem's last word is 'Hell'. It concludes facing posterity, but posterity as apocalypse, an end to place and time.

CHAPTER 6

'Letting the Past be Past': The English Poet and the Irish Poem

Celtic Demos

Alfred Tennyson's 'Locksley Hall Sixty Years After' was written and published in 1886, as Tennyson's long-time friend and rival William Gladstone was struggling with the first Home Rule Bill that was to split English liberalism in two. As his speech veers around Christ, Imperial Rome and Roman Catholicism, the poem's unnamed speaker turns next to the ideals of the French Revolution. Thus, he lands on democratic and Catholic Ireland:

> France had shown a light to all men, preached a Gospel, all men's good;
> Celtic Demos rose a Demon, shrieked and slaked the light with blood.
>
> Hope was ever on her mountain, watching till the day begun–
> Crowned with sunlight – over darkness – from the still unrisen sun.
>
> Have we grown at last beyond the passions of the primal clan?
> 'Kill your enemy, for you hate him,' still, 'your enemy' was a man.
>
> Have we sunk below them? Peasants maim the helpless horse, and drive
> Innocent cattle under thatch, and burn the kindlier brutes alive.
>
> Brutes, the brutes are not your wrongers – burnt at midnight, found at morn,
> Twisted hard in mortal agony with their offspring, born-unborn,
>
> Clinging to the silent mother! Are we devils? Are we men?
> Sweet St Francis of Assisi, would that he were here again,
>
> He that in his Catholic wholeness used to call the very flowers
> Sisters, brothers – and the beasts – whose pains are hardly less than ours!¹

The 'bluster' of the earlier 1842 'Locksley Hall' has barely died down. The older speaker compresses a century of Irish unrest into a French-inspired 'Celtic Demos', from the atrocities of the rising of the United Irishmen in 1798 up to the Land League and Parnell. Bemoaning the loss of an ancien régime from which he has been disinherited by a progressive liberal age that promises only anarchy and degeneration, a sinking below 'the passions of the primal clan', the speaker is led by his own anarchic and passionate speech. In his excitement he reveals rather more than intended, and Tennyson employs a favoured monologue technique, the seemingly passive propulsion of speech through the sonic not semantic association of words. 'Celtic Demos rose a Demon': Demos (from Greek *demos*, 'the people') runs into Demon (from Greek *daimon*, 'deity'), and the associations are picked up in the false etymology later, 'Are we devils? Are we men?'

The effect is unsettling and not entirely accounted for by Tennyson's insistence that the poem was mere prosopopoeia: 'The whole thing is a dramatic impersonation.... Some of my thought *may* come into the poem but am I therefore the hero? *There is not one* touch of *autobiography in it from beginning to end*² (Tennyson's emphasis). The later 'Locksley Hall' is not quite autobiography, but saying it is an impersonation does not entirely remove from it the views of its English author, and its specific address to the times in which it was written. Tennyson's disinherited aristocratic speaker turns with some disgust to the atrocities of those new Catholic democrats who had been granted representation in the Emancipation won by O'Connell more than fifty years previously. The beast-burning Catholicism of more recent Irish political unrest is not the ascetic religion of Saint Francis, whose fraternity was with the animals. Freed by the fiction of monologue, Tennyson allows his speaker to add sectarian bite to the indictment of Irish Catholic degeneration, inhumanity and impiety. Matthew Bevis has shown that Tennyson's image of the maiming and burning of animals can be traced to an earlier conversation recorded in the diary of the Irish poet William Allingham. In 1880, Tennyson was working on his version of the Irish *immram*, or medieval Christian journey poem, 'The Voyage of Maeldune'. In an entry for 29 August, Allingham recorded in his *Diary* a discussion with Tennyson about Ireland and the empire, Catholic emancipation, the 'glorious constitution', Afghanistan and India. Ireland was then the subject of much outraged reporting over the violence of the Land League:

> Speaking of the Irish agitator who said, 'I think their cattle will not much prosper,' – a speech followed by the maiming of many animals, – he [Tennyson] exclaimed, 'How I hate that man – Ireland's a dreadful country! I heartily wish it was in the middle of the Atlantic.'
> 'Below the surface?' I [Allingham] asked.
> 'No, no, a thousand miles away from England. I like the Irish–I admit the charm of their manners–but they're a fearful nuisance.'³

Tennyson's consistent ribbing of his Irish guest Allingham here runs the un-Franciscan maiming of animals into something else: the floating of the island of Ireland away from the Western coasts of Europe. Allingham's part in these conversations is to ask questions in ways that are always slightly more knowing than his host may grasp. The amateur antiquarian who innocently asks, 'Beneath the surface?' would have known of the more extravagant theories of the new Irish ethnography, and one in particular, that the indigenous people of Ireland may have come from the sunken island of Atlantis. Colin Graham has introduced Atlantis into his reading of this conversation, invoking a classic of Irish-American fiction, published two years later, Ignatius Donnelly's 1882 *Atlantis: The Antediluvian World*. In Graham's account, this text makes much fantastical use of earlier Victorian Irish ethnographical research to suggest that Ireland was colonised from the West, by the Atlanteans. Seeking points of origin or identity, an argument for an ethnicity separate from Britain or Europe is based on a call to the reconstruction of a past, whatever the empirical flaws of that reconstruction. But this is the same sort of argument that Tennyson's speaker has made, albeit on slightly safer documentary ground, calling on the Christian example of St Francis to set against that of the latter-day violent Catholic peasant. The present and uncertain future, by contrast, exchange the imagined chivalry of the tribal or familial allegiances of what 'Locksley Hall Sixty Years After' calls 'the primal clan' for the modern atrocities that Allingham, for one, knew had French revolutionary associations of 'terror', and would soon be called 'terrorism'.[4]

Where the older Tennyson allows his speaker to imagine a future of an eventual, French anarchy into which democracy and the ever-extending franchise may fall, other readings might envisage a utopian future. Graham's gloss on Donnelly also looks to the future. For the Irish writer and reader, Tennyson's 'a thousand miles away from England' might be the location of the imagined places to the Atlantic West of Ireland: Tir na nOg, Hy Brasil or even New York. These places all share in filling the problems of origin in the national past with the fullness of a unified future. Graham says:

> So Tir na nOg is not exclusive, it is simply one among many metaphoric declensions of Atlantis. Ignatius Donnelly has a utopian drive which is complicated because the emptiness at the heart of his evidence is not the absent island of Atlantis but the unfulfillable desire to make the past converge on the present just as the present converges on the Atlantean past[5]

Graham pictures utopian nationalism as founded on extravagant fictions of origin and desired return. Whereas these fictions may be composed in the conditions of emigration and loss, they also seek the inadequate compensation afforded by a flawed interpretation of the evidence suggested by the acts of retrieval in history, antiquarianism, archaeology or even geology. The argument asks that the desire for unified or emancipated futures be exposed as based in fictions of the past. Graham thus reverses a critique of imperial claims for an authority based in a settled national agreement about a shared past. He turns it round into a critique of a similar nationalist appeal to a utopian future. So, both past and future are sites of contention, at the level of interpretation as much as fact. This may be a familiar dilemma in contemporary Irish studies, caught between the revisionist and virtual. Nineteenth-century English poems on Irish material, however, did not necessarily seek to expose fictions in the past, but rather to maintain an ambivalence, caught between sounding the echoes of the past through the losses of the present and the desire to forget it altogether. Facing change, the future of the union of the countries within which these poems were written depended on the desire either to forgive or forget. For the poets discussed in this chapter, whether English –Tennyson, William Wordsworth or Matthew Arnold – or Irish – Allingham, Mary Tighe, Thomas Moore, Aubrey de Vere, D.F. McCarthy, T.D. Sullivan or W.B. Yeats – the complications arise when that country is not just Ireland, but also the state of which it formed a part, the United Kingdom of Great Britain and Ireland. That United Kingdom was one troubled by its failure to fully integrate with Ireland. It is one thing to expose national or imperial fictions in the past. It is another to call for their oblivion. But through exploring the Irish matter of poems of travel, voyaging and discovery in the contexts of the integration of the United Kingdom, these poets play between forgetting and hearing the seemingly endless echo of the lost languages, mythologies and beliefs of a shared Celtic and pre-Reformation past.

   Sounding such echoes in the English Victorian poem, the achievement is never quite what might be imagined in the circumstances, the colonist's quelling of the echoes of an insurrectionary history through the rewriting of the culture of the colonised. The very forms of the English poem begin to sound the echoes of the past again, finding new form for the English poet in the Irish poem, just as the Irish poem finds new form in the English language. In conventional accounts of this process as hybrid, the result will be a merging of different cultural registers, languages or genres into a unity of form. In the account put forward in this book, it resulted in Victorian poems that sound ambiguity within themselves, the persistence and never integration of their various sources. This is neither hybridity nor quite translation. These poems never quite achieved those outcomes, and they may thus tell us much about the unravelling of union, just as their forms sought to weave it together.

Passion of the Past

In September 1849, Tennyson concluded a series of journeys round the fringes of the United Kingdom that had taken in Cornwall and Ireland, by visiting the Highlands of Scotland. Returning, he visited Kirk Alloway and the Burns monument. There, he told Edward Fitzgerald, he sat down 'by the banks of Doon' and 'not thinking of Burns (but of the lapsing of the Ages) ... all of a sudden I gave way to a passion of tears.' In more guarded mood, Tennyson wrote to his friend, the Irish poet Aubrey de Vere, that 'I made a pilgrimage thither out of love for the great peasant; they were gathering in the wheat and the spirit of the man mingled or seemed to mingle with all I saw.'[6] This is a complex emotional event, but also a giving in to a very literary sort of nostalgia. It is redolent of the circumstances of the composition and the sentiments of 'Tears, Idle Tears', in which the tears had come when thinking of 'the lapsing of the Ages'. That poem of the 'passion of the past'[7] was written on the Welsh border at Tintern Abbey, and is like a lyric continuation of Wordsworth's blank verse ode on the passing of time.

Tennyson's literary tourism by the banks of Doon is reminiscent, too, of Wordsworth's Scottish touring poems, particularly those on the grave of Burns[8] or the river Yarrow, a place that was as rich in literary or folk-loric association as it was famed for its natural beauty. The poems carry echoes of the ballad inheritance of the river, the most famous being John Logan's 'The Braes of Yarrow'. These are echoes of the sentiment of place. Throughout their twenty-eight-year process of composition, they tell of the future (the unconsummated anticipation of 'Yarrow Unvisited', 1803), present (initial disappointment turns to knowledge and appreciation in 'Yarrow Visited', 1814) and passing of time and change ('Yarrow Revisited', written 1831 and published in 1835):

> Nor deem that localised Romance
> Plays false with our affections:
> Unsanctifies our tears – made sport
> For fanciful dejections:
> Ah, no! the visions of the past
> Sustain life as she is – our changeful Life,
> With friends and kindred dealing.

For both Tennyson and Wordsworth, there is a mixture of at-homeness and foreignness beside these Scottish rivers, of recognisable feelings in locations within their own state that are nevertheless available to them only through literary tourism. The sentiment of place – or 'localised Romance', as Wordsworth puts it here – should not be an object of suspicion or bad faith. More than just 'sport/For fanciful dejections', it provides a means of registering change, both across a personal history and the historical and geographical differences of the United Kingdom. The third Yarrow poem is a tribute to the hospitality of his host, Walter Scott, and as such can claim friendship and kindred between Scottish and English. To do so, however, Wordsworth must acknowledge 'our changeful Life'. The 'Celtic' matter of Wordsworth and Tennyson's tourism is rustic and spiritual and acquaints both of them with the loss of poems, poets and past time. It tells of the 'lapsing of the Ages' through a modernising United Kingdom that is leaving behind the customs and traditions that the conservatism of both poets cherished.

Both Wordsworth and Tennyson record their experience in border or liminal places, and these do tend to have a knack of upsetting the centre. Among other readers of Celticism, Joep Leerssen has placed a Celtic epic foremost in the literary history of the liminal, James Macpherson's *Ossian*. In prose as well as poetry, what Leerssen terms 'Ossianic liminality'[9] is written in such transitional places, not only places through which the traveller passes but also places where an apocalypse may occur. As in the eventual defeat of King Arthur by the Cornish Sea in the Great Battle of the West in 'The Passing of Arthur' (revised for *Idylls of the King* in 1869), such epics remember Ilion rather than Ithaca, battle and eventual defeat rather than quest and homecoming.[10] From the mid- to late nineteenth century, Celtic revival writers recolonised, as it were, these liminal locations. In his classic poem, William Allingham sited 'The Fairies' (1850) on rocky shores and in lake reeds, and Allingham's follower, W.B. Yeats, placed his fairies there, too, in 'The Stolen Child' (1889). The places in which the self-consciously Celtic imagination can find remnants of beliefs that are both unsettling and liberating and imaginatively connected with liminal space are also places where the imperial imagination – that of the English Victorian poet such as Tennyson – can find the forgotten and obscure doing battle with the history and geography of place and culture. The Victorian poetry of these places can mark long geological time as well as the more temporally compacted specifics of a passing language and culture. For all Tennyson's deliberate medievalism, these are places of change, modernity even, a challenge to the late Victorian writer of empire and the United Kingdom.

Three years before Tennyson had placed the unravelling of the Arthurian epoch at the Great Battle of the West, Matthew Arnold had begun his lectures on the *Study of Celtic Literature* at a similarly Western fringe. Arnold's lectures quite self-consciously ape and demur from some of the conclusions of Ernest Renan's 1854 essay 'La poésie des races celtique'. Renan had begun his essay travelling through victorious Normandy to his defeated native Brittany:

> Every one who travels through the Armorican peninsula experiences a change of the most abrupt description, as soon as he leaves behind the district most closely bordering upon the continent, in which the cheerful but commonplace type of the face of Normandy and Maine is continually in evidence, and passes into the true Brittany, that which merits its name by language and race. A cold wind arises full of vague sadness, and carries the soul to other thoughts; the tree-tops are bare and twisted; the heath with its monotony of tint stretches away into the distance; at every step the granite protrudes from a soil too scanty to cover it; a sea that is almost always sombre girdles the horizon with eternal moaning.[11]

Renan seems to pass through time backwards to a pre-Norman and then some primal, geologically stubborn landscape. Of course, in 1854, Brittany was a mere province, which, along with Galicia, held the last Celts of mainland Europe.

By contrast, Arnold's lectures of the following decade begin on his holidays. He is in North Wales, in Llandudno, looking north to the austere and arid English coast around Liverpool (from whence the modern-day Saxon invaders, the city-dwelling tourists, come). He then looks west to the sublime mountain- and sea-scape of Snowdonia and Anglesea. Arnold is caught between the bourgeois – Victorian holidaymakers – and sublime – the seemingly uncontainable memories of the place, history and culture of a land brought to submission by England's first fully successful war of conquest. Consequently, he strolls up and down Llandudno's liminal Victorian promenade, and hears a recognisable language through the Welsh spoken by the voices surrounding him; it is that of a French nursery-maid. For Arnold she is incontrovertibly 'Gaulish', unknowingly a representative of the Celts who thrived – the French – in the midst of those who are facing extinction – the Welsh. The nursery-maid is partly a riposte to Renan and France, either to separatist republicanism or the revival of a French Empire under a new Napoleon. But it also leads to a conception of the modernity of a Europe that promises to swallow up the languages of those at its Celtic fringe:

> But his [the Welshman's] land is a province, and his history petty, and his Saxon subduers scout his speech as an obstacle to civilisation; and the echo of all its kindred in other lands is growing fainter and more feeble; gone

in Cornwall, going in Brittany and the Scotch Highlands, going, too, in Ireland; – and there, above all the badge of the beaten race, the property of the vanquished.[12]

Welsh, Cornish, Breton, Gaelic, Irish: Arnold hears only echoes of speech, and where it has distinction it is only as 'the badge of the beaten race'. He echoes, too, Shylock, who had expressed deracinated and persecuted identity thus: 'Suffrance is the badge of all our tribe.'[13] Next, Arnold tells us that he attended that year's Llandudno Eisteddfod, which had only been revived as recently as 1860. It is, needless to say, a damp affair, dominated by the Methodism as much at odds with Arnold's conception of culture as the philistinism of the Liverpudlian middle classes. For Arnold, Celtic revivals cannot take place alone, and his lectures go on to posit their famous, some might say notorious, conception of the culture of the United Kingdom thriving only when the Celt and Saxon marry, as it were, their respective feminine and masculine racial virtues.[14]

In its best light, Arnold's is an argument about the need to complete the cultural union of the modern Victorian state, the yet-to-be-settled Union of England and those Celtic nations that fringe it. It sees the loss of distinct cultures as inevitable, and views the triumph of Victoria's newly assimilated, United Kingdom. Here, the Celtic past can rest securely as a subject of dispassionate aesthetic or academic study in a new British culture powerful and enlightened enough to enjoy the many cultural treasures of its past. Alfred Tennyson was Poet Laureate of this state, but was long opposed to what he saw as Arnold's Olympian idealism.[15] Tennyson had a much more pessimistic view of culture than Arnold, as well as a longer experience of the destabilising effects of such forgotten peoples and their demands that they be heard across the Union. Always on the conservative, anti-Gladstonian wing of the Liberal Party that ennobled him in 1883, Tennyson feared that the clinging of a defeated Celtic culture to past practice (such as the Irish language, 'the property of the vanquished') threatened catastrophe for the United Kingdom and the empire. And that threat of catastrophe came from Tennyson's own experience of Ireland.

In 1848, Tennyson stayed with Aubrey de Vere at his home at Curragh Chase, outside Limerick. Ireland was in the midst of Famine, and Tennyson's visit was a mixture of tourism to recuperate after depression and sublimated response to the horrors around him. Visiting Killarney, the echoes over the Lakes were demonstrated by the sounding of a bugle, and the poet subsequently composed the lyric beginning, 'The splendour falls on castle walls', also known as 'The Bugle Song':

> The splendour falls on castle walls
> And snowy summits old in story:

> The long light shakes across the lakes,
>   And the wild cataract leaps in glory.
> Blow, bugle, blow, set the wild echoes flying,
> Blow, bugle; answer, echoes, dying, dying, dying.
>
>   O hark, O hear! How thin and clear,
>   And thinner, clearer, farther going!
>   O sweet and far from cliff and scar
>   The horns of Elfland faintly blowing!
> Blow, let us hear the purple glens replying:
> Blow, bugle; answer, echoes, dying, dying, dying.
>
>   O love, they die in yon rich sky,
>   They faint on hill or field or river:
>   Our echoes roll from soul to soul,
>   And grow for ever and for ever.
> Blow, bugle, blow, set the wild echoes flying,
> And answer, echoes, answer, dying, dying, dying.[16]

The poem was composed in the library of de Vere's house and later introduced into the 1850 edition of *The Princess*. The experience of listening to the echoes sounded from a trumpet or cannon from the Eagle's Nest over the Upper Lake at Killarney was an essential part of the Killarney experience for tourists seeking the sublime. For Scottish travel writer Henry David Inglis, in an account of a visit in 1834 reproduced approvingly in the classic *Historical and Descriptive Notices of Cork and Vicinity* by Jeremiah Joseph Callanan's friend and editor – the Cork antiquarian John Windele – the experience of listening to the echoes triggered off thoughts of Edmund Burke with which Tennyson would have concurred:

> The hills seem, alike, to call to each other; and although it would have puzzled Burke to trace the emotion of sublimity to terror, it may be traced to its truer origin – power; for – when we hear the call repeated and answered, from mountain to mountain – sometimes loud, and without interval, and then fainter and fainter – and, after a solemn pause, again rising, as if from some far distant glen – our imagination endues the mountains with life; and to their attributes of magnitude, and silence, and solitude, we, for a moment, add the power of listening, and a voice.[17]

If Tennyson's 'Bugle Song' borrows much from accounts he might have read in guide books such as Inglis's or Windele's to add to his actual experience of the echoes in De Vere's company, these echoes had been a subject for Irish lyric seeking the sublime in Killarney for at least fifty years, in poems by Mary Tighe and Thomas Moore. Tighe wrote three sonnets on the subject, and her 'Written at Killarney' (published in 1811, but dated in the first year of the century, 'July, 29 1800') finds the experience of pausing to listen to echo matched by that of the reflection of moonlight in water:

> The fanning west-wind breathes upon our cheeks
>> Yet glowing with the sun's departed beams.
> Through the blue heavens the cloudless moon pours streams
> Of pure resplendent light, in silver streaks
> Reflected on the still, unruffled lake.
>> The Alpine hills in solemn silence frown,
>> While the dark woods night's deepest shades embrown.
> And now once more that soothing strain awake!
> Oh, ever to my heart, with magic power,
> Shall those sweet sounds recal this rapturous hour![18]

The sonic contrast of echo and silence mingles with the contrasts of moonlight and shadow, establishing a pulsing image of the synaesthetic workings of perception and memory. In the most daring line in the poem, Tighe works this up to such sibilant excess that the reading voice needs to take care in order to avoid the vocal slur that might match an indistinctness in the scene: 'the dark woods night's deepest shades embrown'. If Tennyson's version of this experience faces a similar indistinctness, it also suggests extinction. His is a lyric of history and the fading of memory, suited to a land where in 1848, the people may have appeared to be fading into immortality before his eyes and ears: 'Our echoes roll from soul to soul,/And grow for ever and for ever.'

Tennyson's 'Bugle Song' is a poem about immortality: it views the eternity of both the soul and memory. Yet, to borrow from Wordsworth, its 'localised Romance' is of a place subliminally aware of its immediate context (Famine) and geology, history and politics ('The splendour falls on castle walls/And snowy summits *old in story*'). As a poem about echoes, these echoes are sounded in the present, invoke the past, but also look into the future. One of Tennyson's English Idyls of 1842, 'The Golden Year', is a poem that frames a song of progress within a walking tour in Wales. It ends with the sound of the blasting of a slate quarry through the Llanberis Pass, as the reverberations of 'the great echo flap/And buffet round the hills from bluff to bluff'. Roger Ebbatson has said that this echo matches 'a loss of voice by the local workforce' that is 'answered by the literally unreadable counterblast from the slate quarry, rendered with supreme rhythmic, assonantal and alliterative virtuosity'.[19] As in 'The Bugle Song', Tennyson holds the ending in balance, as 'the great echo' can be both Arnold's faint remaining sounds of the English tourist's Welsh kindred and an echo that sounds into an enlightened future.

Yet the predominant echo through 'The Bugle Song' is of the past, of specific Irish antecedents. Although echoing Tighe, the most pointed allusion is to three of Moore's *Irish Melodies*, 'At the Mid Hour of Night' (1813), 'Echo' (1821) and ''Twas One of those Dreams' (1824). The latter, coming at a rather late and thus fairly optimistic phase of the composition of the *Melodies*, is about the poet hearing his own work (or at least 'The wild notes ... /He had taught to sing Erin's dark bondage and woes') played by the bugle over the Eagle's Nest. Like many of the *Melodies*, it is a lyric about history and time, but also about time passing into the future of a culturally recovered land. Moore imagines the immortality of literary fame, as the national poet of Ireland:

> Oh forgive, if, while listening to music, whose breath
> Seem'd to circle his name with a charm against death,
> He should feel a proud Spirit within him proclaim,
> 'Even so shalt thou live in the echoes of Fame:
>
> Even so, tho' thy memory should now die away,
> 'Twill be caught up again in some happier day,
> And the hearts and the voices of Erin prolong,
> Through the answering future, thy name and thy song.'[20]

Moore was writing at the height of a fully consolidated fame, but the conceit – in both senses of the word – is typical of him. It turns the expected into the novel: the echo is not just of the past, but an anticipation of the future. The lyric plays with end rhyme and internal rhyme around its subject, the 'fame' of the 'name' of the poet. 'Name ... proclaim ... Fame ... name', the echoes cluster in close semantic as well as sonic association around the poet's afterlife. Moore also borrows effects of internal rhyme from Irish-language prosody to represent the persistence of his subject, the recreated Irish lyric. And in the four-line wait for the final rhyme, the repetition of the word 'name', the delay suggests the faintness of the echo of the immortal poet himself. Echo thus becomes a figure for the consolations of belief, both of the Irish poet's fame and of Irish music's rescued immortality.

'The Bugle Song', however, echoes other echoes of the past. At Tennyson's request, Francis Turner Palgrave included Moore's 'Echo' and 'At the Mid Hour of Night' in the first edition of his *Golden Treasury of the Best Songs and Lyrics in the English Language* (1861). That anthology's full title does more than gesture in the direction of a language spoken by more than just the English. Christopher Ricks has told us that the *Golden Treasury* was inspired by William Allingham's 1860 anthology of

English-language lyric, *Nightingale Valley*.[21] Although Wordsworth and
Tennyson, as might be expected, are presiding geniuses of Allingham's
anthology, the tradition of Robert Burns and Walter Scott is strong, too, as
from its eighteenth-century section on, it is filled full of ballads and lyrics
from Scotland, Ireland and the United States.[22] Palgrave, as well, felt that
it was the Scottish ballad that had invigorated the English-language lyrical
tradition in anticipation of the innovations of Wordsworth and Coleridge.
In the second part of his two-part critical history of English poetry in the
Quarterly Review (1861–1862*)*, he had credited Allen Ramsey with publishing before 1720 'the earliest published collections of truly national songs'.
No matter how Ramsey's *Miscellany* and *Evergreen* had their synthetic
inauthenticities ('much dross mingled with purer metal, and not a few
ancient poems alloyed with modern matter'), they were attuned to the
needs of their time, 'an age already prepared to turn an ear to ancient
melodies, and a race alive with just sensitiveness to their national glories'.[23]
More than a century after Ramsey, while acknowledging the contribution
of Burns, Palgrave's *Golden Treasury* could present the antecedents of that
revival of English-language lyric at the beginning of the nineteenth century in which Moore occupied such an important place.

Palgrave said Tennyson chose Moore's 'Mid Hour of Night' because,
in terms we have already seen echoed by Yeats in Chapter 2, he 'much
admired its long drawn music'.[24] The second stanza suggests just which
Celtic source Tennyson used for his image of echo as intimation of immortality in the 'Bugle Song':

> Then I sing the wild song 'twas once such pleasure to hear!
> When our voices commingling breath'd, like one, on the ear;
>> And as Echo far off through the vale my sad orison rolls,
>> I think, oh my love! 'tis thy voice from the Kingdom of Souls,
> Faintly answering still the notes that once were so dear.[25]

For a critic such as Arnold, literary history participates in a sort of
innovatory or modernising process, where a number of differing cultural forms fuse (to use an Arnoldian word) into new literary forms. This
is because an old literary language dies, leaving a linguistic culture in
need of compensation: according to Arnold, 'the echo of all its kindred
in other lands is growing fainter and more feeble'. Moore's echoes bear
a nationalist weight, because they are of the Irish melodies that prompt
the 'long drawn music' of the poem's metre. The English lyric carries
echoes of the recovered Irish music that in turn has lent to the English
poem its metre. It thus attempts to recuperate in metre and symbol the

imagined cultural and legislative freedom of the past. Tennyson echoes Moore's echoes, drawn to them by this element of loss and recuperation, the elegiac subject of lost love reunited in immortality. Yet history is not to be emptied out of the music of the poems, even given that there is a long tradition of dismissing both Tennyson and Moore, in Britain as in Ireland, as mere facile metrists. Given the violent history of the fusion of the four nations of the United Kingdom, in which the imposition of the English language was but one result of centuries of cultural assimilation and coercion, Victorian poetry often shows the writing that attempts to commemorate such fusion carries with it conflicting formal echoes of conflict and rebellion.

Immrama

English and Irish poets writing in English were drawn to one of the most remarkable literary genres of early Irish Christianity, the immram or voyage tale. In these texts, written in Latin or Irish, voyages of conversion, pilgrimage and absolution bring their sailors across the Atlantic, through adventures and visions on imaginary islands, and then back to Ireland or Europe. The *Navigatio Sancti Brendani*, for instance, discovers an Edenic land of plenty far to the West, thought in legend to be Hy Brasil. For the Victorian Irish, seeking a prophetic typology to account for the emigration of thousands from post-Famine Ireland, this land could also be America. The best-known Victorian poetic version is by an English poet, Tennyson. 'The Voyage of Maeldune' was published in *Ballads and Other Poems* in 1880, the year in which Allingham recorded Tennyson's suggestion about floating the island of Ireland far to the west. Tennyson's version of the story is taken many removes from its source, Patrick Weston Joyce's 1879 version of the Latin *Immram Curaig Máele Dúin*.[26] More than translating a translation, Tennyson did what he was accustomed to doing with classical myth, taking a third-person epic narrative and casting it into the genre of prosopopoeia or dramatic monologue. However, this was an established Irish translating practice, as earlier English poetic versions of immrama – Denis Florence MacCarthy's 'The Voyage of St Brendan' and T.D. Sullivan's 'The Voyage of the O'Corras' (which Joyce recommends in his introduction) – are told in the first person.[27] Tennyson also follows Irish poets such as James Clarence Mangan or Aubrey de Vere in experimenting with Irish matter in English hexameter.

The form was adaptable: W.B. Yeats adapted prosody and genre for lyric purposes in 'The White Birds' (1893), adding the imagery of the

Maelduin immram to Tennyson's English experimental metre. Its final stanza runs:

I am haunted by numberless islands, and many a Danaan shore,
Where Time would surely forget us, and Sorrow come near us no more;
Soon far from the rose and the lily and fret of the flames would we be,
Were we only white birds, my beloved, buoyed out on the foam of the sea![28]

The loss of time is also the loss of memory, where the unusual lyrical use of the hexameter exchanges strife on land for a directionless bobbing about at sea. The lover in the lyric seeks the transformation of himself and the loved one into birds in order to secure eternity. But he also asks for forgetfulness of 'the fret of the flames' of the land left behind. In a typical 1890s move, Yeats adopts the conventions of the voyage poem to suggest both the unavoidable conflicts of the land that echo through the past and the desire for an oblivious escape from them, of which more will be said in Chapter 7. Given the context of English versions of Irish immrama, the poem's desire is that the patterns of voyaging and return in the genre be exchanged for perpetual forgetting, from which there will be no return.

Nevertheless, Victorian English-language versions of the immram sought to establish contemporary forms for the remembering of the medieval material contained in the originals. P.W. Joyce, for instance, says that his intention was to translate the romances in his collection into 'simple, plain, homely English',[29] and in Tennyson's hands, the predominant anapests of the rhythm of the synthetic Celtic lyric are carried in monosyllabic English couplets that tend to the archaic:

I was the chief of the race – he had stricken my father dead –
But I gathered my fellows together, I swore I would strike off his head.
Each of them looked like a king, and was noble in birth as in worth,
And each of them boasted he sprang from the oldest race upon earth.
Each was as brave in the fight as the bravest hero of song,
And each of them liefer had died than have done one another a wrong.[30]

In this first stanza, the syntactic and prosodic units close together at the end of the sentence. But the prosodic success in achieving these difficult hexameter couplets is also won by retaining an echo of an anapaestic alternately rhyming ballad or English common measure within the long lines. Caesural or phrasal pauses are emphasised or hinted. We can hear this ballad metre more strongly if we imagine the first four lines lineated thus:

I was the chief of the race –
he had stricken my father dead –
But I gathered my fellows together,

> I swore I would strike off his head.
> Each of them looked like a king,
> and was noble in birth as in worth,
> And each of them boasted he sprang
> from the oldest race upon earth.

The formal trace of a three-stress English-language ballad line sounds within the epic hexameter. In the prosodic experiments in the 1840s of Longfellow (*Evangeline*) and Clough (*The Bothie of Tober-na-Vuolich*, *Amours de Voyage*), the hexameter is either a synthetic metre adapted from Greek for the purposes of an artificial regularity (Longfellow), or a loose and irregularly scanned line that lends itself so well to narrative and speech that many readers heard little distinction between it and prose (Clough). Tennyson himself uses an eight-beat trochaic metre for his Locksley Hall poems. In those poems, the distinctive music of the metre retains a sonic trace of an indigenous oral British tradition. Take the lines on St Francis in 'Locksey Hall Sixty Years After', discussed earlier:

> Sweet St Francis of Assisi, would that he were here again,

> He that in his Catholic wholeness used to call the very flowers
> Sisters, brothers – and the beasts – whose pains are hardly less than ours!

The trochees are allowed to settle into their medieval matter, perhaps a hint at the speaker's Tory nostalgia for Catholic spirituality, one nostalgia in which Tennyson himself did not share. The form of 'The Voyage of Maeldune' also implies tradition and experiment, a conservative attachment to the old as well as an innovatory concern with the new. The form assists in the portrayal of a dilemma about the past that faces the mariners in his poem. Allegiances to tribe or brotherhood are evidence of a loyalty beyond reason, a loyalty that boasts itself as coming from 'the oldest race upon earth'. The boasts are carried in the language of forefathers: they 'liefer had died' than contemplate betrayal and change. The eytmologies are those of the English language (for instance, *Oxford English Dictionary* traces the archaism 'lief' back to Old Saxon, High German and Norse); the hurt is a long-standing Irish one.

In *The Realms of Verse*, Matthew Reynolds has written about Tennyson's early involvement with the Victorian interest in etymologies, and the older poet's preference for an 'English' as opposed to Latin or French diction. So, the poem (from the mid-point of the poet's career) for which 'The Bugle Song' was written, *The Princess*, contains rival Northern and Southern armies, and in Reynolds's delicate phrasing, 'southern and northern phraseology' in which 'the distinction between them might,

on particular occasions, take on expressive salience'.[31] Reynolds sugges-
tions are valuable for a poem such as 'The Voyage of Maeldune' because
Tennyson takes the translator Joyce's lead, 'simple, plain, homely English',
and imports an Anglo-Saxon lexis into his version in order to recreate
a medieval tone. The invention is synthetic, and for at least one reader,
was just too successful. According to one of Tennyson's best early critics,
Stopford Brooke, the fault with the poem is that it makes its Irish monastic mariners too English. Tennyson's monologue takes quite extraordinary
liberties with its source, by turning its voyagers into violent and drunken
buffoons. Allingham records that in another argument with Tennyson
over Ireland, he had the temerity to suggest that England leave the Irish
to themselves. 'Civil War!' was the Laureate's considered (and prophetic)
response.[32] It was perhaps in the spirit of such opinions that Tennyson
originally planned that the sailors in the poem kill each other, and that
Maeldune return alone.

Such English caricatures of a supposed Irish propensity to violence
prompted the Anglo-Irish Brooke to return the compliment:

> Tennyson loses all the sentiment of the original by imposing on the voyag-
> ers his own conception of the Irish character. The warriors who sail boast
> loudly of their descent; the slightest thing flusters them with anger; they
> shout, and hate, and wallow in flowers and tear them up in a blind passion,
> and gorge, and madden, and chant the glories of Finn, and fight with one
> another, and slay, and only a tithe of them return. This is the English form
> which he gave to the story – the English pleasure in rough and tumble
> killing for amusement, the Anglo-Saxon *brutalité* imposed upon the Irish
> nature [...] There is not one trace of this in the original. All are faithful,
> loving and tender comrades. Not one of them acts like a drunken sailor at
> Portsmouth fair.[33]

Brooke's objection, however, is not to the metre or diction of the poem;
rather, it is to the translation of the Irish into English character, a travesty in which the Anglo-Saxon behaviour of enlisted men is 'imposed' on
selflessly questing mystical Celtic warriors. Thus, rather than translation,
'The Voyage of Maeldune' carries a number of unaccommodated formal
echoes of etymologies or poetic forms, matched by the attempted translation into one another of two of the imagined sets of national characteristics of two nationalities within its contemporary United Kingdom.

One of the synonyms of 'Celtic' for the English Victorian poet and
critic is 'poetic'. In an earlier conversation with Allingham in the same year
as the publication of 'The Voyage of Maeldune', Tennyson had contrasted
the acquiescence of the English to Norman rule with the recalcitrant Irish,

who are 'raging and foaming to this hour'. Allingham pointed out that only in the previous century Ireland had to suffer 'the penal laws, and the deliberate destruction' of Irish industry by the English. 'What do you say to that?' he asked, and the Laureate replied: 'That was brutal! Our ancestors *were* horrible brutes! And the Kelts are very charming and sweet and poetic. I love their Ossians and their Finns and so forth – but they are most damnably unreasonable!'[34] The Irish Question, as intemperately elucidated by Tennyson, was both political and cultural, where the 'charming and sweet and poetic' was offset by centuries of 'raging and foaming'. Although nineteenth-century Irish poems in English after Moore frequently seek recompense for traumatic loss in the past, an English poet such as Tennyson also explores the corollary of such recompense, the seeming impossibility of forgiveness. What could not be resolved for this Englishman was that the past not only carried great cultural richness but also seemed unable to give consolation for its losses, as shown by an apparently ungovernable and irreconcilably divided latter-day 'Celtic' country, Ireland.

The other side of poetic mysticism was held to be the political fanaticism that cultural commentators with a more metropolitan cast of mind than Tennyson felt it was their duty to attempt to understand. So Matthew Arnold's 1860 'Saint Brandan' – perhaps more 'Ancient Mariner' than immram – opens with a spirituality that takes little note of personal safety or the decorum appropriate even for saints:

> Saint Brandan sails the northern main;
> The brotherhoods of saint are glad.
> He greets them once, he sails again;
> So late!–such storms! The Saint is mad![35]

One source for Arnold's use of the St Brendan material was Renan's account of the pacifying influence of Christianity on the Irish, an influence that had resulted in the surrender of self:

> Credulous as a child, timid, indolent, inclined to submit and obey, the Irishman alone was capable of lending himself to that complete self-abdication in the hands of the abbot, which we find so deeply marked in the historical and legendary memorials of the Irish Church [...] the legend of St. Brandan is the most singular product of this combination of Celtic naturalism with Christian spiritualism.[36]

The result is exotically un-English and definitely un-Protestant: both 'Celtic naturalism' and 'Christian spiritualism' appeal to a Romantic and Victorian medievalism drawn both to the evidences of textual or ethnographical research and nostalgia for a pre-Reformation Christian unity.

Although attracted to the mystical alliance of naturalism and spiritualism, Arnold is also taken by one episode in the story of Brendan's voyage, which toys with the heterodox notion of momentary relief from eternal damnation. St Brendan is granted a meeting with Judas, who appears to be out of hell. In the Latin *Navigatio Sancti Brendani*, an act of kindness to a leper has enabled Judas to be granted both weekly and seasonal respite – every Sunday and all through Christmas and Easter.[37] Arnold gives him one hour every Christmas. 'St Brandan' becomes a lyrical ballad of eternal suffering and small forgiveness:

> 'Once every year, when carols wake,
> On earth, the Christmas-nights repose,
> Arising from the sinners' lake,
> I journey to these healing snows.
>
> 'I staunch with ice my burning breast,
> With silence balm my whirling brain.
> O Brandan! To this hour of rest
> That Joppan leper's ease was pain.'
>
> Tears started to Saint Brandan's eyes;
> He bowed his head, he breathed a prayer –
> Then looked, and lo, the frosty skies!
> The iceberg, and no Judas there!

By contrast, in a later poem such as 'The Voyage of Maeldune', spiritualism appears only grudgingly to be allowed to overcome fanaticism, as Tennyson strives to make his Irish characters forgive and forget the past. The final meeting of Tennyson's mariners with a 300-year-old relic of the earlier voyages of St Brendan acquaints them with more than the usual lessons of shore leave. The Saint asks:

> 'His fathers have slain thy fathers in war or in single strife,
> Thy fathers have slain his fathers, each taken a life for a life,
> Thy father had slain his father, how long shall the murder last?
> Go back to the Isle of Finn and suffer the Past to be Past.'
> And we kissed the fringe of his beard and we prayed as we heard him pray,
> And the Holy Man he assoiled us, and sadly we sailed away.

Of all the English poets, Tennyson is the supreme elegist, drawn to 'the passion of the past'. The atavistic Irish sailors here are given counsel of deliberate forgetfulness, asked to 'suffer the Past to be Past'. There is no penance or special pleading, and certainly not the admonition of the hermit in Joyce's version: 'As God has delivered you from the many dangers you have passed through, though you were very guilty, and well deserved death at His hands; so you forgive your enemy the crime he committed against you.'[38] Even the immram that might appear closest to Tennyson's contribution to the genre, *Immram Ua Corra*, the tale of three sons who have been given to childless parents after they asked help of the devil, can only find absolution for violence and wanton destruction in repentance, pilgrimage and a voyage of conversion.[39]

In these early Christian tales, forgiveness is rather harder to earn than any post-Reformation prejudice that the sacrament of confession is a matter of swift absolution after a sudden change of mind. But in Tennyson's contribution to these tales, the moment of reciprocal forgiveness, which may in other versions be partial or complete, needs to be accompanied by a disavowal of the past. Asking that the past be suffered to be past is a phrase not used without irony elsewhere in Tennyson's work. A version of it appears in *The Princess*, when Princess Ida castigates one of her maids for singing that great blank-verse lyric of the passion of the past, 'Tears, Idle Tears'. The feminist progressive Ida asks 'let old bygones be,' and repudiates lyric nostalgia as she looks forward to 'that great year of equal mights and rights'. She adds, 'Nor would I fight with iron laws, in the end/Found golden: let past be past.'[40] The patriarchy that was formerly held to be historical and social necessity will be replaced by social and scientific progress, if not evolution: this section of the narrative of *The Princess* takes place on a geological field trip.

Tennyson's phrase, 'let past be past', commonplace as it has become, may only have hardened into cliché throughout the nineteenth century.[41] The sentiment might not have been much recognised in an eighteenth-century culture concerned to found its constitution on claims of tradition and antiquity. Its import is that forgetting will be accompanied by forgiving, and all the better to stave off tragedy. Published along with 'The Voyage of Maeldune' in *Ballads and Other Poems*, 'The First Quarrel' is another monologue about islands and sea journeys, this time written in the dialect of the Isle of Wight. It is spoken by a widow whose last memory of her husband is of a row over a premarital love affair. The chastised husband pleads that his wife forgive and forget: '"Let bygones be!"' he asks. '"By-gones ma' be come-agains"' she retorts (ll. 67–69). The poem ends with the unforgiven husband leaving for farm work on the mainland, and the magnificent flatness of its precipitate final line: 'An' the boat went down that night – the boat went down that night.' (l.92) Conversely, in the final version of 'The Voyage of Maeldune' forgiveness is granted,

and the saint administers absolution because the mariners have allowed
the past to be past. Maeldune can meet again, 'The man that had slain my
father. I saw him and let him be.' (l.128)

In asking that the Irish should suffer the past to be past, Tennyson may
also be alluding to the weight the phrase is made to bear in two poems
written by Aubrey de Vere. The first is from de Vere's best-known poem,
'The Year of Sorrow; Ireland 1849.' Its composition and publication were
contemporaneous with the publication and revision of *The Princess*, and
it is preoccupied in its own way with Victorian notions of 'progress' and
'necessity'. In the 'Autumn' section, the Tory landlord de Vere blames a
political economy that allowed only acquiescence in the return of famine:

> The roof-trees fall of hut and hall;
> 　　I hear them fall, and falling cry, –
> 'One fate for each, one fate for all!
> 　　So wills the Law that willed a lie.'
>
> Dread power of Man! What spread the waste
> 　　In circles hour by hour more wide,
> And would not let the past be past? –
> 　　That Law which promised much, and lied.[42]

De Vere's internal rhyming and repetition ('fall ... hall ... fall ... falling
... all', 'one fate ... one fate', 'circles hour by hour more', 'past be past'),
slight modulations in sound and syllable ('wills the Law that willed a lie')
and the half-rhyme of effect with its cause ('waste'/'past?') move with
some skill around the monotonous force of the iron laws of liberal economics that have held nothing can be done to interfere with such catastrophe. It is all that de Vere can do in such apocalyptic circumstances to
hold off accusations of genocide: after these stanzas he turns to God that
He might offer consolation to the Irish dead, who are 'the afflicted race,/
Whom Man, not God, abolished.' Needless to say, de Vere shows little
patience with the providential justifications of Famine prevalent in the
British defense of their part in administering Ireland during this time.[43]

The power of the past in de Vere's poem caused Ireland and its governors
to cling on to old practices, places and beliefs in the face of a stern economics that could not conceive how contemporary conditions demanded
interference. The responsibilities are shared within the 'Dread power of
man!' between the Law and the wasted people: to adapt the title of de
Vere's 1848 economic and political contribution to the aftermath of the
Great Famine, the fault lies both with *English Misrule and Irish Misdeeds*.
This was not only Ireland's but the Victorian United Kingdom's greatest

catastrophe, the result of a brush with economic modernity that resulted
in wholesale depopulation and the creation of a landscape and society for-
ever changed from what it was in the 'past'. De Vere's solutions were not
just government intervention, but a sort of conservative modernising that
would benefit from the establishment of exclusively Irish emigrant colo-
nies in Canada or Australia, in which the uprooted culture could be replicated in conditions of plenty. Whether the Irish were voluntarily willing
to contemplate such a drastic solution, it might be said that something
similar occurred anyway. The prospect of mass emigration has a brief
counterpart in Denis Florence MacCarthy's 1848 immram, his version of
'The Voyage of St Brendan,' which ends with an angel from a far Western
land telling Brendan to go home to saintly, scholarly Ireland. In the future
though, this place will provide help to the Irish again:

> 'But in the end upon that land shall fall
>   A bitter scourge, a lasting flood of tears,
> When ruthless tyranny shall level all
>   The pious trophies of its early years:
> Then shall this land prove thy poor country's friend,
>   And shine a second Eden in the west;
> Then shall this shore its friendly arms extend,
>   And clasp the outcast exile to its breast.'[44]

The America to which the Victorian Irish voyaged in their millions is
prophesied in Brendan's voyage and carried through these voyage poems.
Tir na nOg or Hy Brasil are found again in conditions of necessity.

De Vere said that his sequence *Inisfail* (1861) was 'a National Chronicle
cast in a poetic form'. It has the dubious distinction, according to Chris
Morash, of being 'the longest single poem by an Irish writer in English'.[45]
In the preface to the poem, first added in 1877 but subsequently much
revised, de Vere stops short of suggesting emigration as the solution to
Ireland's problems. However, he does counsel the forgiveness that, if it
does not come through forgetting, might come when memory gains from
the 'long run' of history:

> In these days few are so biassed by party or sectarian bitterness as to grudge
> an epitaph to virtue and calamity in times gone by. A timid caution may
> shrink from Historical Studies (as if the most interesting studies could be
> suppressed), but a manly prudence will enjoin them, provided that they be
> conducted with justice. Ireland is bound to acknowledge that it was not
> England alone, that persecuted. On the long run Truth is a peacemaker.
> What is to be feared from historical studies in connection with Ireland?
> The spirit of vengeance? A man must be half-witted to sigh for vengeance

when the offenders have been for centuries dead. He must be an idiot not to perceive that on the long run, whatever a just cause may have gained for time through the use of unjust means, it has invariably lost ten times as much through injustice.[46]

In its way, this is the perfectly conventional plea that history itself will provide the temporal distance from the past that will enable its violent disruptions to be understood. The individual, party or sect will, in time – that is viewing past time from a time looking to a peaceful future – leave off their desire for vengeance. Like a latter-day revisionist historian, de Vere looks to 'times gone by' with 'manly prudence' and 'justice', and sees that 'Truth is a peacemaker.' The long run of 'Historical Studies' will salve the hatreds of the past, not through forgetting, but certainly through forgiveness. Thus, the impartial study of history itself as a detachment from the hatreds of the past might allow the Catholic saint in the Protestant Tennyson's poem to absolve the vengeance-driven Maeldune.

Inisfail was first published in 1861, and in the same volume de Vere's *The Sisters; or Weal in Woe*,[47] a blank verse narrative, had also requested that the past be allowed to be past. There, however, he looked to a future for Ireland. Between 'The Year of Sorrow' and the *Inisfail* volume, de Vere had converted to Catholicism in 1851, and as a consequence *The Sisters* tells a contemporary tale of famine, emigration, return and death all transcended by ascetic self-sacrifice. The narrative is framed within a condition-of-Ireland debate between the narrator and a young Oxford visitor, 'A man of tender nerve though stubborn thought' (p. 192), who is impatient about the lack of material progress in the countryside around him. Sitting in an ancient churchyard, the Englishman is courteously corrected by a retelling of the brutal history of Ireland by the narrator who speaks, 'Words few but plain, grim rubric traced in blood' (p.194). The visitor then presses the narrator for the significance of one of the graves.

Frame and tale together give us a poem about sympathies shared through a story of poverty, emigration and unnecessary early death. As such, *The Sisters* bears the influence of another English Laureate friend of de Vere, Wordsworth. The poem is strongly reminiscent of the tale of the Wanderer in the first book of *The Excursion*, where the story of Margaret and her ruined cottage effects sympathy in its poet-listener for suffering that has distinct economic causes: rural unemployment, European war and abandonment.[48] Margaret pines and dies because she cannot allow herself to get over her abandonment; she cannot let the past be past.[49] In de Vere's poem, the Wordsworthian mode enables the narrative to work on the sympathies of an English listener, one who is not so alien that he

cannot be brought to a better understanding of the reasons for the seeming lack of progress of England's poorer neighbour. His dialogue turns
from the failure of Ireland's rulers of the previous 700 years, and the lack
of affection felt for them by their supposed imperial partners, to a possible
future. The narrator states:

> 'No country loved they:
> Her least, the imperial realm! 'Tis late to mourn;
> Let past be past'. 'The Past,' he said, 'is present;
> And o'er the Future stretches far a hand
> Shadowy and minatory.' 'Come what may,'
> I said, 'no suffering can to us be new;
> No shadow fail to dew some soul with grace.
> The history of a Soul holds in it more
> Than doth a Nation's! In its every chance
> Eternity lies hid; from every step
> Branch forth two paths piercing infinity.
>
> (*The Sisters*, p. 237)

The two paths are those of the spiritual and secular, and de Vere goes on
to counsel the theme of his later years, that Ireland's contribution to the
history of the world has been and will continue to be spiritual, Catholic
and quiescent. The 'phantom image of my country,/Vanquished yet victor,
in her weal and woe' (p. 197) is an image of solace given only by a belief in
immortality as illustrated by the story of the ascetic surviving sister, Mary.

The events remembered in 'The Voyage of Maeldune' are linked quite
specifically not only with de Vere's Irish poems of the previous three
decades, but also with the position of Ireland within the United Kingdom
at the time of its writing. In the 1880s, Tennyson's poem might even have
been intended as a direct allegorical intervention, as Victoria's Laureate
turned his attention to that part of her kingdom convulsed by the activities of the Land League, the rise of Parnell and the first parliamentary
test of the UK itself in the increased agitation for Home Rule. Indeed, in
the sections of *The Realms of Verse* that deal with the poetry of the United
Kingdom, Matthew Reynolds reads Tennyson's Irish poems allegorically,
and de Vere's *The Sisters* as an allegory of Catholic Ireland and Protestant
England.[50]

Whatever he felt about his Catholicism, Tennyson would have seen
in de Vere's mysticism a more general concern with a spiritual belief in
the future of an immortal self, or at least the coming historical conditions in which spirituality might have a future. This was tempered only
by a reactionary concern that the coming times might lose all that a

glorious imperial past had gained for an imperial present intent on putting its material prosperity before its spiritual responsibilities. These are responsibilities to church, state, constitution and past. The 1852 version of Tennyson's great funeral ode for Wellington momentarily allowed its grief to overcome its public responsibilities as it foresaw an end to empire and the Union: 'a darkening future yields/Some reverse from worse to worse'.[51] Even if for the individual – Alfred Tennyson, say – the future did contain an eternity illuminated by the prospect of an immortal continuation of the identity of self, then for his country the future also promises chaos and the dissolution of the Union, empire and all.

Given such a prospect, forgiving and forgetting not only suffer the past to be past but also bring about the forgetting of identity – spiritual as well as cultural – in the future. Even in his dealings with the unforgiving Irish, Tennyson could not do that. The central tale of his Irish dialect monologue 'Tomorrow' (1884) is about a woman, Molly Magee, whose inability to get over the disappearance of a long-lost love is ended only by the discovery of the loved one preserved youthful and intact in a bog for forty years. It is when the English poet turns to the past, then, that his borrowing – from himself as well as de Vere or Irish epic – connects the mythic advice to forget with events that cannot be absolved, as it were, from his own memory. These are events that are linked generally with the Celticism that Tennyson knew was well accustomed to remembering the losses of the past, indeed for which the past frequently seemed only to be loss. The echoes of that loss, though heard through the losses of vanquished nations, Tennyson could hear sounding through eternity.

If we cannot grasp eternity as a movement forwards or backwards, we might think of it as circular or repetitive. Such eternal repetition of self-perpetuating revenge, whatever the power of eventual absolution, is implicit not only in the Maelduin story, but throughout those parts of the immram genre that see deliverance from seemingly eternal journeying comes not just through personal repentance but, crucially, through sacramental absolution. Just as Arnold allowed his Judas out of hell once a year, the *Navigatio Sancti Brendani* gave structure to its seemingly directionless voyaging by a miraculous annual return to the same island for Easter. Without compass or map, these early Christian legendary voyagers were described as finding their way only with supernatural intervention, and never solely through their own efforts. It is just this Christian redemptive aspect of the genre from which Yeats later sought to be delivered. He suggested to the loved one in 'The White Birds' a future in a place 'where Time would surely forget us, and Sorrow come near us no more'.

Another poetic version of the myth published a century later, Paul Muldoon's 'Immram' (1980), lends critical as well as poetic distance from what had attracted Renan and Arnold to this material, 'the combination of Celtic naturalism and Christian spiritualism'. These had become alternatives: 'Celtic naturalism' is manifest in Yeats's lovers as wandering birds; 'Christian spiritualism' is found in the absolution and personal immortality that preoccupies the versions by Tennyson, Arnold and MacCarthy. Muldoon's poem ends in a hotel penthouse confronting a figure who is part hippy-mystic, part Howard Hughes: '"I forgive you", he croaked, "And I forget."' The images of the final stanza are images of repetition and circularity. The narrator (Maelduin/Muldoon) leaves the hotel behind two of the characters in the poem, 'Mr and Mrs Alfred Tennyson'. Tennyson had circulated through this material before, and as the characters flow through revolving doors, the poem ends up back in 'Fosters pool room', where it had begun.[52] Forgiveness is granted but eternity is still manifest as repetition.

Tennyson, along with Arnold before him and Yeats after him, participates in the nostalgia of a peculiarly Victorian form of British poetic Celticism. The diction and prosody of English poetry is implicated in personal loss, and through that the large cultural losses of the Scottish, Welsh and Irish languages and their attendant literary and musical traditions. Drawn to what remains of those traditions, the personal inability to let the past be past places the nostalgia of such poetry unrepentantly in the present as it appears stubbornly determined to echo through the future of its increasingly disunited kingdom. As English poets skirt around the fringes of the matter of the United Kingdom, poetic form itself is transformed in the contact of margin with centre. The artistic gains, we can suggest with hindsight, are substantial. But the gain is grounded in loss, no matter that it is a loss that cannot be forgotten.

CHAPTER 7

'Spelt from Sibyl's Leaves': Hopkins, Yeats and the Unravelling of British Poetry

Two Irish Evenings

For a brief period of time, between 1883 and 1889, the English Jesuit poet and Professor of Greek Gerard Manley Hopkins, and the young Irish poet and mystic William Butler Yeats, lived in the same city – Dublin. For Hopkins it was a period of internal exile, estranged at what he called 'a third/remove' from family, religion and homeland, in an increasingly dis-united United Kingdom and British Empire.[1] He sent out the *tristia* of his last Dublin poems to a small band of sympathetic, if frequently exas-perated, readers. While the Yeats family, following their financially inse-cure artist father, shuttled between Dublin and London, the early poetic promise of oldest son William appeared in the pages of the *Irish Monthly*, edited by Hopkins's colleague Fr Matthew Russell, as well as the incipient moment of national revival marked in the publication in 1888 of *Poems and Ballads of Young Ireland* edited by the old Fenian John O'Leary. If Hopkins arrived in Dublin obsessed with twilight of a sort, of the sunsets and evenings on which he contributed rare published letters to the popu-lar scientific journal *Nature*, Yeats sought twilight at other times of day, of the morning and of the dawn. As one poet fashioned increasingly ago-nised late Victorian rhythms of will into subject matter of extreme physi-cal and spiritual instress, another fashioned a rewritten Irish Ossianism and Victorian fairy poetry into the more recognisably fin de siècle calm of 'those wavering, meditative, organic rhythms which are the embodiment of the imagination, that neither desires nor hates, because it has done with time, and only wishes to gaze upon some reality, some beauty'.[2]

Of course, these imagined opposites will easily interchange in the read-ing of actual poems, but this brief contact of the English and Irish poet living in the same place at the same time is written from what looked like the beginning of the decline of the Union and a seemingly unimaginable revival in the national aspirations of one of its parts. For both poets a third figure, the dominant Irish political personality of the time, Charles Stewart Parnell, galvanised their view of the historical moment through which they lived. Hopkins viewed Parnell's seduction of British Prime Minister William Ewart Gladstone to the cause of Home Rule as the end of the Union, perhaps even the precipitate end of a British commonwealth on earth. He didn't live to see Parnell's eventual destruction by a grim alliance of Irish Catholicism and the English Tory party. But in that moment, two years after Hopkins's death, Yeats sought a national rebirth in the midst of personal distress and public suffering.

This chapter begins with a pair of poems written from two Irish evenings, roughly eight years apart, between the arrival of Hopkins into Dublin in 1883 and the death of Parnell in 1891. To take the second evening poem first, William Butler Yeats's 'Parnell's Funeral' was published first as 'A Parnellite at Parnell's Funeral' in the London *Spectator* in 1934, before its retitling as the opening poem in *A Full Moon in March* the following year. It recalls the events of the evening of 11 October 1891, in Glasnevin cemetery in Dublin:

> Parnell's Funeral
> I
> Under the Great Comedian's tomb the crowd.
> A bundle of tempestuous cloud is blown
> About the sky; where that is clear of cloud
> Brightness remains; a brighter star shoots down;
> What shudders run through all that animal blood?
> What is this sacrifice? Can someone there
> Recall the Cretan barb that pierced a star?
>
> Rich foliage that the starlight glittered through,
> A frenzied crowd, and where the branches sprang
> A beautiful seated boy; a sacred bow;
> A woman, and an arrow on a string;
> A pierced boy, image of a star laid low.
> That woman, the Great Mother imaging,
> Cut out his heart. Some master of design
> Stamped boy and tree upon Sicilian coin.
>
> An age is the reversal of an age:[3]

This is a rugged enough performance: the symbols seem merely thrown into the poem as prophetic baggage, cut up into the abrupt syntax of a list. The strange astronomical event, the meteorite, is just one of a number of images from a range of systems and cultures – Greek, Christian, hermetic and astrological – not to mention an Irish crowd witnessing its latest tragic under 'the Great Comedian' Daniel O'Connell's tomb. Rhyme and repetition jar with a roughness unusual even for the older Yeats: in the first four lines, 'crowd' cross-rhymes with 'cloud'; to be followed by a near eye-rhyme 'blown'; the eventual full rhyme, on 'cloud' again; and then the half-rhyme, 'down'. In the second stanza, half-rhyme strikes sonic dissonance, both in sense and its sounds: 'sprang'/'string'/'imaging', or the distinctly bum note as 'design' is given only an off-pitch echo against 'coin'. 'I thirst for accusation' the elderly poet later taunts in the poem, as much giving aesthetic as political offense. It is an example of something Malcolm Brown called 'Literary Parnellism'[4] in 1972, the deliberate courting of the aloofness of the hero Charles Stewart Parnell. In James Joyce's case, the Parnellite artist set himself against the two masters of 'an imperial British state and the one holy Roman, Catholic and Apostolic Church'.[5] In Yeats's case, he set himself against the 'animal blood' of the mob, or (as later in the poem), 'the contagion of the throng'.

'Parnell's Funeral' seems in certain ways quite deliberately to be not answering the rhetorical challenge of the extraordinary event it remembers. It is no 'Easter 1916', nor even 'To Ireland in the Coming Times'. First published the following year, 1892, as 'Apologia Addressed to Ireland in the Coming Days', the latter poem invoked the stirrings of cultural revival in the seeming political vacuum created in the aftermath of Parnell's disgrace and death, rewritten in 1924 to face the challenges of a post-civil war Irish Free State free state. Yeats was not one of the 200,000 Parnellites who followed the funeral cortege, although he had published a polemical elegy, 'Mourn – And Then Onward!' in the Land League newspaper *United Ireland* the day before the funeral (it is a crude poem he went to some lengths to suppress in later life).[6] He says that a 'friend', Maud Gonne, had told him of the atmospheric events of that evening and of the falling star.[7] The observation was corroborated in Standish O'Grady's extraordinary 1894 synopsis of Irish history *The Story of Ireland*, where pathetic fallacy was exceeded by the telepathic hysteria of the crowd:

> While his followers were committing Charles Parnell's remains to the earth, the sky was bright with strange lights and flames. Only a coincidence possibly; and yet persons not superstitious have maintained that there is some mysterious sympathy between the human soul and the elements, and that storms and other elemental disturbances have too often succeeded or accompanied great battles to be regarded as only fortuitous. Truly the souls of men were widely and deeply troubled that night, electrical and highly-wrought in the extreme.[8]

Yeats reviewed O'Grady's book the year after it was published, and he initially dismissed such claims as 'whimsical impressionism'. For all that the mystic in O'Grady could go so far as to link the atmospheric disturbances recorded at the time of death of St Columba in the sixth century with the events of the burial of Parnell in the nineteenth, Yeats's praise of him could ultimately go no higher than to say he was Ireland's first modern cultural historian:

> I am confident that, despite his breathless generalisations, his slipshod style, his ungovernable likings and dislikings, he is the first man who has tried to write [the true history of Ireland], for he is the first to have written not mainly of battles and enactments, but of changing institutions and changing beliefs, of the pride of the wealthy and the long endurance 'of the servile tribes of ignoble countenance'.[9]

For O'Grady, those servile tribes had become O'Connell's people,[10] whose loyalty to the 'Liberator' was to show again as they gathered round his grave in their hundreds of thousands for the funeral of his successor, 'the Chief'.

Forty years later, O'Grady's account of the sky from Glasnevin graveyard was to be found quoted by Yeats in the gloss to the first printing of 'A Parnellite at Parnell's Funeral' in *The Spectator,* inserted between the poem's two sections as 'evidence' of the events of that day.[11] The evidence provided by Maud Gonne was tainted by other, personal matter – namely her suffering in the aftermath of the death of her son, a child she at first told Yeats had been adopted. 'An age is the reversal of an age', Yeats could say, and much happened in the forty years between the burial of Parnell and the publication date of the poem that remembered it, by which time Maud Gonne and O'Grady's prophetic falling star could be read in one way from the 1890s as what Brown calls 'eschatological meteorology'.[12] In another way, by 1934, it was portent confirmed by the hindsight of the subsequent course of an Irish history charged in its way, along with those electrical and highly wrought souls who saw a meteor on that day.

In the months following this event, an aftermath in which Parnell and Gonne were to be inextricably linked in his writing, Yeats gave a notebook to his doubly grieving friend, *The Flame of the Spirit,* and also wrote a number of love lyrics, including the unpublished 'Cycles Ago', which mixes a fantasy of reincarnation with these signs of portent. It begins looking back to an evening spent with Gonne the previous July:

The low crying curlew and peewit, the honey pale orb of the moon,
The dew covered grass in the valley, our mother the sea with her croon
The leaping green leaves in the woodland, the flame of the stars in the skies,
Are tossed in Love's robe for he passes, and mad with Love's feet for he flies.[13]

A. Norman Jeffares suggests that the better-known 'The White Birds' also
dates from the same day, after Gonne expressed a desire to be reincarnated
as a seagull, tiring of the flame of the meteor.[14] 'The Sorrow of Love' was
also drafted in these fraught months of summer to autumn 1891, and it
also indulges in an astrology made manifest in the meteorological events
of that day of Parnell's funeral. Yeats had met Maud Gonne from the ship
that brought Parnell's body back to Dublin, the evening before the funeral,
10 October 1891. The first version of 'The Sorrow of Love' unpacks loved
one and dead hero from the 'labouring ships':

> The Sorrow of Love
>
> The quarrel of the sparrows in the eaves,
> The full round moon and the star-laden sky
> And the loud song of the ever-singing leaves,
> Had hid away earth's old and weary cry.
>
> And then you came with those red mournful lips
> And with you came the whole of the world's tears,
> And all the sorrows of her labouring ships,
> And all burden of her myriad years.
>
> And now the sparrows warring in the eaves,
> The crumbling moon, the white stars in the sky,
> And the loud chanting of the unquiet leaves,
> Are shaken with earth's cold and weary cry.[15]

The 1924 revision of this poem makes explicit what the young Yeats is
content to leave as mere suggestion here, a Homeric theme, of a history
turned askew by adultery, given supernatural shape by the astrology of
moon and stars:

> A girl arose that had red mournful lips
> And seemed the greatness of the world in tears,
> Doomed like Odysseus and the labouring ships
> And proud as Priam murdered with his peers;

Perhaps it is easy to see Maud Gonne as that girl, and less easy to imagine Parnell's lover Kitty O'Shea as Helen of Troy or the hapless Captain
O'Shea as Menelaus. But the revision effects a temporal telescoping, as it
were, of the events of an October evening out through national upheaval,
and thirty years or so of its aftermath, into rebellion, post-civil war retrospect and another set of portents, a world historical upset by no means
quelled by the ending of the Great War. At the very least, this is typical of a Yeatsian text changing form as it alters in its own shifting contexts, reading the runes of differing futures, revised in 1924 into an act

of the composition of lament and not just passively shaken chanting leaves. The girl

> Arose, and on the instant clamorous eaves,
> A climbing moon upon an empty sky,
> And all that lamentation of the leaves,
> Could but compose man's image and his cry.

Yeats's October evening was to last from 1891 to the great post-civil war revisions of his *Poems* of 1924, in which the necessity of composition or composition as necessity ('Could but compose', as in could *only* compose) was added to 'The Sorrow of Love'. Like the 'measured quietude' imported into 'To Ireland in the Coming Times',[16] also revised in 1924, the tenses were turned to control achieved over the past and lull of another uncertain future.

Moving backwards in time to the first of these two Irish evenings, the body of Gerard Manley Hopkins had been interred for two years in the Jesuit plot in Glasnevin by the time Parnell was to be buried a few yards away. In the five years he lived in Dublin he experienced the full pomp of Parnellism. Tracking back seven years before Parnell's funeral, to the arrival of Hopkins to the post of Professor of Greek in University College Dublin in February 1884, the poet had had one of his rare excursions into print in the months preceding his appointment. These took the form of a series of letters to the journal *Nature* in which he had contributed descriptions of sunsets, and then to one of the great preoccupations of *Nature* at that time, the extraordinary phenomena observed in northern hemisphere skies in the aftermath of the eruption of Krakatoa in Indonesia in August 1883. The fascination was widespread: for William Allingham, out walking with his friend Alfred Tennyson in the autumn of that year, these 'strange, rich, volcanic sunsets' were a 'floating ghost, perhaps, of a mountain blown to atoms'.[17] The vast volumes of volcanic debris circulating in the atmosphere were the cause of the strange atmospheric effects, and both Catherine Philips and Kate Flint have recently enlisted the story as an example of the Victorian preoccupation with dust.[18]

On 3 January 1884, a month before his arrival in Dublin, Hopkins's third and final letter to *Nature* described with Ruskinian particularity six ways in which a sunset he had observed at Stonyhurst in Lancashire on 16 December 1883 differed from normal sunsets. At first, he ventured a definition:

> Sunset proper is, I suppose, the few minutes between the first dipping and the last disappearance of the sun's disk below the true horizon; the pageant

or phenomena we call sunset, however, includes a great deal that goes on before and after this. The remarkable and specific features of the late sunsets have not been before or at sunset proper; they have been after-glows, and have lasted long, very long after.

This sounds more like an artist than a scientific reporter, and Hopkins cannot resist the notion that these sunsets are some sort of artwork, as here, on their intensity and lustreless glow:

> These two things together, that is, intensity of light and want of lustre, give to objects on the earth the peculiar illumination which may be seen in studios and other well-like rooms, and which itself affects the practice of painters and may be seen in their works, notably Rembrandt's, disguising or feebly showing the outlines and distinctions of things, but fetching out white surfaces and coloured stuffs with a rich and inward and seemingly self-luminous glow.[19]

Only Gerard Manley Hopkins would turn the phenomena caused by volcanic dust thrown across the atmosphere of the globe into a Dutch interior, but he does this beautifully. The description is of artificial light – a description of art – in which there is a play of the glimmer of the indistinct against objects that appear not to be reflecting surfaces but a source of light in themselves, a 'self-luminous glow'. He won't say it in *Nature*, but the Krakatoan sunsets provide perfect atmospheric conditions for instress, by which things can show their inscape.

Hopkins returned to sunsets later in 1884, a year in which he attempted to complete the (unfortunately now lost) Gregorian musical setting of William Collins's 'Ode to Evening', a project he had begun in his last days in Stonyhurst and continued to work on in his early days in Ireland. He wrote from Dublin to Robert Bridges in November 1884: 'Quickened by the heavenly beauty of that poem I groped in my soul's very viscera for the tune, and thrummed the sweetest and most secret catgut of the mind.'[20] A few weeks later, he imported a brogue cadence into a letter to Bridges on New Year's Day 1885, saying of his musical setting of Collins that it was 'a new departure and more like volcanic sunsets or sunrises in the musical hemisphere than anythin ye can concave'.[21] Collins's 'Ode' is, very strictly speaking, a poem of sunset as conceived by Hopkins: 'the few minutes between the first dipping and the last disappearance of the sun's disk below the true horizon'. That is, unlike its celebrated contemporary poem, Thomas Gray's 'Elegy in a Country Churchyard' ('The curfew tolls the knell of parting day'), day does not part, the sun does not go down in his poem.

In its opening fifteen lines it uses the word 'now' three times. These temporal modifiers of the scene give way to the words 'when', and 'then' and 'while':

> Then lead, calm *Vot'ress*, where some sheety Lake
> Cheers the lone Heath, or some time-hallow'd Pile,
>   Or up-land Fallows grey,
>   Reflect its last cool Gleam.
> But when chill blustering Winds or driving Rain
> Forbid my willing Feet, be mine the Hut
>   That from the Mountain's Side
>   Views Wilds and swelling Floods,
> And Hamlets brown, and dim-discover'd Spires,
> And hears their simple Bell, and marks o'er all
>   Thy Dewy Fingers draw
>   The gradual dusky Veil.
> While *Spring* shall pour his Show'rs, as oft he wont,
> And bathe thy breathing Tresses, meekest *Eve!*
>   While *Summer* loves to sport
>   Beneath thy ling'ring Light;
> While sallow *Autumn* fills thy Lap with Leaves,
> Or *Winter*, yelling thro' the troublous Air,
>   Affrights thy shrinking Train,
>   And rudely rends thy Robes;
> So long, sure-found beneath the Sylvan Shed,
> Shall *Fancy*, *Friendship*, *Science*, rose-lipp'd *Health*,
>   Thy gentlest Influence own,
>   And hymn thy fav'rite Name![22]

As the moment of sunset is prolonged indefinitely, the poem is sustained in a perpetual present tense, eventually paralleling all four seasons, which follow each other but appear to be concurrent: 'Then lead ... when chill ... While *Spring* ... While *Summer* ... While sallow *Autumn* ... or *Winter*'. The poem only uses the future tense at its end when envisaging the peace and security of all possible sunsets in the continuity of a pastoral British scene. For all that 'Dewy Fingers draw/A gradual dusky Veil', no night follows this graduation of evening. Like Gray's 'Elegy', Collins's 'Ode' was also a poem of the 1740s, published in December 1746, and following events that might have been as challenging to the Union of Scotland and England as the events of the 1880s would be to the larger United Kingdom of Great Britain and Ireland. Both poems found their way into Thomas Warton's post-Culloden anthology of 'British' poetry, his 1753 *The Union: or Select Scots and English Poems*.[23]

Hopkins's preoccupations with volcanic dust, Dutch interiors and mid-eighteenth-century evening poems written at a time of crisis for the Union merged in the sunset poem of the autumn of his first year in Ireland, the first draft of which Norman MacKenzie dates to October 1884:

Earnest, earthless, equal, attuneable, vaulty, voluminous…stupendous
Evening strains to be time's den, world's delf, womb-of-all, home-of-all, hearse-of-all night.
Her fónd yellow hornlight wound to the west, her wild willowy hoarlight hung to the height
Waste; her earliest stars, earlstars, stars principal, overbend us,
Firefeaturing heaven. For earth unpenned her being; her dapple is at an end – a-
Stray or aswarm, all throughther, in throng; self ín self steepèd and pashed – flush; quite
Disremembering, dismembering all. My heart rounds me right
Then: Evening is here on us, over us; our night whelms, whelms, when will it end us?
Only the crisp boughs beakèd or dragonish damask the toolsmooth bleak light – black
Ever so black on it. O this our tale too!²⁴

Here, as in Collins, 'Evening' begins as 'the few minutes between the first dipping and the last disappearance of the sun's disk below the true horizon', and like Collins, holds off moving to night. As such it is a first sketch of an eventual sonnet, later called 'Spelt from Sibyl's Leaves', except here it breaks down at its volta, or turn to night.

The poem begins in an 'even-ing', that is, a moment of balance between day and night, and also a stilling of time in the vast interiority of an autumnal night sky. 'Stupendous/Evening' is worked out from that great run of adjectives that narrow into enclosed space, the ethical or political shading into the scientific. Earnestness we might expect from an English Victorian poem. An 'earnest' is also a promise to pay, figuratively, a contract with the future.²⁵ Equality might be slightly more problematic for the conservative Hopkins, but 'equal' is being offered also as a synonym for even-ing, in the sense of day and night becoming 'even'. Earnest and equal go first into equilibrium and then into night. Hopkins invokes Rudolf Clausius's second law of thermodynamics, of the entropy of the universe increasing to its maximum, entropy being a measure of the equilibrium or evening out of energy in any closed physical system. Those closed physical systems will eventually dissipate as their energy must: the sun will burn out and the entropy of the solar system will ensure its end. Such enclosures continue through the 'vaulty' (the well-like room of the volcanic sunsets) and the voluminous (literally, an extensive but limited volume of space, but possibly also a library, full of volumes). As interior space swells, it bursts out into the ineffable, the empty space in the line denoted in print by an ellipsis and the voice by a pause of a full stress or foot. 'Stupendous' might sound a little too colloquial to be up to the task set by the preceding adjectives, but in the ratcheting up of the sublime here, the stupefaction of death and nature before the second law of thermodynamics and the last judgement of the *Dies Irae*, or days of wrath, lurks in the word.[26] 'Stupendous' also sets off the great double-syllable rhymes, of the two quatrains here: 'overbend us' (I imagine the body bending back looking at the sky, not bent over, as with age); 'end as-', 'end us'. Before the word that is the sonnet's subject matter, 'Evening', its end is imagined, and it must thus resolve these sublime interiors into the spaces of womb, home, and the hearse (not tomb, which might be expected) of 'night'.

Collins's 'Ode', perhaps Hopkins's setting of the ode, is still playing in the background here,[27] but where Collins's even-ing remains equal, never giving us the end of the 'gradual dusky Veil', Hopkins's evening cannot sustain itself as such. It 'strains to be', that is, it is in process of beginning or, to borrow a coinage from 'To seem the stranger' a Dublin sonnet of multiple estrangements, is a 'lonely began'.[28] This is about becoming, but becoming night, this Dublin night, and in its first draft it resists that night. Christopher Miller, in his book on *The Invention of Evening* in English poetry, says of the 'Ode to Evening' that it is 'patterned on a kind of double-time: it occupies both one finite twilight in which the poet can see and address his subject and the endlessly extrapolated evening beyond his finite experience'.[29] 'Evening' in its Old English origins is the 'coming of even' (as in eventide or evensong). According to Miller this is an obsolete usage, but it is still in its dialect sense 'a becoming even', a sense that Norman White tells us in relation to 'Spelt from Sibyl's Leaves' is still current in Ireland.[30] And that notion of what might be current in Ireland and not in the tradition of unifying British evening poems that Hopkins knows he is working in is something that the very word 'evening' opens out through this poem. It will become not so much a poem of night as one of last things, as the human world processes not to evening but beyond to eternity, and the ultimate difference of judgement in the days of wrath. Hopkins, unlike William Collins, is a poet of particularity, of *this* evening, indeed in the autumn of 1884, this *Irish* evening. The English word 'evening', if heard in its Irish dialect sense, then sets off Hopkins's rounding on his phrase in the letter to Bridges, 'anythin ye can conçave'.

English poetry meets various British vernaculars in writing about an Irish sunset with the debris of Krakatoa still scattered over it. Take two

words that appear later in this draft, 'throughther' and 'disremembering'.
These are Irish dialect words, the first from *throughother* meaning 'to be
mixed-up or confused'. Patrick Weston Joyce, in his *English as We Speak
It in Ireland* of 1910, suggests it is an Ulster translation from Irish, *trí n-a
chéile*, 'through each other'. Of 'disremember', in a tundish moment worthy of his novelist namesake, Joyce tells us it is 'Good old English; now
out of fashion in England, but common in Ireland'. [31] Or take this line:
'Only the crisp boughs beaked or dragonish damask the toolsmooth bleak
light – black.' In the final version, with caesurae marked on the line, it
echoes the Welsh *cynghanedd* line, where alliterative patterns in one part
of the line must be repeated in its second half, as here: 'boughs beaked,
bleak black or dragonish damask' (where 'damask' will in the final version be placed after one of the heavily marked caesurae). Hopkins's three
years in Wales were much happier than his five years in Ireland. He actually learnt Welsh. He didn't learn Irish, and what views he had of Irish
poets such as Samuel Ferguson seem based in part on his reading of Yeats's
tributes to Ferguson after his death in August 1886.[32] Hopkins was a con-
tributor to his colleague Fr Matthew Russell's seminal pre-revival journal, *The Irish Monthly*, in which many of the lyrics of John O'Leary's 1888
anthology *Poems and Ballads of Young Ireland* were first to appear. More
significantly, Norman MacKenzie and Catherine Philips have found fifty
or so contributions of Hiberno-English words attributed to 'GMH', 'Rev.
Gerard Manley Hopkins', in Joseph Wright's *English Dialect Dictionary*.
The best is 'blarney-stone': 'A certain stone in the walls of Castle Blarney
in Co. Cork, the kissing or licking of which is fabled to convey the gift of
Blarney'. And that blarney, as Francis Sylvester Mahony could have told
Wright or Hopkins, is defined as 'Persuasive talk, flattery, humbug'.[33]

   'Spelt from Sibyl's Leaves', like 'Parnell's Funeral', is not just a poem
set in Ireland, but an Irish poem. Its subject matter, lexis and elements
of its prosody come in the widest sense from 'British' poetry, that is a
synthese of the various poetic languages that its author wrote – English,
Welsh, Hiberno-English, petrarchan, old English – and its author's many
late Victorian imperialist and Catholic preoccupations, scientific as much
as theological or political. Above all, the poem, like others written by
Hopkins in Ireland, transplants a tradition of English poetry into a place
where it should be at home, part of its own United Kingdom, but finds it
cannot work in peace. In Matthew Reynolds's terms, the poem is aware of
its position as a British poem occupying a 'realm of verse', even though,
pace Reynolds, it tells not so much of 'Nation-Building', but more of
its aftermath, if not imminent disintegration.[34] Previous subjects in that

realm – Thomas Gray, William Collins or indeed William Wordsworth – could celebrate the even-ing of British evenings. In Wordsworth's beautiful sonnet addressed to a child who does not see the beauty of an evening:

> Listen! the mighty Being is awake,
> And doth with his eternal motion make
> A sound like thunder – everlastingly.[35]

Miller remarks of this poem, evening is 'a pause within a larger narrative … the respite of a truce writ small'.[36] Hopkins was denied the truce of evening in Ireland, and saw only fear in what should be a consolatory extension of time after strife, the eternal. For all his technique, he refuses himself anything like the little triumph of technique over the temporal in Wordsworth's caesural dash followed by a five-syllable, half-line present participle adverb, 'everlastingly'. After the enunciation of the second law of thermodynamics, for one thing he would have to come to terms with the impossibility of 'eternal motion'. Hopkins was also denied the extraordinary events that followed his own early death, the evening of Parnell's funeral among them – even given that he was in a way, there, in the graveyard. Between the working out of entropy and the last judgement, Wordsworth's 'everlastingly' must come to an end, but there is an ahistoricism in these British evening poems, which Hopkins – writing at the end of empire – refused. Ireland told him that; and his Irish contemporaries knew that to write for the morning might be more in keeping with their 'realms of verse'.

The Commonweal

To move forward a couple of years, towards the time when 'Spelt from Sibyl's Leaves' would be finished. Many English perceptions of the Irish in the political crisis that would mount during Hopkins's time in Ireland diagnosed a surfeit of Blarney. On 30 June 1886, Algernon Swinburne published his broadside 'The Commonweal: A Song for Unionists' in *The Times*. On 8 June, the second reading of William Gladstone's Home Rule Bill had been defeated in the House of Commons, thanks to a rebellion of both Unionist and liberal Whigs led by the former radical Joseph Chamberlain. Gladstone immediately dissolved parliament and called a general election, confronting not only the Tories but his own rebel MPs. Of course that election would take place across the United Kingdom, in Ireland as well as Great Britain, but Swinburne's broadside ended with a direct address to an English electorate: 'Yet an hour is here for answer;

now, if here be yet a nation,/Answer England, man by man from sea to sea!' The 1886 'Commonweal' (Swinburne's 1887 'Jubilee Ode for Queen Victoria' was later given the same title) is not so much a party political broadside, as one based in a single constitutional issue, the Irish Question, and the events of May–July 1886 that were to contrive twenty years of near-uninterrupted Tory rule and effected the same catastrophic splits in late nineteenth-century liberalism that the constitutional issue of Europe was to have on British conservatism 110 years later.

Swinburne's contribution was typical of the middle-aged controversialist, now turned into a monarchical Unionist, accusing Gladstone of the apostasy of which many accused him: it was pointed out in the satirical columns that Swinburne himself had produced a Republican broadside, 'An Appeal to England', twenty years before in 1867, in an attempt to influence the debate over the execution of the Manchester Martyrs, three Fenian-aligned Irish immigrants accused of killing a policeman. 'The Commonweal,' by way of contrast, does appear rather like the savage picture of Gladstone in another Swinburne poem of the period, 'Apostasy', in which Gladstone was 'proven apostate in the apostate's eyes'. 'The Commonweal' also pours scorn on the Parnellite faction in Ireland, and the treachery of a Gladstone who dared to change his mind on the matter of Home Rule. These are the first three stanzas:

Men, whose fathers braved the world in arms against our Isles in union,
    Men, whose brothers met rebellion face to face,
Show the hearts ye have, if worthy long descent and high communion,
    Show the spirits, if unbroken, of your race.

What are these that howl and hiss across the strait of westward water?
    What is he who floods our ears with speech in flood?
See the long tongue lick the dripping hand that smokes and reeks of slaughter!
    See the man of words embrace the man of blood!

Hear the plea whereby the tonguester mocks and charms the gazing gaper -
    'We are they whose works are works of love and peace;
Till disunion bring forth union, what is union, sirs, but paper?
    Break and rend it, then shall trust and strength increase.'[37]

Reading the poem in *The Times* in Dublin, Gerard Manley Hopkins reported to Richard Watson Dixon that someone called it a 'rigmarole', but then had to say, 'Everything he [Swinburne] writes is rigmarole.'[38] Hopkins's objections were aesthetic as well as political. The letter to Bridges two years previously about sunsets and Collins's 'Ode' had also dismissed the description of a sunset in Swinburne's 'Evening on the

Broads': 'Either in fact he does not see nature at all or else he overlays the landscape with such phantasmata, secondary images, and what not of a delirium tremendous imagination that the result is kind of bloody broth: you know what I mean. At any rate there is no picture.'[39] The bullying tone of the older Swinburne, half-achieved sarcasm and pitting of stout English heroism against mere Irish blarney had its say in the defeat of Gladstone's party. The talkative Irishman 'floods our ears with speech in flood', and then casuistically holds up the sacred, we might say sacramental, Union of Great Britain and Ireland within the British Constitution as mere paper. The alliance of Parnell with Gladstone brings violence and lies to the heart of a great empire, so the poem quickly forsakes any disguise of allegory, naming the Irish politician riding on the back of the English Prime Minister: '"Parnell spurs his Gladstone well!"'

Swinburne's broadside has both the vocal and cartoon quality of political satire. But it is also an instance of a British unionism complaining of the loss of a purity of voice and purpose as it faces the disunity of its own United Kingdom. There is quite a gulf between Swinburne and Hopkins, and in fact both changed their minds on Ireland, in Hopkins's case to become convinced of the pragmatism of home rule. However, both shared an anxiety about kingdom and empire dramatised through this anxiety about voice. Whereas Swinburne's solution might be to shout louder than those who shouted for home rule, Hopkins's view was shared only with a few, frequently baffled, friends, and now and again the congregations who heard some distinctly odd sermons. Although his poetry and devotional writing has much to say about the kingdom of heaven, frequently using common – if not in his hands quite conventional – parables of earthly kingdoms for the divine, he was no less concerned with the 'public,' with the civic realm or the word both poets shared, the 'commonweal'. That commonweal, the United Kingdom, was seen under great strain, personal as well as political in the mid- to late 1880s, as nationalists in Ireland strove to detach themselves from it. Hopkins reaches for a stock analogy, figuring the Union undergoing the setting from near the centre of an empire on which the sun never sets. Stock the figure might be, but that setting sun was creating distinctly odd atmospheric effects.

Through his last years in Dublin up to his death in 1889, Hopkins's political positions changed due to his growing understanding of the artificially created 'oneness' of the 'United' Kingdom, which marked nothing but its own 'difference'. Regardless of his own principles he came, by 1887, to understand the practical necessity of Home Rule, no matter how abhorrent it was to him. Early in 1887, he complained to Robert Bridges about the Irish Catholic hierarchy's support for the Parnellite Plan of Campaign and the non-payment of taxes: 'One archbishop backs robbery, the other rebellion.'[40] His upset through 1887 manifested itself as a sort of hysteria edging into pragmatic despair. In July he wrote to Bridges again:

> The will of the nation is divided and distracted. Its judgement is unin-formed and misinformed, divided and distracted, and its action must be corresponding to its knowledge [...] then recognise with me that with an unwavering will, or at least a flood of passion, on one, the Irish, side, and a wavering one, or indifference on the other, the English, and the Grand Old Mischief-maker loose, like the Devil, for a little while and meddling and marring all the fiercer for his hurry, Home Rule is in fact likely to come and even, in spite of the crime, slander, and folly with which its advance is attended, may perhaps in itself be a sort of equity and, considering that worse might be, of a kind of prudence.[41]

This was the final resigned position he held before his early death in 1889 – even if, with Swinburne in 1886, he believed the Grand Old Mischief-Maker Gladstone had been forced into acting treacherously under the cynical influence of Parnell. Indifference causes the 'wavering' English will; it is a small step from 'unwavering will' into a 'flood of passion', and liberal English misunderstanding is no match for the fanaticism that appalled Hopkins, and in the face of which he knew acquiescence might be both equity and prudence. For a poet whose work exists to celebrate difference, and to record his perceptions of distinct identities, the Irish experience could be said to have been positive. Still, Hopkins felt that a social and political arrangement that could not assimilate all into an ideal state he, like Swinburne, called a 'Commonweal', was failing its citizens. Hopkins felt that literature should lend its strength to empire. Against this, we have to place the baffling obscurity to which his later work tends, a work that finds its wisest word banned and thwarted even by the tiny uncomprehending audience that populated his ideal commonwealth of friends, colleagues and correspondents.

Hopkins wrote to his friends that he found in Ireland an invigorating set of arguments for the centrality of culture and literature in the exten-sion of the freedom and civilisation that was the great duty of the British empire. He found consolation in his own estrangement. This is from a letter to Coventry Patmore, written on 4 June 1886, four days before the defeat of Gladstone's first Home Rule Bill in the House of Commons.

> It is good to be in Ireland to hear how enemies, and those rhetoricians, can treat the things which are unquestioned at home. I know that to mere injus-tice and slander innocence and excellence themselves stand condemned,

but since there is always in mankind some love of truth and admiration for good (only that the truth must be striking and the good on a great scale) what marked and striking excellence has England to shew to make her civilisation attractive? Her literature is one of her excellences and attractions and I believe that criticism will tend to make this more and more felt; but there must be more of that literature, a continued supply and in quality excellent. This is why I hold that fine works of art, and especially if, like yours, that are only ideal in form but deal with high matter as well, are really a great power in the world, an element of strength even to an empire.[42]

Hopkins has no doubt that art can be 'a great power in the world' and can even lend its strength to an empire. Because the freedoms offered by the British empire are the best available to the world that Hopkins views, English Literature must take on and propagate the freedoms of that empire. In the Ireland of June 1886, and the events of the Home Rule Crisis, what Hopkins and his Conservative friends saw as the unravelling of a United Kingdom resulting in the unravelling of the empire, 'fine works of art' needed to stand up and be counted in support of the reaction against the violent disunion of the Kingdom. Arnoldian Sweetness and Light is not phrased here as the usual plea for transcendence above historical imperatives that narratives of Imperialism are said to make. This is a placing even of the idealist poetry of Coventry Patmore at the centre of the Imperial project. 'It is good to be in Ireland', the displaced Hopkins says, and speaking back to the English centre of the Union, he relays the errors and slanders of the enemies of his class.

This resulted in characteristically strange patriotic poetry. One of Hopkins's last poems was written after watching the garrison parade in Phoenix Park, the marching song 'What Shall I Do for the Land that Bred Me.' Sending it to Robert Bridges, Hopkins said it was an attempt 'to write a patriotic song that shall breathe true feeling without spoon or brag. How I hate both!' As a result, the poem is characteristically odd for the genre. What soldier might happily consider himself 'England's fame's fond lover', or declare 'Immortal beauty is death with duty'?[43] Hopkins had been this way before, two or three years earlier, in a sonnet titled by Bridges 'The Soldier', which was possibly written in late 1885 at the same time as the failure of the Sudan relief expedition (the failure to support Gordon adequately was another of Gladstone's betrayals, for Swinburne as well as Hopkins[44]):

Yes. Whý do we áll, seeing of a | soldier, bless him? bless
Our redcoats, our tars? Both | these being, the greater part,

But frail clay, nay but foul clay. | Here it is: the heart,
Since, proud, it calls the calling | manly, gives a guess
That, hopes that, makesbelieve, | the men must be no less;
It fancies, feigns, deems, dears | the artist after his art;
And fain will find as sterling | all as all is smart,
And scarlet wéar the spirit of war thére express.
Mark Christ our King. He knows war, served this soldiering through;
He of all can handle a rope best. | There he bides in bliss
Now, and séeing somewhére some mán | do all that man can do,
For love he leans forth, needs | his neck must fall on, kiss,
And cry 'O Christ-done deed! | So God-made-flesh does too:
Were I come o'er again' cries | Christ 'it should be this'.[45]

In its way, as Norman MacKenzie helpfully glosses, this is a poem about
categories and essence. It is a sort of updated Carlylean clothes philosophy,[46] where the poet begins by reproving those who might mistake the
nobility of the individual soldier or sailor for the nobility of their calling.

By the end of the octave, however, just as it has discriminated between
the counterfeit and real, it also becomes attracted to men in uniform.
Smartness itself is sterling, the genuine currency of the empire, so the red-
coats become a moment beyond analogy, beyond the parable of uniform:
'And scarlet wéar the spirit of war thére express.' The minimal vowel modulations – 'scar-', 'wear', 'spir-', 'war', 'there' – run achieved unity of outward form and expression of spirit close to monotone through the line.
But this is the achieved unity, of oneness, of an army together, at war. The
bringing together of form and expression, transcending analogy, is then
replayed as a parable for Christ. Just as the man in uniform attracts the
onlooker, so, too, does Christ, whom Hopkins usually figured as manly.
The poem is a Catholic disquisition on metaphor or analogy, of the uniform expressing the man, and the reality, not mere idealism, of God made
flesh. So there are two earthly kingdoms, and both the Roman Catholic
Church (the Church militant) and the British empire are granted authenticity of expression, as the desire of the onlooker is vindicated through
parable, where the desire for what is sterling also happens to wear a
scarlet coat.

If Hopkins was to write to Bridges that 'the will of the nation' that
relied on this soldier was 'divided and distracted', we can bring these
soldier poems back into Hopkins's Irish experience through their desire
for unity in metaphor, or of tenor and vehicle. They seek a theological
justification of parable that is at the same time a seeking of the spirit of
the earthly United Kingdom figured through its outward signs of power.
Of course 'The Soldier' must end with a moment out of this earth and

after time, the Church triumphant in eternity, and that needs the coming again of Christ fully to achieve a unity that had existed only once in Judaeo-Christian human history, with Adam before he was joined by Eve. The world and its forms are divided, sundered, in exile from their original state, much like Hopkins in Dublin.

In a series of 1880 Liverpool sermons on the kingdom of God, taking as text 'Thy will be done on earth as it is in heaven', Hopkins had said:

> This very justice, original justice, that was in Adam, who but God freely bestowed it? [...] And all fell, all is gone: it was divided against itself, the subject against the sovereign, man against God, and every kingdom, said the son of God, even God's kingdom divided against itself must come to desolation, no commonwealth or household, not even God's commonwealth, God's household, divided against itself can stand.

The text for the sermon is Matthew XII, 25, and it resonates across the United Kingdom, predicting the desolation that awaits the kingdom divided against itself and God's will, at once the great schism of Christendom after the Reformation and the contemporary division of the United Kingdom. The result for Adam was exile, broached in the following Sunday's sermon in which it is hard not to hear the self-pity of the lonely convert, cut off from 'commonweal, home and country, friends and neighbours, power, the franchise,'[47] preaching to semi-literate Irish immigrants who were themselves suffering an involuntary exile.

The difficulty for Hopkins was in bringing together all into an ideal, ordered commonwealth, or of finding room for all in a society that tolerated disfranchisement or the lack of civil autonomy. 'Tom's Garland', which along with its companion poem 'Harry Ploughman' had been begun while on holiday in Dromore, County Down, in September 1887, is perhaps the most baffling of all of Hopkins's Irish poems. If 'Harry Ploughman' is about the integration of the human, male, body in the social through labour, 'Tom's Garland' attempts to picture a unified commonweal, just as it marks the economic waste of those who might not be assimilated within it.

> Tom's Garland:
>
> upon the Unemployed
>
> Tom – garlanded with squat and surly steel
> Tom; then Tom's fallowbootfellow piles pick
> By him and rips out rockfire homeforth – sturdy Dick;
> Tom Heart-at-ease, Tom Navvy: he is all for his meal
> Sure, 's bed now. Low be it: lustily he his low lot (feel

That ne'er need hunger, Tom; Tom seldom sick,
Seldomer heartsóre; that treads through, prickproof, thick
Thousands of thorns, thoughts) swings though. Commonweal
Little Í reck ho! lacklevel in, if all had bread:
What! Country is honour enough in all of us – lordly head,
With heaven's lights high hung around, or, mother-ground
That mammocks, mighty foot. But nó way sped,
Nor mind nor mainstrength; gold go garlanded
With, perilous, O nó; nor yet plod safe shod sound;
        Undenized, beyond bound
Of earth's glory, earth's ease, all; no-one, nowhere
In wide the world's weal; rare gold, bold steel, bare
        In both; care, but share care –
This, by Despair, bred Hangdog dull; by Rage,
Manwolf, worse; and their packs infest the age.[48]

This irregular sonnet stretches out into two codas in order to contain within its commonweal not only the lustily uncomplaining labourer Tom, but also the unnamed 'Undenized', the homeless and unemployed, those with no place in society. They 'infest the age' due to their inability to be reconciled with the common weal, the common good of the ideal, unified, state. In this state, Tom feels no hunger, is seldom 'heartsore', indeed does little thinking: the garland of steel that he wears, his tools hung around his neck, are not to be matched by the crown of thorns of his suffering, self-conscious intellectual superiors. The governed need not share the cares of conscience of their governors. Given bed, food, clothing and happiness, Tom accepts his 'low lot' in the 'Commonweal'.

The first two senses of 'commonweal' in the *Oxford English Dictionary* work the 'general good', the common well-being, against 'The whole body of the people ... state, community = COMMONWEALTH'. The word describes a political arrangement, but a political arrangement that implies its own ideal form, an analogy in which tenor and vehicle are one. Yet the word 'commonwealth' also carries distinct republican echoes. For Hopkins, 'the noble commonwealth' is that enjoyed by Adam, who possessed unity and was 'all man in one person',[49] later to be joined by Eve and his family, who would have inherited the ideal commonwealth of Eden before their fall. This is Miltonic ground, which Hopkins knew well, the ground of a commonwealth that was a radical Protestant Republic, not that of a world governed by a militant Roman Catholic Church. Politically as well as theologically, the Liverpool sermons of January 1880 had addressed the relationship between God and man in the terms of the relationship between governor and governed. Proceeding by analogy with temporal political and economic organisations, they pictured a commonwealth on earth and in heaven proceeding by a contract, in which man shows his love by 'willing obedience'. Obedience is necessary for order:

> For if the governed had never, neither at first nor after, submitted to be ruled / all would be riot, order could never have come about; if the ruling power had never, neither at first nor after, accepted the task of government how could he or his house or heirs or representatives be now upon the throne? The agreement, the understanding, the contract, must have some-how *come about*, and it will always have been brought about for the good of both parties, governor and governed, for their common good, *common weal*; and this is what we call a commonwealth[50].

This agreement which must have 'somehow *come about*' here is not so much a mystical form of understanding as the Whig history of the British Common Law and Constitution as explicated by William Blackstone or Edmund Burke. But the Act of Union did not 'somehow come about'. Hopkins views a contemporary British social reality through his experience of an Ireland denied access to the identity of the United Kingdom.

Neither Robert Bridges nor Canon Dixon could understand 'Tom's Garland', so Hopkins sent Bridges a crib, a paraphrase of the poem. It ends thus:

> But presently I remember that this is all very well for those who are in, however low in, the Commonwealth and share in any way the Common weal; but that the curse of our times is that many do not share it, that they are outcasts from it and have neither security nor splendour; that they share care with the high and obscurity with the low, but wealth or comfort with neither. And this state of things, I say, is the origin of Loafers, Tramps, Cornerboys, Roughs, Socialists and other pests of society.[51]

There isn't much whiggery here: an utterly unforgiving Hopkins contemplates those who cannot be accommodated within the commonwealth, 'no-one, nowhere/In wide the world's weal'. This prospect of the homeless, the malcontent and the rebellious, all thrown together into a political organisation that will not contain them because it does not understand them, is one that Ireland held out for Hopkins. The sonnet's closing lines strive for form for this insight, a yoking onto the main body of the poem of the coda that will bring the unallotted into order. It cannot succeed: the final 'Rage/age' rhyme is the lot of Hopkin's commonwealth of the 1880s, viewed from one of its outposts. The labourers in 'Tom's Garland' are given resolutely English names, Tom and Dick. Add in the title of its companion poem 'Harry Ploughman', another poem drawn to metaphors of martial manliness, and we have the mythical Tom, Dick and Harry of everyday English life.[52] Both poems were written in County Down, but neither involved Paddy Ploughman.

Finish in Art

Yeats never quite got Hopkins – his views of Hopkins's poetry when eventually published were at best eccentric and at worst boneheaded, though he commented with cruel acuity to Monk Gibbon that Hopkins 'brought his faint theatrical Catholicism to Ireland where [it] is not relished by the sons of peasants and died of the shock'.[53] Hopkins's connection with Catholic Ireland was unavoidably a connection with nationalist Ireland, that of an estranged imperialist, in a sort of internal exile, whose tristia was creatively sounded through the facts of that estrangement. If we look at the characteristic figurative and accentual means by which that tristia found its form, we can see a mode complementing as much as contrasting with the new forms and figures that were soon to gain ground in the incipient Irish literary revival. Literary counter-history might speculate along with Irish poet Austin Clarke, who, Norman Mackenzie tells us, was the first person to wonder about what it would be if Hopkins, not Edward Dowden or John O'Leary, became William Butler Yeats's literary mentor. At least they met: the prospect of Hopkins teaching Greek to James Joyce at the university Joyce attended only ten years after Hopkins's early death at not-quite forty-five is even more tantalising. But the relations we can describe and the texts that were written all share a characteristic moment of historical balance, or of history being in the balance, an evening out of empires passing away and nations yet to come.

In November 1886, five months after the Home Rule Crisis, Fr Matthew Russell brought Fr Gerard Hopkins to the studio of the painter John Butler Yeats, where the portrait of Catholic poet and nationalist Katherine Tynan was being painted. There are a number of accounts of this famous meeting, and its conversation over the question of 'finish and non-finish in art'. Yeats was a notoriously slow worker, which was one reason for the genteel poverty of his family, barely supported by their father's art. MacKenzie quotes the older Yeats's definition of a gentleman: 'one not wholly occupied with getting on',[54] which might also be applied to Hopkins, if not to Yeats's fiercely ambitious son. Yeats had given Hopkins a copy of William's *Mosada: A Dramatic Poem*, but Hopkins had already read and admired, with qualifications, the young poet's work in the *Dublin University Review*. *Mosada* he didn't like, as he wrote to Coventry Patmore:

> Now this *Mosada* I cannot think highly of, but I was happily not required then to praise what presumably I had not then read and could praise

another piece. It ['The Two Titans'] was a strained and unworkable allegory about a young man and a sphinx on a rock in the sea (how did they get there? what did they eat? and so on: [...]), but still containing fine lines and vivid imagery.[55]

As I have said, in 1886 Hopkins shared the pages of the *Irish Monthly* with the twenty-one-year-old rising star of Irish poetry. His translations of Shakespeare's songs into Latin were published in the magazine in November and February 1887. Yeats's first twilight classic 'The Stolen Child' appeared in the magazine between these events, in December 1886. Its lake shores, islands and moonlight carry through a writing half in origin and half in achievement, but speaking of an achievement possible in other worlds. Where Hopkins separates and celebrates particularity and inscape, the key word of 'The Stolen Child' is 'mingling'. If it is not the full call to hybridity, it is at least the moonlit eroticism of the Victorian fairy poem and painting, and the familiar call to come away, to desert the hectic material troubles of the world:

> Where the wave of moonlight glosses
> The dim grey sands with light,
> Far off by furthest Rosses
> We foot it all the night,
> Weaving olden dances,
> Mingling hands and mingling glances
> Till the moon has taken flight;
> To and fro we leap
> And chase the frothy bubbles
> While the world is full of troubles
> And is anxious in its sleep.
> *Come away, O human child!*
> *To the woods and waters wild*
> *With a fairy, hand in hand,*
> *For the world's more full of weeping than you can understand.*[56]

The wave of fairy moonlight illuminates a land of oneness not of difference, of mingling and hybridity and not the synthetic struggling of the made and earthly. That mingling will end after dawn, in the full daylight of the everyday denied both to the poem and its eventual abducted/escaped child. The poem seeks a time out of time, or a time out of mind even, to use one of Yeats's favourite phrases from the 1890s. Above all, this scene is grey, a scene in which naturalistic particularity is washed over by moonlight. Artistic effort is removed by the loss of sunlight, and the finish of the poem is allowed to assume a passive aestheticism and not the vigorous willed rhythmic textural aestheticism of a Hopkins.

'I persuaded myself that I had a passion for the dawn', Yeats says of his youthful night-time Sligo boating trips in his *Autobiographies*. That is, the dawn that follows night never quite gives way to the full light of day. These Yeatsian mornings and Hopkinsian evenings have a compatibility beyond their mere congruity or coincidence in the Dublin of 1886 in these first moments of Irish revival and last moments of empire. A discussion of Hopkins's eventual completion of 'Spelt from Sibyl's Leaves' in November of that year, a month before the publication of Yeats's poem, will conclude this chapter. That poem depicts the great loom of the last moments of human history in which one thread spools on and the other spools off. From the retrospect of 'Parnell's Funeral' of 1934, Yeats might also say of these years and the tumult that followed them up to the death of Parnell, 'An age is the reversal of an age.' Hopkins's spools are not quite Yeatsian gyres, but this conflation of a material political history sounded through aesthetic forms with a mystical, at times prophetic, conception of that history characterises one state of 'British' poetry towards the end of the nineteenth century.

Yeats returned to the dawn in 1891, inflected with the meteorological events of Parnell's funeral and his obsession for Maud Gonne in the *Flame of the Spirit* poems written in the wake of history and a doomed love affair.

The White Birds

I would that we were, my beloved, white birds on the foam of the sea!
We tire of the flame of the meteor, before it can fade and flee;
And the flame of the blue star of twilight, hung low on the rim of the sky,
Has awaked in our hearts, my beloved, a sadness that may not die.

A weariness comes from those dreamers, dew-dabbled, the lily and rose;
Ah, dream not of them, my beloved, the flame of the meteor that goes,
Or the flame of the blue star that lingers hung low in the fall of the dew:
For I would we were changed to white birds on the wandering foam: I and you!

I am haunted by numberless islands, and many a Danaan shore,
Where Time would surely forget us, and Sorrow come near us no more;
Soon far from the rose and the lily and fret of the flames would we be,
Were we only white birds, my beloved, buoyed out on the foam of the sea!

This is a lyric of the imminence of desire, a poem haunted by number-less islands but never actually landing on them. It is carried by an odd metre, an anapaestic hexameter of sorts – that is, a six-stress line, with predominantly triple feet, reminiscent of that thing that is rare enough in English poetry, an alexandrine. The rhythmic effect is a simple mimetic one, a verse alternately dipping and soaring and bobbing about like the gulls Maud Gonne dreamt she had become. When the poem moves from thinking about sea to sky, it then invokes the portent of a sort of astrology, of comets or flaming meteors or the evening star. The poem is one of a typical twilight, but one aware both of the spinning earth and of being spun by it, spun on it. Its astrology gives way to the natural processes of evening and morning: temporally the poem travels from evening star to morning dew, time-bound for two stanzas. Indeed, this is the time-binding of sorrow and sadness, the rhythm of being on this earth and being haunted by numberless islands, the places that are not this one.

The poet asks to be removed from this place, the place of Time and Sorrow, and transformed into another one, the place of which his rhythm tells, of perpetual movement, rhythm as movement, tide yet not of time, cosmic but not of earth. Yeats pushes at the limits of the alexandrine in this virtuoso line: 'Or the flame of the blue star that lingers hung low in the fall of the dew', the slow time of the line resolves only in that pair of seemingly endless concluding anapaests mimicking the imperceptible falling of dew. It is almost too good, so the next line then tries to shuck off rhythm itself: listen to the effect that is common enough in Yeats's 1890s poetry, the unscannable stress line that dares the reading voice to trip over it: 'For I would we were changed to white birds on the wandering foam: I and you!' It is the late caesura that rescues the line, the odd reminder that there is a lover here and not just fantasy, no matter how it affronts the courtesies of good English style: 'you and I' just wouldn't rhyme. As seen in Chapter 6, English verse is usually felt to be numberless beyond the number ten, so the twelve and more syllables of the alexandrine are usually chopped by convention in two with a medial caesura. When Yeats does that here, it is for those lines that repeat the determinism of astrology and human time and suffering: 'We tire of the flame of the meteor, before it can fade and flee' or 'Where Time would surely forget us, and Sorrow come near us no more'.

'The White Birds' is a lyrical ballad of sorts, but one that is neither at sea nor stranded, much as it appears to desire both of those outcomes. On first printing in 1892 it had begun with an extra syllable, the merest hint of the come-all-ye of ballad, 'O I would that we were, my beloved, white birds on the foam of the sea.'[57] It closes with a very similar line, and the effect of such repetition is both closure and the sustaining of perpetual utterance in refrain. It sustains a balancing act, on one hand between a willed recreation of the textured layering of ballad and on the other a desire for transmigration into a timeless existence on the 'foam of the sea'. It had originally borrowed from ballad convention the enacted refrain of an Irish verse that tells only of a deliverance long hoped for but as yet to arrive. As mentioned in Chapter 5, James Clarence Mangan's version of the coming to of 'Kathaleen Ny-Houlahan', for instance, turns its twelve- and fourteen-syllable lines to iambic deliverance: in Joyce's praise of the effect, the iambs go marching through the refrain. There is irony, of course, in the recreation of such textures in a time when the Jacobite day had not come after 1745 or 1841 when Mangan made his version. Nor had it appeared when the young Parnellite Joyce praised the insurrectionary fervour of Mangan's iambic thrust. 'The White Birds', by way of contrast, sounds its fantasy in the forms of a poetic language caught between the two drives of Yeats's late nineteenth-century English verse, conflicting desires to enervate poetry in English and while doing so to invigorate it. Playing with the numberless syllables of stress metres, Yeats sounds his desire for the synthetic rhythms of ballad and song and indeed the rhythm of a particular moment in the poetic history of one very specific island, late nineteenth-century Ireland. Between 'The Stolen Child' and 'The White Birds', Yeats discovers a movement between the desire for the dissolution of difference and its reconciliation with the textural and textured sounds of history sounded through form, no matter how it still appears to want to be rid of that history.

This moment is, as I have said, history in the balance, and it is marked in Hopkins and Yeats by an aesthetics of texture. A textured art is of course a Ruskinian virtue, and although Yeats's father was an artist of obsessively layered textures, his Benthamism meant that he disagreed with his son over Ruskin, a disagreement that at one stage involved the older Yeats shoving William into a picture with such violence that he broke the glass of the frame with the back of his head. All because he had been discovered reading *Unto this Last*.[58] The debate between Tynan, Hopkins and the older Yeats over 'finish in art' was also a Ruskinian debate. William wasn't there that day, but for the Ruskinians, Hopkins and the young Yeats, but also in the actual practice of the older Yeats, 'finish' was something achieved with great effort and over much time.

Hopkins didn't actually like the portrait of Katherine Tynan when he eventually saw it, after the two more years John Yeats waited before he allowed the picture to be exhibited. But two years had also passed from Hopkins's first draft of 'Spelt from Sibyl's Leaves'. The poem was finished by the end of November 1886, just after Hopkins had visited Yeats's studio, and was sent to Robert Bridges in December, the same month as the publication of 'The Stolen Child'. Its finish demonstrates a typical Ruskinian nostrum: 'Finish does not consist in smoothing or polishing, but in the *completeness of the expression of the ideas.*'[59] 'Every word in the poem has the complex suggestiveness of whole sentence in prose',[60] says Norman MacKenzie, suggesting in one way just how an attention to finish can lead us on to the demands of literary language placed on it by Joyce on Newman: 'the word is used according to the literary tradition: it has there its full value'[61]; or T.S. Eliot on Mallarmé, in terms Ron Schuchard suggests were developed from his contact with Yeats's chanting: 'in poetry the word, each word by itself, though only being fully itself in context, has absolute value.'[62]

Hopkins told Bridges that 'Spelt from Sibyl's Leaves' was 'the longest sonnet ever made and no doubt the longest making'. His instructions to Robert Bridges were that it should be performed in tempo rubato – literally, 'stolen or borrowed time'.[63] It ended up looking like this:

Spelt from Sibyl's Leaves

Earnest, earthless, equal, attuneable, | vaulty, voluminous, … stupendous
Evening strains to be tíme's vást, | womb-of-all, home-of-all, hearse-of-all night.
Her fond yellow hornlight wound to the west, | her wild hollow hoarlight hung
   to the height
Waste; her earliest stars, earlstars, | stárs principal, overbend us,
Fíre-féaturing heaven. For éarth | her béing has unbound, her dapple is at an
   end, as-
tray or aswarm, all throughther, in throngs; | self ín self stéepèd and
   páshed – qúite
Disremembering, dísmémbering | all now. Heart, you round me right
With: Óur évening is óver us; óur night | whélms, whélms, ánd will énd us.
Only the beakleaved boughs dragonish | damask the tool-smooth bleak light;
   black,
Ever so black on it. Óur tale, O óur oracle! | Lét life, wáned, ah lét life wínd
Off hér once skéined stained véined varíety | upon, áll on twó spools; párt,
   pen, páck
Now her áll in twó flocks, twó folds – black, white; | right, wrong; réckon but,
   reck but, mínd
But thése two; wáre of a wórld where bút these | twó tell, each off the óther; of
   a ráck
Where, selfwrung, selfstrung, sheathe- and shelterless, | thóughts agaínst
   thoughts ín groans grínd.[64]

In conclusion and to hazard a paraphrase: as entropy develops to its maximum in the closed system, thus the natural will come to an end. The oncoming of night provides on the one hand a figure for that end. Night brings the loss of variety, the smoothing out, the greying over of difference, a figure for ultimate night, the end of the physical world, the last judgement. That last judgement is figured not as mere change – of two spools, one spooling on and the other off – but of the unravelling of the loom of time on which the linen had received the damasking of its individuality. It is about an end, the end of evening and life, and indeed the ultimate end of time. Whether the last judgement is envisaged at this end is difficult: why does the Catholic priest-poet seem to think he will be going to the eternity of self-consciousness that would be his hell ('thoughts against thoughts in groans grind')? This Irish evening suggests that while thoughts are telling off one another the speaker remains 'ware of a world' on which the poem is still being written, in a state divided against itself. For Hopkins as well as Yeats, this state of division is also a state of change facing a history after evening in a poetry that is unravelling into something new. That poetry winds off one kind of variety to exchange it for the mingling hands and glances of some sort of dawn.

CHAPTER 8

Violence and Measure: Yeats after Union

Farewells to the Harp

By the beginning of the twentieth century, William Butler Yeats was writing primarily for the theatre, and was enthusiastically involved in its management. He had been struggling with his ambitious blank-verse dramatic poem *The Shadowy Waters* for a number of years, so much so that two completely different versions were published between its first appearance in 1900 and its eventual completion – or abandonment – in 1906.[1] Still exploring Irish Mode musicality and symbolist eroticism, the endings of both versions sought loving suffocation and sexual oblivion under the lover's hair, with an erotic symbolism of 'silver fish', 'trembling ... fawn', 'misty border of the wood', and 'hair'. The odd part is the accompaniment of the harp, which plays itself.

In 1900, the poem ended:

> *Dectora. (She bends beside him and puts her arms about him.)*
> > Bend lower, O king,
> O flower of the branch, O bird among the leaves,
> O silver fish that my two hands have taken
> Out of a running stream, O morning star
> Trembling in the blue heavens like a white fawn
> Upon the misty border of the wood, –
> Bend lower, that I may cover you with my hair,
> For we will gaze upon this world no longer.
> *(The harp begins to murmur of itself.)*
> *Forgael.* The harp strings have begun to cry out to the eagles.

And in 1906, in a longer and slightly more measured reciprocation of Dectora's offer:

> *Forgael [gathering* Dectora's *hair about him.]*
> Beloved, having dragged the net about us,
> And knitted mesh to mesh, we grow immortal;

And that old harp awakens of itself
To cry aloud to the grey birds, and dreams,
That have had dreams for father, live in us.[2]

Yeats's passages allude to a number of texts, not least his own recent love poetry. But here a nineties passive eroticism and a no-less passive Irish Mode atavism bear issue as the music of poetry appears to spawn itself. Dreams are begotten of dreams and the harp is metamorphosed out of the net of hair. Yeats recalls the human harp of his own rewriting of the Ossianic in his 1889 'The Wanderings of Oisin'. The harp in that poem had been hurled out of sight by Niamh's people, the Tuatha de Danaan, once Oisin had begun to sing to it: the inherent sadness of its mortality proved just too much for Tír na nÓg.[3]

In 'Oisin', Yeats had the harp of Thomas Moore in earshot, a poet he professed to despise. For Moore, it was an instrument unavoidably drawn to a sadness only amplified by the insistent mournfulness of the national music echoing in its strings, as at the end of the song 'Dear Harp of My Country':

> The warm lay of love and the light note of gladness
> Have wakened thy fondest, thy liveliest thrill;
> But, so oft hast thou echo'd the deep sigh of sadness,
> That ev'n in thy mirth it will steal from thee still.[4]

If Moore's harp is an instrument that insists on making only a sad sound, it does so with an assonance that tells of close sonic relations that operate with a certain indirect furtiveness, stealing around with the stillness of perpetuity. In *The Shadowy Waters*, Yeats's 'old harp awakens of itself', and in Yeats and Moore both net and strings have been formed from lovers' hair enmeshed in the singularity of a music that has given birth to itself in the conditions of amorous rejection and national defeat.

In 'The Origin of the Harp', the national instrument had been metamorphosed from the hair of a jilted 'Syren of old' who lived by 'the green shore' and tells a sub-Ovidian myth of the birth of national music as a new Irish mythology:

> Still her bosom rose fair – still her cheeks smil'd the same –
> While her sea-beauties gracefully form'd the light frame;
> And her hair, as let loose, o'er her white arm it fell,
> Was chang'd to bright chords utt'ring melody's spell.
>
> Hence it came, that this soft Harp so long hath been known
> To mingle love's language with sorrow's sad tone;
> Till *thou* didst divide them, and teach the fond lay
> To speak love when I'm near thee, and grief when away.[5]

The final turn of the lyric's singer to his loved one turns a mythic meta-morphosis beyond the folkloric into the conventional consolations of the poem of parting, or aubade. But the song still tells of division, the instrument formed by rejection.[6] Unlike Joyce, Yeats did not exchange the symbolist metamorphoses of this passive mode for a more experimental modernism. Nevertheless, for Yeats, if passive rejection would not be enough, symbolism, too, had its shortcomings. One eventual formulation of this was in the 1906 *Shadowy Waters*: 'dreams,/That have had dreams for father, live in us'. So, although the self-begotten dream provides its own lineage, it will eventually turn to a living present and not the defeated past. This dream will then be written by a personality who will seek something beyond what Yeats's 1916 poem 'Ego Dominus Tuus' calls 'the common dream'.

This book began with an account of the argument over critical constructions of the 'Celtic note' or 'Irish Mode' as a sort of evanescent sonic irresponsibility founded in the rhythms of both Irish-language poetry and music that were imaginatively – and now and again factitiously – recreated in English verse translation. There were other, rather more concrete contacts of lyric with Irish-English, and the vernacular of British-archipelagic folk and ballad verse and its relationship with British and European romantic and Victorian poetry. The strongest early twentieth-century apologists of the new Irish poetry that thus emerged wrote in one way at its apogee, the coming of revolution after decades of cultural renewal, founding that renewal in the recovery of the lost thing that had previously been heard in the satires or elegies of the seemingly static culture of a hidden Ireland. But in another way, they also wrote after the fact, in the first decades of a twentieth century in which the new art forms of a modernist European culture were contiguous with the state-building of a partially liberated Ireland primarily seeking to consolidate the forms of tradition. As the contrary examples of Yeats and Joyce alone might show, such temporal coincidences and misplacements were in one way accidental, contingent even. What remained behind were the successful results of the experiments necessary to manage so many of the formal challenges of writing a new poetry in a new language, part of the creative interplay of anachronism and incongruity that resulted in the emergence of the synthetic jumble of a new verse in English from the previous century. In the work of Moore, Ferguson or Mangan, and then in redactions of the theme by British as well as Irish poets, the various formal tempi of the verse – rhythm, rhyme, song and ballad as well as the long history revealed in words themselves through trails of etymology and translation – were attuned to a preoccupation with temporality as much as history. A lyricism redeemed from the past seemed to be in the very process of giving way to an uncertain future.

For Thomas MacDonagh and Austin Clarke, the early poetry of Yeats remained as a singular example of an Irish Mode in English poetry. Yeats did indeed continue to find ways of emphasising its importance as bearing the primary responsibility of performance, constructed for the ear as much as the printed page. As Ronald Schuchard has explored, his experiments with Arnold Dolmetsch's psaltery and collaborations with Florence Farr from 1902 to 1912 show him consistently seeking ways of establishing the performative texts of his earlier poems in a sort of chant verse.[7] His work for the theatre is the most sustained attempt at verse drama in English before T.S. Eliot, himself greatly influenced by Yeats's middle-period dramatic experiments. But as so often with Yeats, poetic instinct frequently overrode public dogmatism, and the poems that followed *The Shadowy Waters*, written as the psaltery project was underway, were to explore styles at some remove from the harp-like, the wavering, the chanted or the assonantal. There may be some debate over whether there is an early and late Yeats style,[8] and Yeats was a poet who resisted vers libre and continued to demonstrate a mastery of conventional metric, rhyme and elaborate stanza structures. But his example is the strongest we have of a growing ambivalence towards the alternating achievements of the cultural nationalism and what Terence Brown calls 'The Counter-Revival',[9] times of retrenchment and disillusion, the surprise of revolution and the violence of war, and the changing forms of Irish poetry in pressing conditions in which some poets played roles that were other than poetic.

This chapter will conclude with an account of Yeats's revisions of his early poems at the end of 1924. That was the year of the publication of Corkery's *Hidden Ireland*, a retrospective text from the first years of the newly Free State, which discovered in its strong reading of Gaelic poetry the repressive conditions of the supposed cultural hiatus that preceded a long cultural revival. If 1924 was also the first year of a sort of Irish peace, following on from the ceasefire after civil war that followed the establishment of the Irish Free State, it was a peace still very much in the shadow of the years of a European war fought by a British state in which the Irish also played a part. Similarly, if Irish poetry was to be seen coming out from under the Union along with the Irish State, in the war years it bore witness through a lyricism attuned to the various conflicts in which Irish people found themselves, both in Ireland and further afield.

Through-otherness

Much has been written about the distinctiveness of twentieth-century Irish war poetry. The revolutionary events of 1916 and the Irish wars of independence and civil war that followed were the subject of many and varied poems. Yeats's extraordinary response to the event of Easter week 1916 is the best known of these texts, and even Corkery's *Hidden Ireland* can be read as a reiteration of national purpose in a time of aftermath from the exhaustions of uncertain achievement after immense political change. In the best account of Irish writing of the Great War, Fran Brearton pictures Irish poetry as playing a significant part in the British and European writing of that war and the extraordinary example it provided to posterity, most notably in the war elegies by Michael Longley and Seamus Heaney.[10] In a 2001 lecture, Heaney engages in his own act of retrospect, from the early twenty-first century following the long period of Northern Irish conflict, by holding up Francis Ledwidge as an exemplary case of one who doesn't quite fit in previously settled political or poetic categories. Ledwidge represents at the least a challenge for a nationalist account of Irish poetry and at most a point of contact between archipelagic poets in the last years of the United Kingdom of Great Britain and Ireland and the renewal of poetic and linguistic energy up to that point. Heaney's thinking about Ledwidge has a place called 'Ulster' in mind, part of which remains in the Union. So whether the short career and violent end of Ledwidge represent a traumatic finality for Irish poetry under the union or simply one way of acknowledging that union continues along with its poetry, the 'through-other' relation of poetry in the history of the Hiberno-British archipelago must remain in play.

In Chapter 7, I mentioned Gerard Manley Hopkins's use of the Irish-English word 'throughther' in 'Spelt from Sibyl's Leaves'. The word comes from both the Gaelic 'trí n-a chéile' meaning 'mixed up or confused', and the English word, which both translates it and sonically echoes it: 'through-other'. I viewed Hopkins's use of this word as one example of the linguistic contact with Irish-English in a poem about disintegration of a sort, moving past evening into the end of light and the end of union and empire, spiritual as well as material. The word cropped up again seventy or so years later in a poem by poet, Presbyterian minister and broadcaster W.R. Rodgers, 'Armagh' (1952), written in and about a mixed-up demotic:

> There is a through-otherness about Armagh
> Of tower and steeple,
> Up on the hill are the arguing graves of the kings
> And below are the people.

> [...]
> Through-other is its history, of Celt and Dane,
> Norman and Saxon,
> Who ruled the place and sounded the gamut of fame
> From cow-horn to klaxon.[11]

There is a lovely play here with the 'Here is the church' finger game and nursery rhyme, as a long history is domesticated into childhood play. Heaney reads the poem reassuringly, as one where word, poem and poet are 'analogous to the triple heritage of Irish, Scottish and English traditions that compound and complicate the cultural and political life of contemporary Ulster.'[12] As this book has shown, after the example of Samuel Ferguson – an Ulster poet, writing from Dublin, initially publishing a post-Burns and Wordsworth ballad poetry in Edinburgh – this is not simply an 'Ulster' matter, and the triple and more heritages of Irish poetry through the nineteenth century have all contributed to the through-other complications of its synthetic compound. Heaney's discussion of the word leads him to the example of Ledwidge and his well known 1916 elegy for his friend, 'Thomas MacDonagh', a poem better known as 'He shall not hear the bittern cry'.

In Chapter 1, I quoted from Heaney's lecture about the poet's conception of the importance of reading for poetry as much as for politics. His insights about Ledwidge ensue from registering the political complications of an Irish Home Ruler serving in the British Army in Turkey and France as his increasingly radicalised friends in Ireland opted for armed revolution in his absence. At first sight, Ledwidge's poem looks like an Irish mode poem by rote, filled full of the internal rhyme, cross-rhyme and assonance that those prior to MacDonagh held to be the sonic crossing over from Gaelic into Anglo-Irish poetry. Ledwidge would have known that MacDonagh himself was sceptical on that point, preferring to hear music and an Irish accent speaking English as the main determinant of the aural capabilities of the new Irish mode verse. Heaney heard MacDonagh's English-language translation of Cathal Buí MacGiolla Ghunna's lyric 'An Bunnan Buí' or 'The Yellow Bittern' in Ledwidge's MacDonagh elegy. A sort of integrated homage to the Irish mode, itself through-other in various English-Irish texts as noticed by MacDonagh, the poem is sounded across political differences, conflicting allegiances and the fact of death.

In Ledwidge's 'Thomas MacDonagh', Irish mode wildness, scenery, weather, flora and mythic livestock are recognisable:

> He shall not hear the bittern cry
> In the wild sky where he is lain,
> Nor voices of the sweeter bird

Above the wailing of the rain.

Nor shall he know when loud March blows
Thro' slanting snows her fanfare shrill,
Blowing to flame the golden cup
Of many an upset daffodil.

But when the Dark Cow leaves the moor,
And pastures poor with greedy weeds,
Perhaps he'll hear her low at morn
Lifting her head in pleasant meeds.[13]

Of this lyric Heaney says that 'the idiom of English poetry [...] is being revised in favour of an idiom recommended by the man being elegized.' So, from the beginning of MacDonagh's 'Bunnán Buí' translation, Heaney cites (and I extend the brief extract he gives):

The yellow bittern that never broke out
In a drinking bout, might as well have drunk;
His bones are thrown on a naked stone
Where he lived alone like a hermit monk.
O yellow bittern! I pity your lot,
Though they say that a sot like myself is curst –
I was sober a while, but I'll drink and be wise
For fear I should die in the end of thirst.[14]

These poems are in many ways trí n-a chéile, or through each other, using both the echoing capabilities of end and internal rhyme as well as English-language social-linguistic registers to suggest something that is no longer quite there anymore.

In MacDonagh, the Irish melody to the song has been removed both by translation and print and remains as a mere hint when read aloud, along with the voice of the bird, dead for want of water. In this version the poet tells of his thirst for more than water in the lexis of a vernacular English: 'bout', 'sot', 'curst' or 'For fear I should die in the end of thirst', the odd formality of the English conditional adjusted to the Irish original: 'ar eagla go bhfaighinnse bás den tart' ('afraid I would be getting death from thirst').[15] MacDonagh catches the insouciance of the drunkard poet's resignation to his lot in ways that Ferguson and Yeats had heard in their versions of the speaker of the 'Páistín Fionn' song discussed in Chapter 4, a sort of dramatic monologue version of a voice from the past caught in the animated tenor of a literary milieu recovered from its hiding place. Heaney suggests Wordsworthian lyricism in Ledwidge's reference to the daffodil, a restorative sight for Wordsworth. But in Ledwidge it is an 'upset' flower of spring, and it may have Miltonic echoes: 'And daffadillies fill their cups with tears,/To strew the herse where Lycid lies'.[16] In Ledwidge, though, the narcissus figures loss without offering consolation. Mention of Narcissus suggests Echo, and here the symbolism is part of a multiple synthetic echoing of the not-quite-lost that commemorates the more completely lost: his dead friend and (in 1916 at least) his cause. Indeed, the war poet's own precious subject matter finds echo and reflex in 'many an upset daffodil', the wasted masculinity all around him and the soldier-poet's presage of death in battle. For Ledwidge, this would occur in the following year.

Beautiful and moving as these poems are, even more so given their terrible contexts, they inhabit an Irish mode turned to elegy for that mode itself. Of course, it is impossible, and for all the dangers of the imposition of hindsight, politically irresponsible not to read them as such given the violent end that was to befall their authors. This is no crass causality, as these are poetic as much as historical matters. It is as if the poems are on the verge of extinction, cast into a symbolism (snow, daffodil, bittern) and sounded in a metric that has been borrowed from the stock of tradition for what looks like the last time. But if the circumstances are historical and political, the implications are nevertheless poetic.

A host of questions arise for Irish poetry. Where to now for poetry at the crisis point of a movement in national culture in which it had played such a significant part? Could poetry continue to participate in this movement or should it cast itself in another shape? Should Irish poetry now participate in the concerns of a traumatised wider world and an internationalised and increasingly modernist Anglophone culture in which the Irish poet writing in English now moved with some confidence? Consequently, could the Irish poem in English be effectively extricated from its through-other relations with British poetry? The first chapter of this book ended with the 'freshening and stirring' of the Irish stew of poetry that MacDonagh saw coming in his *Literature in Ireland*, but he envisaged that Irish poetry should imagine the new in the wake of the partial dissolution of the Union, or indeed the moment of 'liberation'. Heaney formulates the matter as an orientation towards the future from the uncertainty of finding oneself alone in a present in which circumstances have changed: 'Poetry moves things forward once the poet and the poem get ahead of themselves and find themselves out on their own.'[17]. The poet contemplates the new both as freedom and as feeling lost.

Out on his own, Yeats had recognised this dilemma since his failed experiment in an Irish symbolist mode in *The Shadowy Waters* and was working through it in his own way, if not as yet heading off in another

direction. His 1914 volume *Responsibilities* famously declared Romantic
Ireland dead and gone, and the volume neared its end by throwing off
'A Coat', 'covered with embroideries/Out of old mythologies'. With contempt, the speaker of the poem watches it being picked up and worn by
both detractors and imitators alike. The little parable poem ends as if it
couldn't care less:

> Song, let them take it
> For there's more enterprise
> In walking naked.[18]

In one way, this is a manifestation of Yeats's need to test again an aspiration dating back to at least 1892, in 'To Ireland in the Coming Times',
to show on his written page the trailing of '*the red-rose-bordered hem/Of
her, whose history began/Before God made the angelic clan*' (6–8). The hem
of the coat is embroidered with the old mythologies of an Ireland of pre-
antiquity, antecedent to divine and human histories, a nationhood that is
both ideal and eternal. 'A Coat' throws off one fantasy of authenticity in
order to return to another, one of the recurrent preoccupations of Irish
poetry: the primitivism of naked song, the thing itself, unaccommodated
man, poet and poem 'out on their own'.

But like 'To Ireland in the Coming Times', 'A Coat' has yet to enact
what thing might emerge from such nakedness. The resolution is provisional to the new style and theme that will – should – follow. The
Responsibilities volume did not end there, but neither did its poems
break through into expression: the final untitled lyric tells of the inter-
mittent message of the poet's occult muse, the 'reed-throated whisperer'
who now speaks 'inwardly' rather than in public. The voice tells only of
the world's disdain for forgotten monuments of antiquity and revival.
Yeats sabotages the Irish mode sonic and rhetorical repetition, internal
rhyme and syntactic looseness along with the Ossianic subject matter of
an 'ancient' poetry, just as he skilfully suggests that these remain parts
of his poetical repertoire. The poem ends in scatology, with a turn to
both the poet's own notoriety and the 'relevance' that the philistines
demand:

> *I can forgive even that wrong of wrongs,*
> *Those undreamt accidents that have made me*
> *– Seeing that Fame has perished this long while,*
> *Being but a part of ancient ceremony –*
> *Notorious, till all my priceless things*
> *Are but a post the passing dogs defile.*   (9–14)

'Notorious', 'priceless', 'post', 'passing': this can't give up the reed-throated whispering music in its sibilant consonants. Poetry's end might be the word the poem sounds but doesn't actually use. The dogs have the right idea.

If one solution for Yeats had been to write verse drama, then that still left him with the problem of continuing to write lyric under a dissolving Union. One response, given historical events, was to rise to the challenge of elegy. The poem composed two years later that names 'MacDonagh and MacBride/And Connolly and Pearse' solves it in that very roll call: 'I write it out in a verse –.'[19] But the extraordinary success of 'Easter 1916' as a public elegy that finds a metric for heroic naming was not consistently matched by Yeats's other war poetry, nor indeed in what was to come. David Pearce estimates Yeats wrote forty-three 'First World War poems', and as public poem or private elegy, they are variously successful.[20] But Yeats was formulating his own question, one that he sought to answer in his own way, often by the promulgation of further questions. As he appeared to move away from Irish poetry under the Union, the question for Yeats was how to write a poetry no longer serving the need either to create a national tradition or to remain in hock to the traditions of dominant neighbours, in Europe as much as England. I have framed this issue here as a matter of taking authenticity seriously – even when the poets had most fun with its seeming impossibility – showing successive examples of poems seeking a sort of singularity, as the thing itself, something seeking to persist on its own terms.

In 1916, as both the United Kingdom and continental Europe faced times of war and modernity in which they appeared to have begun a final unravelling, Yeats revisited this as a small-scale thematic matter, facing the new day in the singularity of possible achievement in the future:

> 'Before I am old
> I shall have written one
> Poem maybe as cold
> And passionate as the dawn.'
>
> ('The Fisherman', 37–40)

The wish remains unresolved in an ambiguity that shades into an unusual hesitancy around that crucial word 'maybe': '*one*/Poem maybe …' or 'one/*Poem* – maybe as cold/And passionate…'? Even if that ambiguity were to be resolved, the establishment of an oxymoron familiar in the later Yeats – cold passion – shows no small ambition. This little speech comes at the end of 'The Fisherman', a late Romantic self-conscious lyric

about creativity and boorishness Yeats had been writing in the wake of
the disappointments that followed times of revival and counter-revival,
the death of his friend John Millington Synge, the Hugh Lane pictures
debacle, the failure of his and Florence Farr's psaltery project: 'The beating
down of the wise/And great art beaten down' (23–24). But it is mostly a
simple alternate-rhyming trimeter ballad, which with immense skill is still
sounding a hint of anglicised Irish (the place name 'Connemara' is used
twice) through a poem written in the plainest English syntax and diction.
It also admiringly recreates another simple art, as in these lines, which are
part exquisite observation of sporting skill and part symbol of an integrated aesthetic mastery. Here it imagines an integration of human body
and fishing rod, poem and poet:

> Imagining a man,
> And his sun-freckled face,
> And grey Connemara cloth,
> Climbing up to a place
> Where stone is dark under froth,
> And the down-turn of his wrist
> When the flies drop in the stream;   (28–34)

There is a pointed simplicity and no little prosodic artfulness in the mim-
icry of the simple skills of the fisherman, particularly those hyphenated
double-syllable stresses on 'sun-freckled', or the sonic flick on the spondee
'down-turn', which turns the verse swiftly down with the wrist. 'And the
down-turn of his wrist' acts as narrative presage to the metrically near-
identical but infinitesimally slower response to that wrist movement in
the following line: 'When the flies drop in the stream' (x x / / x x /; the
'slowing down' in performance is achieved by the removal of the hyphen
between 'flies' and 'drop' and thus the slight lengthening of duration on
the word 'flies'). The symbol recreates the marriage of form and function
in art (poetry, fly-fishing) from which the 'one/Poem' should emerge.
Only that word 'maybe' suggests that this might not be so easily achieved
with the required sprezzatura.

The initial writing of 'The Fisherman' predated the Great War,[21] and
its initial publication in Chicago, in Harriet Monroe's *Poetry*, in February
1916 occurred two months before the events of Easter week of that year. It
would take some ingenuity to connect the poem with events about which
Yeats was given no inkling, but afterwards his view of his contemporaries
would change utterly. The poem's eventual gathering together with the
poems published in the great 1919 volume of coldness and passion, *The*

Wild Swans at Coole, bespeaks its position in the work of poet seeking not just a theme but a poetry coming out from under union in a shape and style always wary of the challenge of its own adequacy when facing that theme. At the very least it seeks to reconnect with the plastic art celebrated in 'The Fisherman', to 'find myself and not an image' and offset one mistake, finding 'the gentle, sensitive mind' and thus losing 'the old nonchalance of the hand' ('Ego Dominus Tuus', 10–13).

The Common Dream

'The Fisherman' is one of a number of Yeats's poems immediately prior to, concurrent with or reflective of war, Rising and Independence struggle, both anxious to break from a style in the past and wary of speaking about events in the present. If the 1914 'On Being Asked for a War Poem' was a notorious privileging of the poet above the merely contemporary ('I think it better that at times like these/We poets keep our mouths shut'), the points at which Yeats engaged head-on with current events were not always successful. The extraordinary 'Reprisals' of five years later, which imagines the ghost of the war hero Robert Gregory returned to Coole to witness the killing of Eileen Quinn by Black and Tans, remained unpublished. With its invocation of Gregory's 'good death' and his 'battle joy', it was destined to offend its subject's bereaved mother, Augusta Gregory.

Quinn's murdered body also lies at the centre of 'Nineteen Hundred and Nineteen', a poem that allows the event and the murdered one to attain a specificity that resists one version of the Yeatsian, that is, an inevitable ratchet into a heroic or symbolic mode. In a bravura book-length reading of the linguistic and ethical achievement of that poem, Michael Wood says, 'Yeats's recourse is not only to his own considerable powers but to something like the powers of the English language itself'. Thus, when it comes to writing about Eileen Quinn's death (unlike that of Robert Gregory), 'It is not possible to lose her, to convert her into a simple instance, and in this case the allegory would not be at odds with the specificity of one mother's dying.' In Wood's account the issue is both stylistic ('powers of the English language') and ethical ('the specificity of one mother's dying'), and political violence emerges out of the polishing of priceless things or ancient ceremony into the present, in the present tense: '*Now* days *are* dragon-ridden; the nightmare/*Rides* upon sleep; a drunken soldiery/*Can* leave the mother murdered at her door,/*To crawl* in her own blood, and *go* scot-free' ('Nineteen Hundred and Nineteen', I, 25–28 [my emphasis]). On that 'Now' that opens the passage and recurs a few lines later, Wood says, 'What's interesting about *now* is how it shifts in time; and how it is never without a *then*'.[22]

Unlike Moore or Mangan before him, the question raised by Yeats's 'Now' is of his intuition in the decade before 1920 that the Irish poem had yet to rise to its occasion. To do so, his poetry must then continuously reconsider itself as the aspired-for 'one / Poem' of 'The Fisherman': that is, a succession of 'one poems', unencumbered by the crippling backwards look, the *then* of the temporality of Irish poetry, consistently renewed since it will be 'cold / And passionate as the dawn'. The task comports with the impossible throughout, an embrace of the accidental and the contingent we have seen so closely involved in the 'thing itself' in this book. At the very least, it might involve throwing out history. Whatever the aspiration Yeats sets himself in 'The Fisherman', the present continues to comport with the past in his poetry of this period, and the question of what the future holds (for poetry, Ireland and Irish poetry) is always uncertain.

The blank-verse dialogue poem 'Ego Dominus Tuus', written in 1915 and first published by Monroe in *Poetry* in October 1917, is best known for Yeats's eccentric testing of the models offered him by the lives of Dante and Keats. Yeats also approaches one version of his relation to a recent history by addressing a nameless coterie from the past in a statement that is part assertion and part question:

> *Hic.* Yet surely there are men who have made their art
> Out of no tragic war, lovers of life,
> Impulsive men that look for happiness
> And sing when they have found it.
> *Ille* No, not sing,
> For those that love the world serve it in action,
> Grow rich, popular and full of influence,
> And should they paint or write, still it is action:
> The struggle of the fly in marmalade.
> The rhetorician would deceive his neighbours,
> The sentimentalist himself; while art
> Is but a vision of reality.
> What portion in the world can the artist have
> Who has awakened from the common dream
> But dissipation and despair?
>
> (38–51)

This abjures both rhetorical and sentimental poetry. The public poetry of 'those that love the world' is haughtily dismissed in that extraordinary image of the fly in marmalade. If Yeats was later to say that the poet is 'never the bundle of accident and incoherence that sits down to breakfast',[23] the marmalade is both the quotidian and his disdain for it. It is on the one hand bathos, an observation from breakfast on any given morning; on the other, it is an image remembered by Yeats from an 1894 conversation with Paul Verlaine about Paris when Verlaine told Yeats he 'lived in it like a fly in a pot of marmalade'.[24] Between these registers, the blank verse is roughened, shoved to the verge of free verse before its iambic straightening up in alternating four- and five-beat lines: 'the struggle of the fly in marmalade' (x / x x / x / x /) or the intonationally ambiguous, 'But dissipation and despair?'; either a cadenced calming in regular iambs (x / x / x / x /) or a final heavy stress as the voice rises to the question mark after 'despair?' (x / x / x x x /). This is a verse edging into new content by trying out a new style, careless of the odd bum note in image or tone, as the everyday is employed as symbolic form for the failings of an art that seeks historical impact.

The subsequent publication of the poem at the head of *Per Amica Silentia Lunae* in 1918, the first part of which acts as gloss on this dialogue poem, names the source of the dissipated and despairing 'artist/Who has awakened from the common dream' as Yeats's 1890s contemporaries, 'The Tragic Generation' of 'last romantics',[25] such as Edward Dowson and Lionel Johnson.[26] In comparison with these fast-living poets, victims of addiction or suicide, the historical person of Keats offers bathos again: 'I see a schoolboy when I think of him/With face and nose pressed to a sweet-shop window' (55–56). If this school boy is without interest for Yeats in the poem and in *Per Amica*, it is only slightly redeemed by an overstatement of negative capability: 'Those men that in their writings are most wise/Own nothing but their blind stupefied hearts' (68–69). But the question is, what insight was gained by those failed artists, who in their dissipation and despair were neither Dante nor Keats, yet had nevertheless awakened from the common dream?

Even strongly sympathetic readings of the poem bring out the difficulty here with Yeats's conception of 'the common dream' and its relation to the statement, 'art/is but a vision of reality'. Of the phrase 'vision of reality', Helen Vendler says, 'In 'bringing together two words [...] that normally form an antithesis, Yeats makes them mirror each other.' Elsewhere in her discussion of the poem she opposes 'common dream' with 'vision'.[27] For Denis Donoghue, 'The common dream is the assumption that reality is as it is supposed to be, according to the dictates of common sense and science.' He quotes one of Yeats's fellow workers in '90s symbolism, Arthur Symons, who had expounded 'a literature in which the visible world is no longer a reality and the unseen world no longer a dream'.[28] Michael

O'Neill brings out this imprecision in the phrase with a hint of exaspera-
tion: '"Vision" bespeaks the student of Shelley and Blake, even as "reality"
swithers between a quasi-occultist sense of the real and a glance at would-
be unillusioned modernism.'[29] Earlier than these readings, Harold Bloom
glosses the dissatisfactions in the phrase as a result of finding style as much
as vision: 'What has begun in Yeats is that marvellous style one fights in
vain, for it can make any conviction, every opinion even, formidable out
of all proportion to its actual imaginative validity.'[30]

As Stephen Dedalus might say, these may be 'big words which make us
so unhappy' – 'world', 'vision', 'reality', 'common', 'dream' – and maybe
not that removed from the vocabulary of the 'rhetorician [who] would
deceive his neighbours'. If they aren't quite oxymoronic or antinomial
concepts, they do play with widely diverse meanings. For instance, what
is 'common' for Yeats is not necessarily in opposition to the visionary, and
the relation of the poet to the 'reality' of various common artistic traditions, French symbolist and English as well as Irish, is recast through
the lines. If we substitute the 1890s memories of Verlaine and the poets
of the Cheshire Cheese with a figure further in the past, such as James
Clarence Mangan or the authors of the eighteenth-century amhrán and
Jacobite lament, then the common dream of poets in a national tradition
seemed always to be working against the dissipation of their lives. As far
back as 1895, in the introduction to his *Book of Irish Verse*, one of the first
victims of Yeats's critique of a certain kind of rhetorical cultural nationalism, Thomas Davis, showed his weakness as a poet because he was 'in
the main an orator influencing men's acts, and not a poet shaping their
emotions'. Yeats said that, 'No man was more sincere, no man had a less
mechanical mind', but the insincerity crept into Davis's poetry. If in his
verse Davis felt the temptation to become the rhetorician who deceives his
neighbours, Yeats had excused only Mangan among Davis's Young Ireland
compatriots, as one who was 'kept out of public life and its half-illusions
by a passion for books, and for drink and opium'.[31] Cathal Buí MacGiolla
Ghunna, or Samuel Ferguson and Yeats's conception of the anonymous
author of 'Páistín Fionn' or Mangan's 'Nameless One': all are in troubled
relation with the common dream if it is understood as a rhetorical tradition out of which the poet awakes at his peril, a coat thrown aside along
with its 'embroideries/Of old mythologies'.

Take these stanzas from 'The Nameless One', about which Yeats noted
in *The Book of Irish Verse*: 'This poem is an account of Mangan's own life,
and is, I think, redeemed out of rhetoric by its intensity.'[32] Late in his life,
the extraordinarily prolific Mangan appeared still to be pouring out poetry

in dithyrambic fervour ('Roll forth, my song, like the rushing river'), but the poem addresses rejection, abjection even, within the cultural climate of 1840s Ireland and in the terms of writerly dissipation and despair – his models were William Maginn and Robert Burns. The editor of *The Irishman* who first published it in 1849, just after Mangan's death, introduced it as 'the soul-harassing consciousness that tortured our friend in his reflective moments'.[33] If it was not quite Mangan's last-written poem,[34] it certainly fits that legend:

> IV
> Roll on, my song, and to after-ages
>   Tell how, disdaining all earth can give,
> He would have taught men, from Wisdom's pages,
>   The way to live.
> V
> And tell how trampled, derided, hated,
>   And worn by weakness, disease, and wrong,
> He fled for shelter to God, who mated
>   His soul with song –
> VI
> With song which alway, sublime or vapid,
>   Flowed like a rill in the morning-beam,
> Perchance not deep, but intense and rapid –
>   A mountain stream.
> VII
> Tell how this Nameless, condemned for years long
>   To herd with demons from hell beneath,
> Saw things that made him, with groans and tears, long
>   For even death.
> VIII
> Go on to tell how, with genius wasted,
>   Betrayed in friendship, befooled in love,
> With spirit shipwrecked, and young hopes blasted,
>   He still, still strove.

This is one antecedent in the common dream from which Yeats sought to awake. Its relation to poems such as 'The Fisherman' or 'Ego Dominus Tuus' is that it shares a similar preoccupation with the temporality of song, a poetry speaking from a recently dissipated past while facing a posterity over which it claims the aspiration of ethical example: 'He would have taught men, from Wisdom's pages,/The way to live'. Mangan's personal solution to 'dissipation and despair' was in one way through a recourse to his Catholicism and a redemption of his fluency through temperance, of poetry after the pledge. Yet it is still a fluency addicted to sonic extravagance at the end of the lines, where the sound of the poem reiterates a double-syllable rhyming and repetition. Throughout the extract, Mangan points up consistent oppositions to the official ethics of his reformed expression: 'hated'/'mated'; 'vapid'/'rapid'; 'years long'/'tears, long' (the comma is a Browningesque stroke, obscuring and reinforcing rhyme at the same time, where 'long' initially seems to refer to the length of the speaker's tearfulness but then becomes a longing for death as we see that the word is actually a verb). The near-triple rhymes on 'Genius wasted'/'young hopes blasted' carry the temporal biographical span of its poet, both of long time and the cruel doubling of self as it views unfulfilled aspiration. The poem is also doubled, combining the rolling flow of Mangan's undammed song and a wilful play of instability and indeterminacy of expression. The verbal unity granted through grace by 'God, who mated/His soul with song – ' inevitably surrenders that unity in the very act of its poetic execution, doubling itself in the ambiguity of the sonic oppositions thrown up by rhyme.

Given such typical Mangan virtuosity on the verge of doggerel, in Yeats's opposition of rhetoric and sentiment in 'Ego Dominus Tuus', for all that he was 'redeemed out of rhetoric', Mangan may very well be the self-deceiving sentimentalist. As early as 1887, the young Yeats approvingly viewed Mangan as the poet who 'can never be popular like Davis, for he did not embody in clear verse the thoughts of normal mankind'.[35] Mangan now does service for the middle-aged Yeats seeking a way past the common dream of normal mankind. Regardless of the limited symbolic stock of marmalade, Yeats's relation with other images in the extant common-dream symbolism was at question, repudiating another common question, the need in time of 'tragic war' to serve the world through the action of rhetoric or sentiment. Written before the events of 1916 but still published before the end of the Great War, if the 'modern hope' (11) of 'Ego Dominus Tuus' is to stare at dissipation and despair as the consequence of repudiating a common symbolism, it needed to seek a new one.

Yeats's solution in this poem is similar to Mangan's, though more explicit, and borrows from another Romantic precursor. Taking a lead from Shelley's *Laon and Cynthia*, Hic questions Ille about why he draws in the sand.[36] The response imagines the poet's own double ghosting by the stream of expression itself:

> I call to the mysterious one who yet
> Shall walk the wet sands by the edge of the stream
> And look most like me, being indeed my double,
> And prove of all imaginable things

The most unlike, my anti-self,
And, standing by these characters, disclose
All that I seek; and whisper it as though
He were afraid the birds, who cry aloud
Their momentous cries before it is dawn,
Would carry it away to blasphemous men.

(70–79)

This flirts with gothic and returns to a more recognisable Yeatsian occultism via a psychic vision of doppelganger or archetype. The double is not quite an anima – it is male, usually associated with Yeats's séance communicator Leo Africanus.[37] But as we have seen, there are other candidates, including those unnamed yet present in the poem, Verlaine, Dowson, Johnson or Mangan. Bloom adds in Arnold and Wordsworth.[38] O'Neill, who sums up a tradition of reading Romantic precursors in Yeats that stretches back to Bloom and George Bornstein, concludes, 'The longer one looks at "Ego Dominus Tuus" the more Shelley's features obtrude.'[39] And Shelley for Yeats represents not just the writing on the sand but a double poetics, writing out of self and writing in history, the lure of the unacknowledged legislator. O'Neill also intriguingly suggests that there is unresolved Parnellism in the worry over division and doubling in the poem. If the brief unity that Parnell brought to Irish nationalism was split by his adultery and Catholic bad faith, such unity can also be bad cultural politics for Yeats: as he said in 1910, 'No land lives out a wholesome life, full of ideas and vitality, that is not fighting out great issues within its borders.'[40] Those borders are both the imagined borders of the Ireland of 1910 and the actual borders of the United Kingdom, of which Ireland was still constitutionally a part.

Artistic and political precursors are brought together in the dramatic solution of the dialogue poem, so that the 'anti-self' emerges as another 'reed-throated whisperer', whether it be Shelley as rhetorician or Mangan as sentimentalist or both subsumed with Charles Stewart Parnell into Yeats's own 'mysterious one' alter ego. This is company of a sort for the solitary artist, if not quite the lover-companion of the Joycean 'high unconsortable one', nor even the love-bird swans who 'paddle in the cold/ Companionable streams' in the title poem of *The Wild Swans at Coole* volume. This whisperer or 'mysterious one' walks by the poetic stream of Mangan's rushing river of song or the 'living stream' of history, in the midst of which Yeats would place a stone in order to figure the historical events of Easter 1916. Quite what the whispered message from the anti-self is, the poem never tells us. The ending here is again provisional, clearing the ground, setting up the opposites in preparation for some new style or subject matter that hasn't quite come around yet. Like Mangan's 'Nameless One' it is poetics and not yet poetry.

That summoning up of other possible poetic positions – all tested and failed – is followed here by the invocation of 'the birds who cry aloud/ Their momentous cries before it is dawn'. These crying birds are familiar in many guises in Yeats's own past. They present the wished-for metamorphosis of the lovers in 'The White Birds', and appear at the end of the original 1898 version 'The Song of Mongan' from *The Wind Among The Reeds*, eventually collected as 'He thinks of his Past Greatness when a Part of the Constellations of Heaven', which the ending of 'Ego Dominus Tuus' echoes:

> Although the rushes and the fowl of the air
> Cry of his love with their amorous cries.

The answer to the question is a double utterance and not just overheard, but it is the doubleness of tautology not paradox: the birds are crying their cries. By the 1909 collection of his *Poems*, Yeats had rephrased this as a question:

> O beast of the wilderness, bird of the air,
> Must I endure your amorous cries?[41]

Now, after 1914, trading the endurance of 'amorous cries' for the imminence of 'momentous cries before it is dawn' would make it appear to be time to answer a question that had looked merely rhetorical, or at least to prepare to answer the question. Yeats's literary Parnellism needed more than tautology or paradox. It needed to find something in division that would move this poetry past mere endurance of 'the common dream' into that 'vision of reality'.

To Ireland in the Coming Times

For twenty-five years after 1914 until his death in 1939, Yeats sought increasingly heterodox diversions from the common dream in order to achieve his 'vision of reality'. From *Per Amica Silentia Lunae* in 1917 through the two versions of *A Vision* (1925 and 1937), he developed ideas of poetry and history that both worked from the division and the doubling of the self into the outright and persistent conflict of the wars that went on around him. The procedure, and the solution it presents, was grounded in Romanticism, as a number of the critics mentioned in this chapter have suggested. But for all his desire to move towards the dawn of one cold and passionate poem, Yeats maintained a consistent look backwards to precursors closer to home. A vision of reality cannot resist the pressure of history or the common dream. Wallace Stevens is frequently invoked as another late Romantic, and one who had Yeats in mind as 'the sensitive poet, conscious of negations', who in his struggles with 'affirmations of nobility' is granted 'that occasional ecstasy, or ecstatic freedom of mind, which is his special privilege'. In Stevens's formula, the privilege that brings artistic freedom and insight comes from two sources of 'violence': 'It is a violence from within that protects us from a violence without. It is the imagination pressing back against the pressure of reality.'[42] Stevens was writing in 1942, after Yeats's death but more significantly after Pearl Harbour, and thinking of a second world war that the United States had just joined. The contexts are interchangeable. For his predecessor Yeats, in Fran Brearton's words: '*A Vision* is a poetics of war [...] Its "violence ... within", the doctrine of conflict at its centre, liberates Yeats's poetic response to the "violence without" – the Great War, the Anglo-Irish War, the Civil War.'[43]

Stevens's formula travels in two directions for the marked disunions that Irish poets saw when contemplating poetry's purpose in times and places of violence. Much later in the twentieth century, Seamus Heaney returned to Stevens in his own thinking about the usefulness of poetry and 'how poetry's existence as a form of art relates to our existence as citizens of society'. Before introducing Stevens's violence from within and without as one model of the redress of poetry, he essays a modified Platonism in his own heterodox response: 'Poetic fictions, the dream of alternative worlds, enable governments and revolutionaries as well. It's just that governments and revolutionaries would compel society to take on the shape of their imagining, whereas poets are typically more concerned to conjure with their own and their readers' sense of what is possible or desirable or, indeed, imaginable.'[44] For Yeats, Stevens and Heaney, the proper stuff of poetic fictions amounts to one vision of reality. Heaney's ethical discriminations of that vision ('possible or desirable or, indeed, imaginable') are less assertive and certainly more liberal minded than those of Yeats, who, for David Bromwich, embraces destruction:

> If 'art / Is but a vision of reality', as Yeats said once and always believed, in some of the strongest of his later poems art offers a vision achieved by exposure to a violence that the poet or someone like him can magnificently outlast. The artist earns the privilege of submitting to the violence outside by the strength of his detachment within.[45]

This is maybe seeking too much consolation in one version of the recourse to permanence in Yeats's later poetry: the perpetual song of golden birds in the Byzantium poems, the little Chinese objet d'art and the glorious misreading of Shakespearean tragedy in 'Lapis Lazuli'. But Yeatsian 'violence', like that contemplated by Stevens and Heaney in their own times, was the violence attendant on holding the violence of poetic form against that of historical destruction.

Such achievements are beyond the scope of this book, which is concerned with bringing Irish poetry up to the point where the United Kingdom of English poetry suffered a partial dissolution at the difficult founding of the Irish Free State. That 'Free State' was in part founded on poetic fictions and alternative worlds that were in no small part of Yeats's devising. These were no longer acted in 'embroideries/Out of old mythologies', in fairy worlds or by long- and soon-to-be-gone aristocracies, Gaelic or Anglo-Irish. Those powerful recreations played their part in the versions of culture that persisted into Ireland's peculiar modernity. For all that they faced responsibilities in an uncertain present and an even less secure future, synthetic modern Irish fictions remained powerfully founded in fictions of the past, grounding themselves in their own sense of authenticity and self-authentication. For Declan Kiberd, Stephen Dedalus in another text from 1916, Joyce's *A Portrait of the Artist as a Young Man*, 'immodestly equates self and nation' claiming to 'incarnate the uncreated conscience of his race'. That is in his millionth encounter with reality, and according to Kiberd, Yeats had 'made the same pact' more than twenty years before Joyce. In 'To Ireland in the Coming Times', Yeats asks:

> Nor may I less be counted one
> With Davis, Mangan, Ferguson,
> Because to him who ponders well
> My rhymes more than their rhyming tell
> Of things discovered in the deep
> Where only body's laid asleep.[46]

'Nation-building can be achieved by the simple expedient of writing one's autobiography' Kiberd writes, after invoking Walt Whitman. He goes on:

The republican ideal was the achieved individual, the person with the courage to become his or her full self. The imperialists were not to be thought of as different, so much as aborted or incomplete individuals. By a weird paradox, their incompleteness was evidenced by their polished surface, their premature self-closure which left them at once incomplete and *finished*. The glossy, confident surface indicated a person immune to self-doubts and therefore incapable of development. The Irish self, by contrast was a *project* and its characteristic text was a process, unfinished, fragmenting. [...] Such openness, such freedom is not nobly chosen by an artist who might otherwise have sought the cowardly safety of closure; it is, rather, the inevitable result of the pressure under which the artist places him- or herself.[47]

Those words – 'freedom', 'pressure', 'finish', 'closure' – come round with slight variations again. Here, they propose a decolonising politics conveyed in the decolonising aesthetic of the artist, addicted to style and an openness to change that can never allow the finish of the achieved postcolonial moment. This maybe sounds more like middle Joyce than Yeats's wish, also first published in 1916, to write his 'one/Poem'. Closure and finish remained among Yeats's poetic concerns. 'The correction of prose, because it has no fixed laws, is endless,' he famously wrote to Dorothy Wellesley in 1935, 'a poem comes right with a click like a closing box.'[48]

That sense of the aesthetic artefact in process before its closing down is nevertheless very much part of Yeats's vision of reality. And that is when it became a re-vision of reality. Kiberd quotes from the text of 'To Ireland in the Coming Times', revised at the end of 1924 to be published along with other significant revisions of Yeats's *Early Poems* in 1925. The revisions occurred in Coole Park, in the calm of ceasefire immediately following civil war, in a period of personal illness for a poet nevertheless also completing *A Vision* at the same time. The great roll call of the names of Davis, Mangan and Ferguson had, for the first thirty or so years of the publication history of a poem written in 1892, been followed here by an earlier version of the reed-throated whisperer. If the 1924 revision asserts that the poet's 'rhymes' tell of 'things discovered in the deep', the 1892 version had spoken 'Of the dim wisdoms old and deep/That God gives unto man in sleep'.[49] If the later Yeats is rather more self-authenticating about his own process of discovery, he was also more circumspect about what Kiberd calls, the Irish '*project*'.

Kiberd holds Matthew Arnold in view throughout his discussion of Irish style, possibly as one of the glossy finished ones. Arnold, of course, notoriously held that for all its stylishness, Celtic literature could never be Greek:

> Balance, measure, and patience, these are the eternal conditions, even supposing the happiest temperament to start with, of high success; and balance, measure, and patience are just what the Celt has never had. Even in the world of spiritual creation, he has never, in spite of his admirable gifts of quick perception and warm emotion, succeeded perfectly, because he never has had steadiness, patience, sanity enough to comply with the

conditions under which alone can expression be perfectly given to the finest perceptions and emotions. The Greek has the same perceptive, emotional temperament as the Celt; but he adds to this temperament the sense
of *measure*; hence his admirable success in the plastic arts, in which the
Celtic genius, with its chafing against the despotism of fact, its perpetual
straining after mere emotion, has accomplished nothing.[50]

'*Measure*', to use the word that Arnold returns to in italics, is what Yeats
added three times to his revised poem: as musical and poetic rhythm; as
the patient quality of a brooding Ireland awaiting significant rebirth; and
as the conditions of unfolding history in which the labour leading to that
birth would take place:

> *And Time bade all his candles flare*
> *To light a measure here and there;*
> *And may the thoughts of Ireland brood*
> *Upon a measured quietude.*
> [. . .]
> *And we, our singing and our love,*
> *What measurer Time has lit above,*
> *And all benighted things that go*
> *About my table to and fro*
> *Are passing on to where may be,*
> *In truth's consuming ecstasy,*
> *No place for love and dream at all.*

If Stevens had this poem in mind, his gloss would mute Yeats slightly, by
tuning '*truth's consuming ecstasy*' down to 'occasional ecstasy, or ecstatic
freedom of mind, which is [the poet's] special privilege'. But neither poet
dismisses the visionary. Whether Yeats's mystic table is a place of séance
or national gathering, it is also the place of violence, reality and common dream, looking uncertainly at its future. And in 1924, its various
pasts, immediate, atavistic and ancient are held in an uncertain present
looking ahead to 'coming times'. I have written about this elsewhere as
Yeats's response to ideas of 'compresence' in the idealist philosophy of
Bendetto Croce and Giovanni Gentile.[51] Suffice to say here that holding
these temporal schema together in the moment of the act of revision of
one of his most prophetic 'republican' poems', the republic of letters, the
Heaneyesque poetic fiction or alternative worlds seem uncertain and very
much still in process. Except that '*measure*' – of poetry, maternity, temporality – is allowed to hold the moment of imminence before poem and
audience, something doing the pressing back against reality while recon-
ciling itself to the common dream. Imagination, to use Stevens's word,

holds the poem in balance. Balance also comes from measure, to use Yeats and Arnold's word, enacting aesthetic and political discrimination facing the coming times of poetry and nation.

Yeats kept 'Davis, Mangan, Ferguson' in play as he revised a post-independence reality. Up until the end of his life, even when reading a text seemingly at many removes from his project (though engaged in its own republicanism), *Paradise Lost,* he could still hear the rhythm of folk song through its synthetic English blank verse:

> The folk song is still there, but a ghostly voice, an unvariable possibility, an unconscious norm. What moves me and my hearer is a vivid speech that has no laws except that it must not exorcise the ghostly voice. I am awake and asleep, at my moment of revelation, self-possessed in self-surrender; there is no rhyme, no echo of the beaten drum, the dancing foot, that would overset my balance. When I was a boy I wrote a poem upon dancing that had one good line: 'They snatch with their hands at the sleep of the skies.' If I sat down and thought for a year I would discover that but for certain syllabic limitations, a rejection or acceptance of certain elisions, I must wake or sleep.[52]

Between haunting and dream, Yeats's aesthetic achievement is balanced between this conception of the sound of poetry and the edging into new form and new subject matter after *Responsibilities.* But the ghost of old forms could never be entirely forgotten, and the uncommon dreams of the common people insisted on their return. As he told a BBC audience the year before the 'General Introduction' in 1936, in any overview of 'modern poetry' the Irish offered a singular case, resisting 'the realism of Eliot, the social passion of the war poets. Because Ireland has still a living folk tradition, her poets cannot get it out of their heads that they themselves, good-tempered or bad-tempered, tall or short, will be remembered by the common people. Instead of turning to impersonal philosophy, they have hardened and deepened their personalities.'[53] The persistence of this folk tradition and the hardening of Yeats's notion of the personality of Irish poetry after the partial end of the Union can be seen in one last poetic example, setting something from the past going again in the present. Over a period of seven days, 6–13 November 1924, a supposedly ill Yeats wrote from his convalescence in Coole to his wife George of his work revising his old poems. The revision of 'To Ireland in the Coming Times' dates from this period, as does that of 'The Sorrow of Love', mentioned in Chapter 7: 'I have just turned an absurd old poem [...] into a finer thing'. Of the revision to his 'Dedication' to his 1891 *Representative Irish Tales,* he says, 'I think that removes the last sentimentality.' About turning the

1892 'The Death of Cuchulain' into 'Cuchulain's Fight with the Sea' he said, 'To rewrite an old poem is like dressing up for a fancy dress ball.' The euphoria extended to the claim made for a poem first published in 1890. Yeats wrote, 'I have made a new poem of the "Song of the Old Pensioner" & a good poem.'[54]

The 'new poem' reads thus:

The Lamentation of the Old Pensioner

Although I shelter from the rain
Under a broken tree,
My chair was nearest to the fire
In every company
That talked of love or politics,
Ere Time transfigured me.

Though lads are making pikes again
For some conspiracy,
And crazy rascals rage their fill
At human tyranny,
My contemplations are of Time
That has transfigured me.

There's not a woman turns her face
Upon a broken tree,
And yet the beauties that I loved
Are in my memory;
I spit into the face of Time
That has transfigured me.[55]

The refashioned ballad speaks back from the wreck of the body and the country as both summation and complete recasting of an English-language poetic tradition that runs from Ferguson's version of 'Páistin Fionn' to MacDonagh's version of Cathal Buí MacGhiolla Gunna, from Moore's 'Last Rose of Summer' to Mangan's 'Nameless One'. The second stanza is an addition of late 1924, an addition that heads back to the 1790s and the persistence of violence through the song tradition. Whether or not this 'new poem' is the elusive 'one/Poem maybe as cold/And passionate As the dawn', its response is the insouciance of the ageing pensioner-poet who speaks the poem in an impersonality that is filled with the cold and passionate personal obsessions of its author. The refrain in the first stanza originally ran, 'And therefore do I wander on/And the fret is on me' (though that Irish-English construction had in 1892 been cleaned up as 'the fret lies on me'). In 1924, Yeats replaced this with transfiguration by time, endurance traded in for change. The poem ends with more than just a pressing back against reality: 'I spit into the face of Time'. A desolate landscape that might later be called Beckettian – a broken tree, memories of beauty and the facing up of the crazy to tyranny – both completes and acts as presage to a historical and aesthetic pattern held in lyric form and lyric sense. It inhabits a ballad form in the present tense of transfiguring time held resolutely out against the certainties of its future, the common dream pressing back against the real.

Notes

1 'The Synthetic Irish Thing'

1 Patrick Kavanagh, 'From Monaghan to the Grand Canal' (in *Studies*, 1959), repr. in *Collected Prose* (London: McGibbon and Kee, 1967), p. 227.

2 Matthew Arnold, *The Study of Celtic Literature* (1867), repr. (Port Washington: Kennikat, 1970), p. 131; William Hazlitt, *The Spirit of the Age*, ed. E.D. Mackerness (London: Collins, 1969), p. 279.

3 William Butler Yeats, 'Popular Ballad Poetry of Ireland' (1889), in *Uncollected Prose*, ed. John P. Frayne, 2 vols. (London: Macmillan, 1970), Vol. I, p. 162.

4 Declan Kiberd, *Inventing Ireland: The Literature of the Modern Nation* (London: Verso, 1995), pp. 115–129. See also, Timothy Brennan, 'The National Longing for Form', in *Nation and Narration*, ed. Homi K. Bhabha (London: Routledge, 1990), pp. 44–70.

5 The phrase comes from Longinus via Standish James O'Grady who used it as a term of praise for Macpherson in O'Grady, *History of Ireland: The Heroic Period*, 2 vols. (London: Sampson Low, 1878), Vol. II, pp. 45–46.

6 Arnold, *Celtic Literature*, pp. 84–85. On the Irish language and national expression, see, for instance, Thomas Davis, 'Our National Language' in *Literary and Historical Essays* (Dublin: James Duffy, 1847), pp. 173–182.

7 William Shakespeare, *King Lear*, act 3, sc. 4.

8 Alfred Tennyson, 'Morte D'Arthur', in *Poems*, ed. Christopher Ricks, 3 vols. (London: Longman, 1987), Vol. I, p. 17.

9 See Daniel Corkery, *The Hidden Ireland* (1924) (Dublin: Gill and Macmillan, 1967), p. 23: 'For Irish Ireland had, by the eighteenth century, then, become purely a peasant nation.'

10 Corkery, *Hidden Ireland*, p.20.

11 Grainne Yeats, *The Harp of Ireland: The Belfast Harpers' Festival, 1792 and the Saving of Ireland's Harp Music by Edward Bunting* (Belfast: Belfast Harpers' Bicentenary, 1992), p. 21.

12 Corkery, *Hidden Ireland*, p. 41.

13 L.M. Cullen, '*The Hidden Ireland:* Re-Assessment of a Concept', *Studia Hibernica*, 9 (1969), pp. 7–47.

14 See, for instance, Seamus Deane, 'Arnold, Burke and the Celts', in *Celtic Revivals* (London: Faber, 1985), pp. 17–27.

15 James Joyce, 'James Clarence Mangan', in *Occasional, Critical, and Political Writing*, ed. Kevin Barry (Oxford: Oxford University Press, 2000), p. 59.

16 *The Variorum Edition of the Poems of W.B. Yeats*, eds. Peter Allt and Russell K. Alspach (New York: Macmillan, 1957), p. 161.

17 James Joyce, 'I Hear an Army Charging on the Land', in *Poems and Exiles*, ed. J.C.C. Mays (London: Penguin, 1992), p. 39.

18 Robert Crawford, *Devolving English Literature*, 2nd edn. (Edinburgh: Edinburgh University Press, 2000); and John Kerrigan, *Archipelagic English* (Oxford: Oxford University Press, 2008), pp. 91–115.

19 Katie Trumpener, *Bardic Nationalism: The Romantic Novel and the British Empire* (Princeton: Princeton University Press, 1997); Maureen McLane, *Balladeering, Minstrelsy, and the Making of British Romantic Poetry* (Cambridge: Cambridge University Press, 2008), pp. 9 and 16–17.

20 The classic account is in the first chapter of Terry Eagleton, *Heathcliff and the Great Hunger* (London: Verso, 1996).

21 Thomas Kinsella, *The Dual Tradition: An Essay on Poetry and Politics in Ireland* (Manchester: Carcanet, 1995), p. 47.

22 Robert Welch, *Irish Poetry from Moore to Yeats* (Gerrards Cross: Colin Smythe, 1980); David Lloyd, *Nationalism and Minor Literature: James Clarence Mangan and the Emergence of Irish Cultural Nationalism* (Berkeley: University of California Press, 1987).

23 Richard M. Dorson, *Folklore and Fakelore* (Cambridge, MA: Harvard University Press, 1976), p. 5. For an overview of the literary import of such fakelore, its forgery and innovation in Dorson's terms, see Anne Markey, 'The Discovery of Irish Folklore', *New Hibernia Review*, 10.4 (2006), pp. 21–43.

24 Kinsella, *The Dual Tradition*, p. 47.

25 Charlotte Brooke, preface to *Reliques of Irish Poetry* (1789), ed. Aaron Crossley Seymour (Dublin: Christie, 1816), p. cxxxiii.

26 Text and translation from Sean Ó Tuama and Thomas Kinsella, *An Duanaire 1600–1900: Poems of the Dispossessed* (Dublin: Dolmen, 1981), pp. 284–285.

27 Brooke, *Reliques of Irish Poetry*, p. 287.

28 Samuel Ferguson, *Lays of the Western Gael* (London: Bell and Daldy, 1865), p. 216.

29 Peter Denman, *Samuel Ferguson, The Literary Achievement* (Gerrards Cross: Colin Smythe, 1990), p. 111.

30 James Hardiman, ed., *Irish Minstrelsy: Or Bardic Remains of Ireland, with English Poetical Translations*, 2 vols. (London: Robins, 1831), Vol. I, p. 263.

31 See Peter McDonald, 'Paul Muldoon and the Windlass-Men' in *Mistaken Identities* (Oxford: Oxford University Press, 1997), pp. 145–148. The discussion is of Michael Longley's poem 'Form' in *The Ghost Orchid* (1995).

32 Angela Leighton, *On Form: Poetry, Aestheticism, and the Legacy of a Word* (Oxford: Oxford University Press, 2007), pp. 168–169.

33 Leighton, *On Form*, p. 29.

34 W.B. Yeats, 'A General Introduction for My Work' (1937), in *Essays and Introductions* (London; Macmillan, 1961), p. 509.

35 Susan Wolfson, *Formal Charges: The Shaping of Poetry in British Romanticism* (Stanford: Stanford University Press, 1997), pp. 19 and 67.

36 Arnold, *Celtic Literature*, p. 87.

37 Kavanagh, *Collected Prose*, p. 223.

38 Kiberd, *Inventing Ireland*, p. 116.

39 See, for instance, Mary Jean Corbett, *Allegories of Union in Irish and English Writing, 1790–1870* (Cambridge: Cambridge University Press, 2000); and Claire Connolly, *A Cultural History of the Irish Novel, 1790–1829* (Cambridge: Cambridge University Press, 2012).

40 Ernest Renan, *The Poetry of the Celtic Races and Other Essays*, trans. William G. Hutchinson (1896) repr. (Washington, NY: Kennikat, 1970).

41 See P.S. O'Hegarty, *A History of Ireland Under the Union, 1801–1922* (London: Methuen, 1952); a project of a different historical hue, the fifth and sixth volumes of Vaughan (ed.), *New History of Ireland, Ireland Under the Union, 1801–1921*, ed. W.E. Vaughan (Oxford: Oxford University Press, 1989); and Bruce Stewart (ed.), *Hearts and Minds: Irish Culture and Society Under the Act of Union* (Gerrards Cross: Colin Smythe, 2002).

42 W.J. McCormack, *From Burke to Beckett: Ascendancy, Tradition and Betrayal in Literary History* (Cork: Cork University Press, 1994), p. 6.

43 Thomas Moore, *Poetical Works*, ed. A.D. Godley (Oxford: Oxford University Press, 1910), p. 182.

44 Samuel Ferguson, 'Mesgedra', in *Poems* (New York: Magee, 1880), p. 42.

45 McCormack, *From Burke to Beckett*, p. 7.

46 Jahan Ramazani, *The Hybrid Muse: Postcolonial Poetry in English* (Chicago: University of Chicago Press, 2001), pp. 17–18.

47 David Lloyd, 'Adulteration and the Nation', in *Anomalous States: Irish Writing and the Post-Colonial Moment* (Dublin: Lilliput, 1993), pp. 90 and 114.

48 Seamus Heaney, 'Through-Other Places, Through-Other Times: The Irish Poet in Britain', in *Finders Keepers: Selected Prose, 1971–2001* (London: Faber, 2002), p. 373.

49 Thomas MacDonagh, *Literature in Ireland* (1916), (Nenagh: Relay, 1996), p. 73.

2 The Ruptured Ear: Irish Accent, English Poetry

1 Samuel Beckett, *Murphy* (1938) (London: Picador, 1973), p. 53.

2 Austin Clarke, *Poetry in Modern Ireland* (Cork: Mercier, 1951), p. 16.

3 Ibid., pp. 19–20.

4 *Paddy's Resource: Being a Select Collection of Original and Modern Patriotic Songs, Toasts and Sentiments Compiled for the Use of the People of Ireland* (n.p. 1795); Thomas Davis, ed., *The Spirit of the Nation* (1845), Repr. (Otley: Woodstock, 1998); Colm Ó Lochlann, *Irish Street Ballads* (Dublin: Three Candles, 1939).

5 Samuel Beckett [as Andrew Belis], 'Recent Irish Poetry', (1934) in *Disjecta: Miscellaneous Writings*, ed. Ruby Cohn (London: John Calder, 1983), p. 71.

6 Seamus Deane and Seamus Heaney, 'Unhappy and at Home', *The Crane Bag*, Vol. I, No.1 (Spring 1977), pp. 64 and 62.

7 Bernard O'Donoghue, 'The Translator's Voice: Irish Poetry before Yeats', *Princeton University Library Chronicle*, Vol. LIX, No. 3 (Spring 1998), pp. 317 and 302.

8 William Larminie, 'The Development of English Metres', *Contemporary Review*, LXVI (Nov. 1894), p. 736; Robert Farren, *The Course of Irish Verse* (London: Sheed and Ward, 1948), pp. 57–61.

9 Larminie, p. 733.

10 *Vision of World Language* is the subtitle of McDiarmid's *In Memoriam James Joyce* (1955) in *Complete Poems*, 2 vols. (London: Martin Brian and O'Keefe, 1978), Vol. II, p. 735.

11 Matthew Hart, *Nations of Nothing but Poetry: Modernism, Transnationalism and Synthetic Vernacular Writing* (New York: Oxford University Press, 2010), pp. 71 and 51–78 *passim*.

12 Thomas MacDonagh, *Literature in Ireland* (1916) (Nenagh: Relay, 1996), pp. 50 and 53.

13 Thomas MacDonagh, *Thomas Campion and the Art of English Poetry* (Dublin: Talbot, 1912), p. 52.

14 George Saintsbury, *A History of English Prosody from the Twelfth Century until the Present Day*, 3 vols. (Macmillan: London, 1906–1910), Vol. III. pp. 457–458. See also, T.S. Omond's classic overview, *English Metrists* (Oxford: Clarendon, 1921), pp. 226–227: he objects to Larminie's praise of Mangan, but acknowledges the recognition of the importance of quantity in his verse.

15 See, e.g., Robert Bridges, *Milton's Prosody* (1889–1921), revd. edn. (Oxford: Oxford University Press, 1921).

16 MacDonagh, *Thomas Campion,* p. 55, relates Yeats reading Patmore to him.

17 Quoted in Ron Schuchard, *The Last Minstrels* (Oxford: Oxford University Press, 2008), p. 308; see also, Ezra Pound, 'Thomas MacDonagh as Critic', *Poetry*, 8 (Sep. 1916), pp. 309–312.

18 MacDonagh, *Literature in Ireland*, pp. 46–47.

19 William Butler Yeats and F.R. Higgins, in Yeats, *Prefaces and Introductions*, ed. William H. O'Donnell (London: Macmillan, 1988), p. 179.

20 MacDonagh, *Thomas Campion*, p. 52. He says he found the idea in a *Quarterly Review* article on Tennyson, 1911.

21 Thomas Moore, *Poetical Works*, ed. A.D. Godley (Oxford: Oxford University Press, 1910), p. 194.

22 Harry White, *Music and the Irish Literary Imagination* (Oxford: Oxford University Press, 2008), p. 7. Deane is quoted from Deane, ed. *The Field Day Anthology of Irish Writing*, 3 vols. (Derry: Field Day, 1991), Vol. II, p. 5.

23 See Leith Davis, *Music, Postcolonialism and Gender* (South Bend: University of Notre Dame Press, 2006), pp. 140–163; here, p. 144, quoting Lloyd and Eagleton.

24 Terry Eagleton, *Heathcliff and the Great Hunger* (London: Verso, 1996), p. 231.

25 Deane, *Field Day Anthology*, Vol. I, p. 1056.

26 See White, pp. 40–41; the reference is to Robert Welch's statement that Moore single-handedly founded Irish verse tradition in English, in *A History of Verse Translation from the Irish, 1789–1897* (Gerrards Cross: Colin Smythe, 1988), p. 56. On Eliot's 'auditory imagination', see White, p. 43.

27 MacDonagh, *Literature in Ireland*, p. 49.

28 Walsh's lyric appears in *The Ballad Poetry of Ireland*, ed. Charles Gavan Duffy (Dublin: James Duffy, 1845), p. 128. The poem was first published in *The Nation* in 1844. See also, Walsh, 'Mo Craóibhinn Aoibhinn Áluin Óg' in *The Spirit of the Nation* (Dublin: Duffy, 1845), where Walsh peppers the fourth stanza with Irish words, allowing him to conserve 'the same dear tongue to curse the stranger'.

29 Thomas Davis, 'The Ballad Poetry of Ireland', in *Literary and Historical Essays* (Dublin: James Duffy, 1846), p. 223.

30 Davis, 'Our National Language', *Essays*, pp. 173–174.

31 See, for instance, Edmund Burke, *Reflections on the Revolution in France* (1790), ed. Conor Cruise O'Brien (Harmondsworth: Pelican, 1968), p. 119:

> You will observe that from Magna Charta to the Declaration of Right, it has been the uniform policy of our constitution to claim and assert our liberties as an *entailed inheritance* derived to us from our forefathers, and to be transmitted to our posterity [...] By this means our constitution preserves a unity in so great a diversity of its parts.

I am grateful to Susan Wolfson for drawing my attention to Davis's allusion.

32 'The Songs of Ireland' in *Thomas Davis: Selections from His Prose and Poetry*, ed. T.W. Rolleston (Dublin: Talbot, 1914), p. 225.

33 Thomas Kinsella, 'The Irish Writer', in W.B. Yeats and Thomas Kinsella, *Davis, Mangan, Ferguson: Tradition and the Irish Writer* (Dublin: Dolmen, 1970), p. 66.

34 Robert Welch, 'Constitution, Language and Tradition in Nineteenth-Century Irish Poetry', in Terence Brown and Nicholas Grene (eds.), *Tradition and Influence in Anglo-Irish Poetry* (New Jersey: Barnes and Noble, 1989), p. 26.

35 Moore, *Poetical Works*, p. 180.

36 Welch, 'Constitution', pp. 14–15.

37 Moore, *Poetical Works*, p. 187.

38 Thomas Moore, *Irish Melodies*, second number (Dublin: Power, 1808). The melody is actually the Scottish-Irish air to 'Pretty Peg of Derby, O' and 'The Bonnie Lass of Fivie'.

39 See Aloys Fleischmann, *Sources of Irish Traditional Music c.1600–1855*, 2 vols. (Garland: New York, 1998), Vol. II.

40 Yeats, *Prefaces and Introductions*, p. 178.

41 Moore, *Poetical Works*, p. 201.

42 Published for a 'Scotch Air' in the first number of *National Airs* (1818–1823); see Moore, *Poetical Works*, p. 238.

43 Yeats, *Prefaces and Introductions*, p. 103.

44 Ibid., p. 178.

45 Moore, Preface to *Melodies, Songs, Sacred Songs and National Airs* (New York: George Long, 1821), p. vi. The passage was known by Yeats and is reproduced in part at the end of Yeats and Dorothy Wellesley's 'Music and Poetry' contribution to the 1937 *Broadsides* collection. See Yeats, *Prefaces and Introductions*, pp. 191–193 and 310.

46 Moore's celebrated retort to Bunting's comments in the preface to his 1840 edition of *Ancient Music of Ireland* was made in a diary entry of July 1840, cited by Harry White, *The Keeper's Recital: Music and Cultural History in Ireland, 1770–1970* (Cork: Field Day, 1998), p. 47.

47 Francis Turner Palgrave, *The Golden Treasury*, ed. Christopher Ricks (Penguin: Harmondsworth, 1991), p. 499.

48 See Davis's chapter on the *Melodies* in *Music, Postcolonialism and Gender*, *passim*.

49 Clarke, *Poetry in Modern Ireland*, p. 43.

50 Sean Lucy, 'Metre and Movement in Anglo-Irish Verse', *Irish University Review* (1978), p. 158.

51 O'Donoghue, 'The Translator's Voice', p. 309.

52 Raymond Hickey, *Irish English: History and Present-Day Forms* (Cambridge: Cambridge University Press, 2007), p. 125.

53 See Hickey, *Irish English: History and Present-Day Forms,* pp. 100–110.

54 O'Donoghue, 'The Translator's Voice', p. 299.

55 MacDonagh, *Literature in Ireland*, p. 36.

56 Ibid., pp. 36–37, where he appears to argue that Moore learnt his rhythm from Callanan and Ferguson, even though the example given was published in 1810 and predates Callanan's Gaelic translations by at least a decade, and Ferguson's by twenty years.

57 Welch, *A History of Verse Translation*, p. 7.

58 Jeremiah Joseph Callanan, *The Irish Poems,* ed. Gregory A. Schirmer (Gerrards Cross; Colin Smythe, 2005), p. 94.

59 MacDonagh, *Literature in Ireland*, p. 38.

60 'Caiseal Mumhan', in Seán Ó Tuama and Thomas Kinsella, *An Duanaire: 1600–1900: Poems of the Dispossessed* (Dublin: Dolmen, 1981), pp. 278–281.

61 Thomas Furlong, in *Irish Minstrelsy: Or Bardic Remains of Ireland, with English Poetical Translations*, 2 vols., ed. James Hardiman (London: Robins, 1831), Vol. I, p. 239.

62 Samuel Ferguson, 'Hardiman's *Irish Minstrelsy*', *Dublin University Magazine*, Vol. 4, No. 23 (Nov. 1834), p. 536.

63 Ó Tuama and Kinsella, *An Duanaire*, p. xxxvii.

64 Breandán Ó Buachalla, 'The Gaelic Background', in Terence Brown and Barbara Hayley, eds., *Samuel Ferguson: A Centenary Tribute* (Dublin: Royal Irish Academy, 1987), pp. 33–34.

65 Ferguson, 'Hardiman's *Irish Minstrelsy*', Vol. p. 154.

66 Edward Walsh, *Irish Popular Songs* (Dublin: McGlashan, 1847), p. 169.

67 Walsh, Preface to *Irish Popular Songs*, pp. 31–32.

3   From Moore to Mahony: The Transmigration of Intellect

1   [Samuel Ferguson], *Hardiman's Irish Minstrelsy,* 4 parts, *Dublin University Magazine*, Vols. 3–4 (April–November 1834), here part II, Vol. 4 (August 1834), p. 153s

2   Francis Sylvester Mahony, 'The Rogueries of Tom Moore' (1834) in *The Reliques of Father Prout* (London: George Bell, 1894), p. 153.

3   According to *The Wellesley Index of Victorian Periodicals*, ed. Walter Houghton, Vol. II (University of Toronto Press: Toronto, 1972), p. 309, Mahony may have assumed the editorship of *Fraser's* and the Oliver Yorke persona when William Maginn fell out with James Fraser in 1836, editing the journal for the next year. *Wellesley* credits Mahony as Oliver Yorke in the Prout papers. In addition to Maginn and Mahony, the pseudonym of Yorke was also assumed by Thomas Carlyle, James Hogg and George Henry Lewes, among others. See also Miriam Thrall, *Rebellious Fraser's: Nol Yorke's Magazine in the Days of Maginn, Thackeray and Carlyle* (New York: Columbia University Press, 1934), pp. 30–32.

4   Mahony, 'Father Prout's Plea for Pilgrimages', *Reliques*, pp. 55–62. On the Hardiman font, see Seamus Deane's classic account in *Strange Country: Modernity and Nationhood in Irish Writing since 1790* (Oxford: Oxford University Press, 1997), pp. 100–109.

5   Mahony, 'The Watergrasshill Carousal', *Reliques*, pp. 100–101.

6   Ibid., p.63. See the refrain to the mid-nineteenth-century ballad 'Finnegan's Wake', where there was also 'lots of fun'.

7   Ibid., p. 63.

8   Thomas Moore, *Poetical Works*, ed. A.D. Godley (Oxford: Oxford University Press, 1910), p. 181.

9   Ibid., pp. 66–67.

10   Terry Eagleton, 'Cork and the Carnivalesque', in *Reviewing Ireland*, eds. Sarah Briggs, Paul Hyland and Neil Sammells (Bath: Sulis, 1998), pp. 20–29. For a riposte to Eagleton's essay, see also Feargal Gaynor, '"An Irish Potato Seasoned with Attic Salt": *The Reliques of Fr Prout* and Identity before *The Nation*', *Irish Studies Review*, Vol. 7, No. 3 (1999), pp. 313–323.

11   Mahony, 'The Rogueries of Tom Moore', *Reliques*, p. 133.

12   The fullest biography to date is by Ethel Mannin, *Two Studies in Integrity: Gerald Griffin and the Rev. Francis Mahony ('Father Prout')*, (London: Jarrolds, 1954). On Mahony's dismissal, see pp. 140–143: the grounds would appear to be a drunken carousal with his students in the course of which Mahony delivered an anti-O'Connell diatribe, and after which they found themselves stranded out of bounds late at night.

13   Mahony, 'An Apology for Lent', *Reliques*, p. 5.

14   The immigrant Irish were to feature in a chapter in Thomas Carlyle's 1839 pamphlet *Chartism* as 'The Finest Peasantry in the World'. For an overview, see Roger Swift, 'Thomas Carlyle, *Chartism* and the Irish in Early Victorian England', *Victorian Literature and Culture*, Vol. 29, No. 1 (2001), pp. 67–83.

15 Henry O'Brien, *The Round Towers of Ireland*, 2nd edn., (London: Parbury and Allen, 1834), pp. 100–110.

16 Joep Leerssen, *Remembrance and Imagination: Patterns in the Historical and Literary Representation of Ireland in the Nineteenth Century* (South Bend: University of Notre Dame Press, 1997), pp. 108–143.

17 Ronan Kelly, *Bard of Erin: The Life of Thomas Moore* (Dublin: Penguin, 2008), pp. 509–510. [Thomas Moore], 'The Round Towers of Ireland', *Edinburgh Review*, Vol. LIX, No. CXIX (April 1834), pp. 153–154.

18 Mahony, *The Reliques of Father Prout*, 2 vols. (London: Fraser, 1836), Vol. I, pp. 262–264; 1894 edn., facing p. 162. *The Wellesley Index of Victorian Periodicals*, Vol. II, p. 348, attributes the obituary to Mahony.

19 Thomas Carlyle, *Sartor Resartus*, Book II, chap. IX, in *Fraser's Magazine*, Vol. IX, No. LII (April, 1834), p. 447.

20 Mahony, *Reliques*, pp. 137–138.

21 John O'Keefe, *The Poor Soldier*, Act II, sc. Iii, retrieved from http://lion.chadwyck.co.uk.

22 Richard Kirkland, 'Questioning the Frame: Hybridity, Ireland and the Institution', in *Ireland and Cultural Theory: The Mechanics of Authenticity*, eds. Colin Graham and Richard Kirkland (London: Macmillan, 1999), p. 219; quoting Homi K. Bhabha, 'Interrogating Identity: Frantz Fanon and the Postcolonial Prerogative', in *The Location of Culture* (London: Routledge, 1994), p. 83.

23 Luke Gibbons, 'Unapproved Roads', in *Transformations in Irish Culture* (Cork: Field Day, 1996), p. 179. On the consolations of hybridity, see also, Declan Kiberd, quoting Salman Rushdie in *Inventing Ireland: The Literature of the Modern Nation* (London: Cape, 1995), p. 163: 'Something was gained rather than lost in the act of translation, one result of which might be "radically new types of human being."'

24 See Robert J.C. Young, *Colonial Desire* (Abingdon: Routledge, 1995), chapter 1, *passim*.

25 Mahony, *Reliques*, p. 151.

26 Joep Leerssen, 'Ossianic Liminality: Between Native Tradition and Pre-Romantic Taste', in *From Gaelic to Romantic: Ossianic Translations*, eds. Fiona Stafford and Howard Gaskill (Amsterdam: Rodoipi, 1998), p. 1.

27 Mangan, 'An Extraordinary Adventure in the Shades' in *Collected Works of James Clarence Mangan*, 6 vols., eds. Jacques Chuto et al. (Dublin: Irish Academic Press, 1997–2002), Vol. 5, p. 18.

28 Ibid.

29 Mahony, *Reliques*, pp. 159–160.

30 Mannin, *Two Studies in Integrity*, p. 186; Mannin prefers to think that it dates from Mahony's disastrous return to Clongowes as Prefect of Studies. As far as I can ascertain, the first publication of the poem was in the Moore piece in *Fraser's*.

31 Ibid., pp. 186–187.

32 The word appears in Scots and Northern English as well as Hiberno-English. See *English Dialect Dictionary*.

33 Eagleton, 'Cork and the Carnivalesque', p. 28.

34 Prout, 'The Rogueries of Tom Moore', p. 257; Moore, 'National Airs', in *Poetical Works*, p. 236.

35 The text here is from the 'Polyglot Edition', in Mahony, 'A Plea for Pilgrimages', *Reliques,* pp. 56–62.

36 Behan, *Brendan Behan's Island: An Irish Sketch-Book* (London: Random House, 1982), pp. 78–80. See Behan's comment after quoting the poem, p. 80: 'And they say that sex is only in its infancy in Ireland!'

37 Mahony, *Reliques*, p. 60.

38 Geoffrey Taylor, *Irish Poets of the Nineteenth Century* (London: Routledge, 1951), pp. 387 and 394–395. See also notes by W.J. McCormack and Seamus Deane in Deane et al. (eds.) *The Field Day Anthology of Irish Writing*, 3 vols. (Derry: Field Day, 1991), Vol. I, p. 1102 and Vol. II, p. 98.

39 Ibid., pp. 297–298.

40 The text is that given in William Henry Curran, *The Life of the Right Honourable William Philpot Curran*, 2 vols. (London: Constable, 1819), Vol. I, p. 211. William Curran dates the song to around 1786.

41 Taylor, *Irish Poets of the Nineteenth Century,* p. 322, prints the lyric in eight-line stanzas, with two-stress lines. See Deane's headnote to 'Preab San Ól', *Field Day Anthology*, Vol. II, p. 93, on the options for printing such texts in long or shorter lines according to conventions of printing lyrics for Irish music.

42 Deane, *Field Day Anthology,* Vol. II, pp. 93–94.

43 Aloys Fleischmann, *Sources of Irish Traditional Music, c. 1600–1855*, 2 vols. (New York: Garland, 1998), Vol. I, p. 223.

44 See Hugh Shields, 'New Dates for Old Songs, 1766–1803', *Long Room*, Vol. 18–19, (1979), p. 41.

45 Moore, *Poetical Works*, p. 202.

46 Moore's celebrated retort to Bunting's comments in the preface to his 1840 edition of *Ancient Music of Ireland* was made in a diary entry of July 1840, cited by Harry White, *The Keeper's Recital: Music and Cultural History in Ireland, 1770–1970* (Cork: Field Day, 1998), p. 47.

47 [William Maginn], 'Parody' ('Tis the Last Glass of Claret'), *London Literary Gazette*, No. 183 (22 July 1820), p. 477. The poem follows Maginn's Hiberno-English squib on the Romantic poem of place, 'Ballidehob'.

4   Samuel Ferguson's Maudlin Jumble

1 W.B. Yeats, 'The Poetry of Sir Samuel Ferguson', *The Irish Fireside*, 9 October 1886, in *Uncollected Prose*, ed. John P. Frayne, 2 vols. (London: Macmillan, 1970), Vol. 1, p. 87.

2 [Thomas Moore], *Memoirs of Captain Rock, the Celebrated Irish Chieftain, with some Account of his Ancestors, Written by Himself* (London: Longman, 1824).

3 Joep Leerssen, *Hidden Ireland, Public Sphere* (Galway: Arlen House, 2002), p. 13. See also, Niall Ó Ciosáin, *Print and Popular Culture in Ireland, 1750–1850* (London: Macmillan, 1997).

4 On the Ulster Gaelic Society, see Robert Welch, *A History of Verse Translation from the Irish, 1789–1897* (Gerrard's Cross: Colin Smythe, 1988), pp. 90–91.
5 [Samuel Ferguson] 'A Dialogue between the Head and Heart of an Irish Protestant', *Dublin University Magazine*, Vol. 2 (Nov. 1833), p. 587.
6 [Samuel Ferguson], 'Hardiman's *Irish Minstrelsy*', 4 parts, *Dublin University Magazine*, Vols. 3–4 (April–November 1834), here Vol. II (August 1834), pp. 153–154. Hereinafter 'Hardiman'.
7 Ferguson, 'Hardiman', Vol. II, p.155.
8 Ferguson, 'Dialogue', p. 591.
9 Ibid., p. 589.
10 Eve Patten, *Samuel Ferguson and the Culture of Nineteenth-Century Ireland* (Dublin: Four Courts Press, 2004), p. 25.
11 Ibid., pp. 29–52.
12 Colin Graham, 'Hireling Strangers and the Wandering Throne: Ireland, Scotland and Samuel Ferguson', *Estudios Irlandeses*, No. 4 (2009), pp. 21–35; here p. 25.
13 Ferguson, 'Hardiman', Vol. II, p. 156.
14 Samuel Ferguson, 'Robert Burns', 2 articles, *Dublin University Magazine*, Vol. XXV, (January and March, 1845); second article, p. 293.
15 See Campbell, 'Davis, Mangan, Ferguson' in *The Blackwell Companion to Irish Literature,* ed. Julia M. Wright, 2 vols. (Oxford: Blackwell, 2010), I, pp. 427–443.
16 Ferguson, 'Robert Burns', Vol. II, p. 293.
17 Ibid.
18 Samuel Ferguson, *Lays of the Western Gael* (London: Bell and Daldy, 1865), pp. 204–206; Douglas Hyde, *Abhráin grádh chúige Connacht: The Love Songs of Connacht* (Baile-Ath-Cliath: Gill, 1893), pp. 49–52; Thomas MacDonagh, *Literature in Ireland* (Nenagh: Relay, 1996), pp. 129–130.
19 W.B. Yeats, *Collected Plays* (London: Macmillan, 1952), pp. 99–100.
20 *The Variorum Edition of the Poems of W.B. Yeats*, eds. Peter Allt and Russell K. Alspach (New York: Macmillan, 1957), pp. 550–551.
21 Ferguson, 'Hardiman', Vol. III, p. 163.
22 James Hardiman, ed. *Irish Minstrelsy: Or Bardic Remains of Ireland, with English Poetical Translations,* 2 vols. (London: Robins, 1831), Vol. I, p. 218. The above follows Hardiman's text, rendered into roman script.
23 Ferguson, 'Hardiman', Vol. III, p. 163.
24 Ferguson, 'Pastheen Finn', in 'Hardiman', Vol. IV, pp. 535–536.
25 Ferguson, 'Hardiman', Vol. III, p. 465.
26 Hardiman, *Irish Minstrelsy*, Vol. I, p. 218.
27 Ferguson, 'Hardiman', Vol. III, pp. 465–466.
28 Brendan Ó Buachalla, 'The Gaelic Background', in *Samuel Ferguson: A Centenary Tribute,* eds. Terence Brown and Barbara Hayley (Dublin: Royal Irish Academy, 1987), pp. 33–34.
29 Robert Burns, *Poems and Songs,* ed. James Kinsley (Oxford: Oxford University Press, 1969), p. 141; John Keats, *The Complete Poems*, ed. Miriam Allott

(London: Longman, 1970), p. 366. The Keats sonnet was not published until 1848. I am grateful to Hamish Mathison for pointing out Keats's allusion to Burns to me.

30 John D'Alton, 'Paistheen Fion', in Hardiman, *Irish Minstrelsy*, pp. 217–219.

31 Ferguson, 'Hardiman', Vol. III, pp. 154–155.

32 Ferguson, 'Hardiman', Vol. III, p. 455n.

33 Charlotte Brooke, preface to *Reliques of Irish Poetry* (1789), ed. Aaron Crossley Seymour (Dublin: Christie, 1816), p. cxxxiii.

34 Ferguson, 'Hardiman', Vol. III, p. 467.

35 [Samuel Ferguson], 'Thomas Davis', *Dublin University Museum*, Vol. 29, No. 170 (February, 1847), p. 197.

36 Ferguson, 'Hardiman', Vol. III, p. 457.

37 David Lloyd, *Nationalism and Minor Literature: James Clarence Mangan and the Emergence of Irish Cultural Nationalism* (Berkeley: University of California Press, 1987), p. 84.

38 Ibid.

39 Robert Welch, *Irish Poetry from Moore to Yeats* (Gerrard's Cross: Colin Smythe, 1980), p. 130.

40 William Wordsworth, 1801 Preface to *Lyrical Ballads*, in *Poetical Works*, eds. Thomas Hutchinson and Ernest de Selincourt (Oxford: Oxford University Press, 1969), p. 739.

41 Ferguson, 'Hardiman', Vol. IV, p. 429.

42 Chapter 2, p. XX.

43 James Johnson, ed., *The Scots Musical Museum*, 6 vols. (Edinburgh: Johnson, 1787–1803), title page.

44 Robert Burns to George Thomson, 26 Jan. 1793, in *The Letters of Robert Burns*, ed. J. De Lancey Ferguson, 2 vols. (Oxford: Oxford University Press, 1931), Vol. II, pp. 148–149.

45 Burns to Thomson, 26 April 1793, *Letters*, Vol. II, p. 259.

46 Burns to Thomson, 8 Nov. 1793, Vol. II, pp. 129–130.

47 Robert Crawford, *Devolving English Literature*, 2nd edn. (Edinburgh: Edinburgh University Press, 2000), p. 106.

48 G. Gregory Smith, *Scottish Literature, Character and Influence* (London: Macmillan, 1919), pp. 146 and 148.

49 Thomas Moore, 'Alarming Intelligence – Revolution in the Dictionary – One *Galt* at the Head of It', *Poetical Works*, ed. A.D. Godley (Oxford: Oxford University Press, 1910), pp. 621–622.

50 'The Fairy Well of Lagnanay' originally appeared as 'The Fairy Well' in *Blackwood's Edinburgh Magazine*, Vol. XXXIII, No. CCVII (April 1833), II, p. 667. Peter Denman, *Samuel Ferguson: The Literary Achievement* (Gerrards Cross: Colin Smythe, 1990), p. 15, recounts that Ferguson intended it to be a companion poem to 'The Fairy Thorn', and also Ferguson's dismay when *Blackwood's* printed only the second poem with a number of mistakes in spelling and lineation. It was retitled by Denis Florence McCarthy as 'The Fairy Well of Lagnanay' on republication in his 1846 *Book of Irish Ballads*

(Dublin: Duffy, 1846), pp. 31–33, which contained a number of Ferguson poems (though not the better-known 'Fairy Thorn'). McCarthy's anthology is dedicated to Ferguson, and the poem has been corrected slightly from the *Blackwood's* version. It was not reprinted in Ferguson's retrospective collection of the first thirty years of his career, *Lays of the Western Gael* (London: Bell and Daldy, 1865). The McCarthy version was printed in Yeats's 1888 *Fairy and Folk Tales of the Irish Peasantry* (Gerrards Cross: Colin Smythe, 1973), pp. 21 and 41, along with its companion poem, though not as a pair.

51 Hemans published the poem first in the *New Monthly Magazine* in 1829 and again in her 1830 *Songs of the Affections* collection. See *Works*, 7 vols. (Edinburgh: Blackwood, 1839), Vol. VI, p. 129.

52 Wordsworth, *Poetical Works*, pp. 127–128.

53 Text from W.B. Yeats, *Fairy and Folk Tales,* pp. 21–23.

54 Hugh Kenner, *A Colder Eye* (London: Allen Lane, 1983), pp. 93–94.

55 *Oxford English Dictionary* is hesitant on the derivation, pointing to a cluster of Irish and Welsh words – *carraig*, or *creag* or *craig* – all bearing small semantic differences.

56 S.F. [Samuel Ferguson], 'The Fairy Thorn', *The Dublin University Magazine*, Vol. III, No. xv (March, 1834), pp. 331–332.

57 Graham, 'Hireling Strangers', p. 28.

58 See the epigraph to this chapter.

59 See Denman, *Samuel Ferguson*, p. 63.

60 [Samuel Ferguson], 'Thomas Davis', *Dublin University Magazine*, Vol. XXIX, No. 170 (February 1847), pp. 190–199; here p. 198.

5 Mangan's Golden Years

1 Oliver MacDonagh, *States of Mind: A Study of Anglo-Irish Conflict, 1780–1980* (London: Allen Unwin, 1983), p. 6.

2 MacDonagh, *States of Mind*, p. 9, as quoted.

3 Chris Morash, *Writing the Irish Famine* (Oxford: Oxford University Press, 1995), pp. 90–95.

4 Clare O'Halloran, 'Historical Writings, 1690–1890', in *The Cambridge History of Irish Literature*, eds. Margaret Kelleher and Philip O'Leary, 2 vols. (Cambridge: Cambridge University Press, 2006), Vol. I, p. 621.

5 David Lloyd, *Nationalism and Minor Literature: James Clarence Mangan and the Emergence of Irish Cultural Nationalism* (Berkeley: University of California Press, 1987), p. 80.

6 Michael Cronin, *Translating Ireland: Translation, Languages and Identity* (Cork: Cork University Press, 1996), p. 107.

7 MacDonagh, *States of Mind*, p. 14.

8 All quotations from Mangan from *The Collected Works of James Clarence Mangan*, 6 vols., eds. Jacques Chuto, Rudolph Patrick Holzapfel, Ellen Shannon-Mangan and Peter Van de Kamp (Dublin: Irish Academic Press, 1997–2002).

9   Seamus Deane, *Strange Country: Modernity and Nationhood in Irish Writing since 1790* (Oxford: Oxford University Press, 1997), p. 165.

10 James Joyce, 'James Clarence Mangan' (1902), *Occasional, Critical, and Political Writing*, ed. Kevin Barry (Oxford: Oxford University Press, 2000), p. 59.

11 Ian McBride (ed.), 'Memory and National Identity in Modern Ireland', in *History and Memory in Modern Ireland* (Cambridge: Cambridge University Press, 2001), p. 1.

12 Matthew Arnold, Preface to the first edition of *Poems* (1853), in *The Poems of Matthew Arnold*, ed. Kenneth Allott, 2nd edn., ed. Miriam Allott (London: Longmans, 1979), pp. 664 and 655–656.

13 *The Poems of Tennyson*, 2nd edn., ed. Christopher Ricks, 3 vols. (London: Longmans, 1987), Vol. II, p. 318.

14 See Lloyd, *Nationalism and Minor Literature*, pp.136–142; and Welch, *Irish Poetry from Moore to Yeats* (Gerrards Cross: Colin Smythe, 1980), p. 99.

15 Welch, *Irish Poetry from Moore to Yeats*, p. 102.

16 Aristotle, *Poetics*, in *Classical Literary Criticism*, trans. T.S. Dorsch (Harmondsworth: Penguin, 1965), p. 65–66.

17 Mangan, *Collected Works*, Vol. V, p. 160.

18 I am grateful to Claire Connolly for drawing my attention to this implication.

19 Mangan, *Collected Works*, Vol. V, pp. 223–224.

20 D.J. O'Donoghue, *The Life and Times of James Clarence Mangan* (Edinburgh: Patrick Geddes, 1897) p. 19.

21 Joyce, p. 15, following John Mitchel, Introduction to James Clarence Mangan, *Poems* (New York, Haverty, 1859).

22 'An Extraordinary Adventure in the Shades' in Mangan, *Collected Works: Prose*, Vol. II, p. 18.

23 Lloyd, *Nationalism and Minor Literature*, p. 199.

24 Joyce, 'James Clarence Mangan', p. 56.

25 William Butler Yeats, 'Clarence Mangan (1803–1849)' (1887), in *Uncollected Prose*, ed. John P. Frayne, 2 vols. (London: Macmillan, 1970), Vol. I, *First Reviews and Articles, 1886–1896*, p. 117. I have corrected Yeats's quotation of the poem.

26 Mangan's Oriental sources were Joseph Freiherr von Hammer-Purgstall's *Geshichte der osmanischen Dichtkunst* (1836), and Barthélemy d'Herbelot's *Bibliothèque Orientales* (1697). See Jacques Chuto, "The Sources of James Clarence Mangan's Oriental Writings", *Notes and Queries*, New Series, Vol. 29, No. 3 (June 1982), pp. 224–228. Also David Lloyd, 'James Clarence Mangan's Oriental Translations and the Question of Origins', *Comparative Literature*, Vol. 38, No. 1 (Winter, 1986), pp. 20–35, here p.26: 'One finds that more often than not the stated sources of the poems themselves – of which Hammer-Purgstall's four-volume work contains thousands – are either non-existent, misattributed, or, when they do exist, have, as Mangan openly avers, completely forfeited their identity.'

27 Frank O'Connor, *The Backward Look: A Survey of Irish Literature* (London: Macmillan, 1967), p. 152.

28 Mangan, *Collected Works*, Vol. II, p. 188 and Vol. III, p. 69.

29 Compare the longer version of this theme in 'Khidder', which takes up most of stanza VIII, ll.115–162. The city is a place of cacophony, as is the verse, where 'the sounding tide of life' finds a rhyme with 'the strife/of sounds', then shown in percussive incessant rhyming in a highly irregular verse. David Wheatley hears its sound effects in Joyce's 'Sirens' and its wandering speaker in Beckett; see the introduction to James Clarence Mangan, *Poems*, ed. David Wheatley (Oldcastle: Gallery, 2003), p. 15.

30 Seamus Deane, 'Arnold, Burke and the Celts', in *Celtic Revivals* (London: Faber, 1985), p. 19.

31 Morash, *Writing the Irish Famine*, pp. 119 and 122.

32 Melissa Fegan, *Literature and the Irish Famine, 1845–1919* (Oxford: Oxford University Press, 2002), pp. 174–175.

33 D.J. O'Donoghue, *The Life and Times of James Clarence Mangan*, pp. 164–165.

34 Ellen Shannon-Mangan, *James Clarence Mangan, A Biography* (Dublin: Irish Academic Press, 1996), p. 207.

35 Welch, *A History of Verse Translation from the Irish, 1789–1897* (Gerrards Cross: Colin Smythe, 1988), p. 105.

36 Mangan, 'John Anster' (*The Irishman*, 1849), in *Collected Works: Prose*, Vol. II, p. 201.

37 Welch, *A History of Verse Translation*, p. 105.

38 Goethe, *Faustus, A Dramatic Mystery*, trans. John Anster (London: Longman, 1835), p. xxi.

39 Anster, pp. xx–xxi.

40 See Adolph B. Benson, 'English Criticism of the "Prologue in Heaven" in Goethe's *Faust*', *Modern Philology*, Vol. 19, No. 3. (Feb. 1922), pp. 225–243.

41 Mangan, *Collected Works*, Vol. II, p. 211.

42 See, for example, the e.g. from Browning's 'Ivan Ivanovitch': 'Chafe away, keep chafing, for she moans: she's coming-to!'

43 Joyce, 'James Clarence Mangan', p. 58.

44 John O'Daly (ed.), *The Poets and Poetry of Munster: A Selection of Irish Songs of the Poets of the Last Century*, trans. J.C. Mangan (Dublin: John O'Daly, 1847).

45 Headnote to 'James Clarence Mangan', *Collected Works: Prose*, Vol. I, p. X. Shaun Ryder, *Selected Writings*, p. 477, points out that Mangan's 'An Ode of Hafiz' (1848) is original.

46 Edgar Allen Poe, 'The Philosophy of Composition' (1846), in *Selected Writings of Edgar Allan Poe*, ed. David Galloway (Harmondsworth: Penguin, 1967), p. 485.

47 Seamus Perry, *Tennyson* (Northcote, Tavistock, 2005), p. 51.

48 See note to Mangan, *Collected Works*, Vol. II, p. 409. I am grateful to Michael Perraudin for much information about Rückert.

49 Lloyd, *Nationalism and Minor Literature,* p. 112. Lloyd also finds an allusion to Tennyson's poem in 'A Vision of Connaught in the Thirteenth Century'.

50 Felicia Hemans, *Records of Woman* (1828) repr. (Woodstock: Woodstock Books, 1991), p. 203.

51 Hemans, *Records of Woman*, pp. 187–193.

52 Chuto made his claim after the publication of the *Collected Works,* in *Selected Poems of James Clarence Mangan*, eds. Jacques Chuto et al. (Irish Academic Press, 2003), p. 378. Jan Jędrzejewski, 'Between Dublin and Siberia: Poland in *The Nation* Newspaper, 1846', *Dimensions and Categories of Celticity: Studies in Literature and Culture*, ed. Maxim Fomin et al. (Lodz: Lodz University Press, 2010), pp. 13–28.

53 Mangan, *Collected Works*, Vol. III, p. 455.

54 Joseph Lennon, *Irish Orientalism* (New York: Syracuse, 2004), p. 162.

55 Tennyson, *Poems*, Vol. I, p. 468.

56 Mangan, *Collected Works*, Vol. III, p. 439.

57 Mitchell, introduction to Mangan, *Poems* (1859), p. 15.

58 John Keats, *Endymion*, Vol. III, 331.

59 Thomas MacDonagh, *Literature in Ireland* (Nenagh: Relay, 1996), pp. 50 and 54.

60 See Robert Browning, e.g,. 'Soliloquy in the Spanish Cloister' and 'Fra Lippo Lippi'.

61 Samuel Ferguson, 'Hardiman's *Irish Minstrelsy*', Vol. III, *Dublin University Magazine*, Vol. 4 (Oct. 1834), pp. 456–460.

62 James Hardiman, *Irish Minstrelsy: Or Bardic Remains of Ireland,* 2 vols. (London: Robins, 1831), Vol. I, p. 351.

63 Ferguson, 'Hardiman's *Irish Minstrelsy*', Vol. II (August 1834), pp. 157–159.

64 'Little Black-haired Rose' was published posthumously in Mangan and John O'Daly's O'Daly (ed.), *The Poets and Poetry of Munster: A Selection of Irish Songs of the Poets of the Last Century*, trans. J.C. Mangan (Dublin: John O'Daly, 1847).

65 John Hollander, 'Breaking into Song: Some Notes on Refrain', in *Lyric Poetry: Beyond New Criticism*, eds. Chavia Hošek and Patricia Parker (Ithaca: Cornell University Press, 1985), p. 74. I am grateful to Rachel Buxton for drawing my attention to this essay.

66 See Chapter 2, p. X.

67 The poem is read explicitly alongside Mangan's *Autobiography* by Shannon-Mangan, pp. 391–395. She dates it to 1848.

6 'Letting the Past be Past': The English Poet and the Irish Poem

1 All quotations from A. Tennyson from *The Poems of Tennyson*, ed. Christopher Ricks, 2nd edn., 3 vols (London: Longman, 1987).

2 A. Tennyson to C. Esmarch in 1888, quoted in A. Tennyson, *Poems*, ed. Christopher Ricks, 3 vols. (London: Longman, 1987), here Vol. III, p. 149.

3 William Allingham, *A Diary, 1824–1889* (1907) (Penguin: Harmondsworth, 1985), p. 293 (29 August 1880). See Matthew Bevis, 'Tennyson, Ireland and "The Powers of Speech"', *Victorian Poetry*, Vol. 39, No. 3 (Fall 2001).

4 In his long poem *Laurence Bloomfield in Ireland: A Modern Poem* (London: Macmillan, 1864), Allingham uses the word 'terror' to refer to political violence four times.

5 Colin Graham, *Deconstructing Ireland: Identity, Theory, Culture* (Edinburgh: Edinburgh University Press, 2001), pp. 1 and 19–23.

6 See Hallam Tennyson, *Tennyson and His Friends*, ed. Hallam Tennyson (London: Macmillan, 1911), p. 143; and Hallam Tennyson, *Tennyson: A Memoir*, (London: Macmillan, 1899), p. 234.

7 A. Tennyson, *Poems*, Vol. II, p. 232.

8 See numbers II–IV of the poems grouped as *Memorials of a Tour in Scotland, 1803*, in William Wordsworth, *Poetical Works*, ed. E. De Selincourt (1904) (Oxford: Oxford University Press, 1969), pp. 225–236.

9 Joep Leerssen, 'Ossianic Liminality: Between Native Tradition and Pre-Romantic Taste', in *From Gaelic to Romantic: Ossianic Translations*, eds. Fiona Stafford and Howard Gaskill (Amsterdam: Rodoipi, 1998), pp. 1–26.

10 See Campbell, 'Poetry in the Four Nations', in *A Companion to Victorian Poetry*, eds. Richard Cronin, Alison Chapman and Anthony H. Harrison (Oxford: Blackwell, 2002), pp. 438–439.

11 Ernest Renan, in *The Poetry of the Celtic Races and Other Essays*, trans. William G. Hutchinson (1896) repr. (Washington, NY: Kennikat, 1970), p. 1.

12 Matthew Arnold, *The Study of Celtic Literature* (1867), repr. (Port Washington: Kennikat, 1970), p. 5.

13 William Shakespeare, *The Merchant of Venice*, act I, sc. iii, p. 107. I am grateful to Christopher Ricks for pointing out this allusion to me.

14 See, for instance, Gerry Smyth, '"The Natural Course of Things": Matthew Arnold, Celticism and the English Poetic Tradition', *Journal of Victorian Culture*, I, i (Spring, 1996).

15 Tennyson told Allingham that he was once asked to dinner and that his host was going to ask Arnold. He refused the invitation: 'I said I didn't much like dining with Gods!' Allingham, *Diary*, p. 288.

16 Tennyson, *Poems,* Vol. II, p. 231.

17 Henry David Inglis, *A Journey Throughout Ireland during the Spring, Summer and Autumn of 1834*, 2 vols. (London: Whittaker, 1835), Vol. I, p. 228. See also John Windele, *Historical and Descriptive Notices of the City of Cork and Its Vicinity* (London: Longmans, 1839), pp. 422–423.

18 Mary Tighe, *Psyche and Other Poems* (1811), repr. (Woodstock: Oxford, 1992), p. 233.

19 Roger Ebbatson, *Tennyson's English Idylls,* Tennyson Society Occasional Paper, 12 (Lincoln: Tennyson Society, 2003), p. 24.

20 Thomas Moore, *Poetical Works*, ed. A.D. Godley (Oxford: Oxford University Press, 1910), pp. 222–223.

21 Francis Turner Palgrave, *The Golden Treasury*, ed. Christopher Ricks (Penguin: Harmondsworth, 1991), pp. 437–438.

22 *Nightingale Valley: A Collection, Including a Great Number of the Choicest Lyrics and Short Poems in the English Language*, ed. Giraldus (William Allingham) (London: Bell and Daldry, 1860). It contains poems by Baillie, Scott, Carlyle, Emerson, Logan, Burns, Poe, Barnes and from Percy's *Reliques*. Irish poets not included in the *Golden Treasury* include Samuel Ferguson, William Kennedy and Allingham himself.

23 F.T. Palgrave, 'English Poetry from Dryden to Cowper', *Quarterly Review*, Vol. 112 (July 1862), pp. 173–174. The first part had appeared as 'The Growth of English Poetry' in October 1861.

24 Palgrave, *Golden Treasury*, p. 499.

25 Moore, *Poetical Works,* p. 201.

26 P.W. Joyce (trans.), 'The Voyage of Maildun', in *Old Celtic Romances* (London: C. Kegan Paul, 1879), pp. 112–176.

27 Denis Florence McCarthy, *Ballads, Poems and Lyrics, Original and Translated* (Dublin: McGlashan, 1850); Timothy Daniel Sullivan, *Poems* (1888) (Dublin: Sullivan, n.d.). See P.W. Joyce, p. xiii.

28 W.B. Yeats, *The Variorum Edition of the Poems of W.B. Yeats*, eds. Peter Allt and Russell K. Alspach, New York: Macmillan, 1957.p. 122. Yeats's stanza alludes to chapter XIX of Joyce's 'Voyage of Maildun', p.143. Yeats had already used the looser form of the same metre for the last section of *The Wanderings of Oisin* in 1889. See also, Yeats on the 'Maeldune' (spelt after Tennyson's version) legend and 'The White Birds', in 'The Message of the Folklorist' (1893), in *Uncollected Prose*, ed. John P. Frayne (London: Macmillan, 1970), Vol. I, p. 286.

29 P.W. Joyce, *Old Celtic Romances*, p. viii.

30 Tennyson, *Poems*, Vol. III, pp. 62–66.

31 Matthew Reynolds, *The Realms of Verse: English Poetry in a Time of Nation-Building* (Oxford: Oxford University Press, 2001), pp. 238–240.

32 Allingham, *Diary*, p. 325.

33 Stopford A. Brooke, *Tennyson: His Art and Relation to Modern Life* (London: Isbister, 1894), p. 471.

34 Allingham, *Diary*, pp. 297–298.

35 *The Poems of Matthew Arnold*, ed. Kenneth Allott, 2nd edn., ed. Miriam Allott (London: Longmans, 1979).

36 Renan, *The Poetry of the Celtic Races*, pp. 49–50.

37 'The Voyage of St Brendan' in *The Age of Bede*, 2nd edn., trans. J.F. Webb (Harmondsworth: Penguin, 1983), pp. 239–240.

38 Joyce, *Old Celtic Romances*, p. 171.

39 See Sullivan, 'Voyage of the O'Corras', pp. 222–248.

40 Tennyson, *The Princess*, iv, Vol. II., pp. 51–58.

41 A scan of *Literature Online* (Chadwyck Healey/Proquest), for instance, records no occurrences of 'past be past', or 'past to be past' in English Poetry before Coleridge, and only fifteen in total from the nineteenth century.

42 *Selections from the Poems of Aubrey de Vere*, ed. George Edward Woodberry (New York: Macmillan, 1894), pp. 224–225.

43 The most notorious statement was that by Trevelyan, on the first page of *The Irish Crisis*, that 'supreme wisdom has educed permanent good out of

transient evil'. See Chris Morash, *Writing the Irish Famine* (Oxford: Oxford University Press, 1995), pp. 30–51.

44 MacCarthy, 'The Voyage of St. Brendan', in *Ballads,* pp. 721–728.

45 Chris Morash, 'The Little Black Rose Revisited: Church, Empire and National Destiny in the Writings of Aubrey de Vere', *Canadian Journal of Irish Studies*, Vol. 20, No. 2 (Dec. 1994), p. 46.

46 Aubrey de Vere, Preface to *Inisfail, A Lyrical Chronicle of Ireland*, new ed. (London: Macmillan, 1897), pp. xxix–xxx.

47 The last published version of the poem in the *Inisfail* volume (1897), the poem has a second title, *The Irish Sisters*. This is the version quoted here.

48 Like Tennyson, the elderly Wordsworth was a friend of de Vere and admirer of the verse of his father, Sir Aubrey de Vere.

49 Wordsworth, *Poetical Works*, pp. 591–602.

50 Reynolds, *The Realms of Verse*, pp. 261–262. De Vere's later retitling of the poem as *The Irish Sisters* may discount Reynolds's reading. See also Morash, 'The Little Black Rose Revisited', pp. 45–52, on de Vere's conversion and his desire to accommodate Catholicism, Unionism and empire while bringing together the historicist and lyrical modes of Irish poetry in his *Inisfail*.

51 Tennyson, *Poems*, Vol. II, pp. 487n.

52 Paul Muldoon, *Poems, 1968–1998* (Faber: London, 2001), p. 102. For Muldoon's critical account of the immram, see also, *To Ireland, I* (Oxford: Oxford University Press, 2000), pp. 87–89.

7 'Spelt from Sibyl's Leaves': Hopkins, Yeats and the Unravelling of British Poetry

1 Gerard Manley Hopkins, 'To Seem the Stranger', in *Poetical Works*, ed. Norman H. MacKenzie (Oxford: Oxford University Press, 1990).

2 W.B. Yeats, 'The Symbolism of Poetry' (1900), in *Essays and Introductions* (London: Macmillan, 1961), p. 163.

3 W.B. Yeats, *The Variorum Edition of the Poems of W. B Yeats,* eds. Peter Allt and Russell K. Alspach (New York: Macmillan, 1957), p. 541.

4 Malcolm Brown, *The Politics of Irish Literature* (London: Allen Unwin, 1972), pp. 371–390.

5 James Joyce, *Ulysses* (London: Bodley Head, 1960), p. 24.

6 R.F. Foster, *W.B. Yeats: A Life*, 2 vols. (Oxford: Oxford University Press, 1997–2003), Vol. I, pp. 116 and 561n.

7 See Foster, *W.B. Yeats*,Vol. I, pp. 115–116; and Yeats, *Variorum*, pp. 834–835.

8 Standish O'Grady, *The Story of Ireland* (London: Methuen, 1894), pp. 211–212.

9 W.B. Yeats, 'Irish National Literature, II: Contemporary Prose Writers' (1895), in *Uncollected Prose*, 2 vols., ed. John P. Frayne (London: Macmillan, 1970), Vol. I, pp. 368–369. O'Grady's *Story of Ireland* is an impressionist narrative of Irish affairs from the coming of the gods to the death of Parnell, which has aroused acrimonious controversy, and is still something of a by-word, for

Ireland is hardly ready for impressionism, above all for a whimsical impressionism which respects no traditional hatred or reverence, which exalts Cromwell and denounces the saints, and is almost persuaded that when Parnell was buried, as when Columba died, 'the sky was alight with strange lights and flames'.

10 Yeats was quoting O'Grady, *Story of Ireland*, p. 185.

11 See Yeats, *Variorum*, pp. 541 and 832–845.

12 Brown, *Politics of Irish Literature*, p. 374.

13 Quoted in Foster, *W.B. Yeats*, Vol. I, p. 116.

14 A. Norman Jeffares, *W.B. Yeats, Man and Poet,* third edn. (New York: Macmillan, 1996), p. 58.

15 The text here is reconstructed from Yeats, *Variorum*, pp. 119–120, as it appeared in *The Countess Cathleen and Various Legends and Lyrics* (1892).

16 See the revisions recorded in *Variorum Poems,* pp. 137–139; and Campbell, 'Yeats in the Coming Times', *Essays in Criticism*, Vol. 53, No. 1 (January 2003), pp. 10–32.

17 William Allingham, *A Diary, 1824–1889,* ed. John Julius Norwich (Harmondsworth: Penguin, 1985), p. 320. I am grateful to Adrian Paterson for pointing out this passage to me.

18 Kate Flint, *The Victorians and the Visual Imagination* (Oxford: Oxford University Press, 2000); and Catherine Philips, *Gerard Manley Hopkins and the Victorian Visual World* (Oxford: Oxford University Press, 2007).

19 Hopkins, *The Correspondence of Gerard Manley Hopkins and Richard Watson Dixon,* ed. C.C. Abbott, 2nd edn. (London: Oxford University Press, 1955), p. 164.

20 Hopkins, *The Letters of Gerard Manley Hopkins to Robert Bridges,* 2nd. edn., ed. Claude Colleer Abbott (London: Oxford University Press, 1955), p. 199.

21 Ibid., p. 202.

22 Thomas Gray and William Collins, *Poetical Works,* ed. Roger Lonsdale (Oxford: Oxford University Press, 1977), pp. 156–157.

23 See Lonsdale, headnotes to Gray and Collins, *Poetical Works,* pp. 33–34 and 156. Lonsdale sets the period of composition of Gray's 'Elegy' as between the summer of 1746 and 1750.

24 'Spelt from Sibyl's Leaves', from drafts of October–November 1884. See Hopkins, *Poetical Works,* pp. 471–472; and Hopkins, *The Later Poetic Manuscripts of Gerard Manley Hopkins,* ed. Norman H. MacKenzie (New York: Garland, 1991), p. 298. See also MacKenzie, 'Hopkins, Yeats and Dublin in the Eighties' in *Myth and Reality in Irish Literature,* ed. Joseph Ronsley (Waterloo: Wilfrid Laurier University Press, 1977), pp. 77–97; here pp. 83–84.

25 I am grateful to Adrian Poole for pointing this out to me.

26 See Hopkins, *Poetical Works,* p. 474.

27 Collins provides a number of images in Hopkins's poem: 'hornlight wound', for instance, comes from Collins's winding of the beetle's horn. MacKenzie, *Poetical Works,* p. 474, suggests more explicit allusions had been revised out by this stage.

28 Hopkins, 'To Seem the Stranger', l.14.

29 Christopher R. Miller, *The Invention of Evening: Perception and Time in Romantic Poetry* (Cambridge: Cambridge University Press, 2006), p. 34.

30 Norman White, *Hopkins in Ireland* (Dublin: University College DublinPress, 2002), p. 29.

31 P.W. Joyce, *English as We Speak It in Ireland* (Dublin: Wolfhound, 1988), pp. 341 and 248.

32 See Colin Graham, 'Hopkins, Yeats and the Death of Samuel Ferguson', *Notes and Queries*, 40.4 (1993), pp. 493–494.

33 Wright, *The English Dialect Dictionary*, 3 vols., ed. Joseph Wright (London: Frowde, 1898), Vol. 1, p. 289. See MacKenzie, 'Hopkins, Yeats and Dublin', pp. 89–90.

34 See Matthew Reynolds, *The Realms of Verse: English Poetry in a Time of Nation-Building, 1830–1870* (Oxford: Oxford University Press, 2001), chapter 8, pp. 203–217.

35 William Wordsworth, 'It Is a Beauteous Evening', in *Poetical Works*, ed. Ernest de Selincourt (Oxford: Oxford University Press, 1969), p, 205.

36 Miller, *The Invention of Evening*, p. 11.

37 Algernon Swinburne, *Poems,* 6 vols. (London: Chatto, 1904), Vol. VI, p. 355.

38 Hopkins, *Correspondence* with Dixon, p. 135.

39 *Letters to Bridges*, To RB, 1 January 1884. Cp. 'bloody broth' with the letter of 4 January relating a sunset observed on 4 December 1883: 'I took note of it as more like inflamed flesh than the lucid reds of ordinary sunsets.'

40 *Letters to Bridges*, pp. 252–252. The references are to the Archbishop of Dublin William Walsh and Archbishop of Cashel Thomas Croke (after whom Croke Park was named).

41 Ibid., pp. 256–257.

42 Hopkins to Coventry Patmore, 4 June 1886.

43 Hopkins, *Poetical Works*, p. 497.

44 The end of Swinburne's 'Apostasy' invokes Gordon's name against that of Gladstone.

45 Hopkins, *Poetical Works*, p. 184.

46 Ibid., p. 458.

47 Hopkins, sermons on 'Thy Will Be Done on Earth as It Is in Heaven,' 11–18 Jan. 1880, in *The Sermons and Devotional Writings of Gerard Manley Hopkins*, ed. Christopher Devlin, S.J. (London, 1959), pp. 55–58.

48 Hopkins, *Poetical Works*, p.171.

49 Hopkins, *Sermons*, p.59.

50 Ibid., pp. 55–56.

51 *Letters to Bridges*, pp. 273–274 (10 Feb. 1888).

52 See White, *Hopkins in Ireland*, pp. 144–157.

53 Monk Gibbon, *The Masterpiece and the Man* (London: Hart Davis, 1959), p. 144.

54 MacKenzie, 'Hopkins, Yeats and Dublin', p. 78.

55 *Further Letters of Gerard Manley Hopkins*, ed. C.C. Abbott (Oxford: Oxford University Press, 1971), pp. 373–374.

56 This is the revised version with italicised refrain from *Poems*, 1895. See Yeats, *Variorum*, p. 86.

57 See Yeats, *Variorum*, pp. 121–122.

58 Yeats, *Autobiography*, ed. Denis Donoghue (London: Macmillan, 1972), p. 19.

59 John Ruskin, *Complete Works*, eds. E.T. Cook and Alexander Wedderburn, 30 vols. (London: George Allen, 1904), *Modern Painters*, Vol. III, p. 155.

60 MacKenzie, 'Hopkins, Yeats and Dublin', p. 83.

61 James Joyce, *Stephen Hero*, ed. T. Spencer, revd. J.J. Slocum and H. Cahoun (London: Jonathan Cape, 1956), p. 32. See also Chapter 8, p. X.

62 Quoted in Ronald Schuchard, *The Last Minstrels: Yeats and the Revival of the Bardic Arts*, (Oxford: Oxford University Press, 2008), p.321.

63 Hopkins, *Poetical Works*, p. 472.

64 Ibid., p. 190–191.

8 Violence and Measure: Yeats after Union

1 W.B. Yeats, *The Variorum Edition of the Poems of W.B. Yeats*, eds. Peter Allt and Russell K. Alspach (New York: Macmillan, 1957), pp. 745–769 (1900) and 221–252 (1906). On Yeats's difficulties with completing and constant revising of the poem, see R.F. Foster, 'The Apprentice Mage', in *W.B. Yeats: A Life*, 2 vols. (Oxford: Oxford University Press, 1997), Vol. I, pp. 218–220 and 336–337.

2 Yeats, *Variorum*, pp. 769 and 252.

3 Yeats, *Variorum*, 'The Wanderings of Oisin', pp. 16–17.

4 Thomas Moore, 'Dear Harp of My Country', in *Poetical Works*, ed. A.D. Godley (Oxford: Oxford University Press, 1910), p. 201.

5 Moore, *Poetical Works*, p. 195.

6 See Matthew Campbell, 'Thomas Moore, Daniel Maclise and the New Mythology: The Origin of the Harp', in *The Voice of the People: Writing the European Folk Revival, 1760–1914*, eds. Matthew Campbell and Michael Perraudin (London: Anthem, 2012), pp. 65–86.

7 Ronald Schuchard, *The Last Minstrels: Yeats and the Revival of the Bardic Arts* (Oxford: Oxford University Press, 2008).

8 For a sceptical linguistic analysis, see Adelyn Dougherty, *A Study of the Rhythmic Structure in the Verse of William Butler Yeats* (The Hague: Mouton, 1973).

9 See Brown's introduction and selection 'Counter Revival' writing in *The Field Day Anthology of Irish Writing*, eds. Seamus Deane et al., 3 vols. (Derry: Field Day, 1991), Vol. III, pp. 129–313.

10 Fran Brearton, *The Great War in Irish Poetry: W.B. Yeats to Michael Longley* (Oxford: Oxford University Press, 2000).

11 W.R. Rodgers, *Collected Poems* (London: Oxford University Press, 1971), p. 91.

12 Seamus Heaney, 'Through-Other Places, Through-Other Times: The Irish Poet and Britain', in *Finders Keepers: Selected Prose, 1971–2001* (London: Faber, 2002), p. 366.

13 Francis Ledwidge, *Selected Poems*, ed. Dermot Bolger (Dublin: New Island, 1992), p. 57.

14 Thomas MacDonagh, *Literature in Ireland* (Nenagh: Relay, 1996), p. 147.

15 Sean Ó Tuama and Thomas Kinsella (eds. and trans.), *An Duanaire 1600–1900: Poems of the Dispossessed* (Dublin: Dolmen, 1981), pp. 132–135. The line appears at the end of the version MacDonagh gives, and at the end of stanza four in Ó Tuama.

16 John Milton, 'Lycidas', in *Poetical Works,* ed. Douglas Bush (Oxford: Oxford University Press, 1966), p. 146.

17 Heaney, *Finders Keepers*, p. 373.

18 Yeats, *Variorum*, p. 320.

19 Yeats, *Variorum*, p. 394.

20 David Pearce, *Yeats's Worlds: Ireland, England and the Poetic Imagination* (New Haven: Yale, 1935), pp. 180–182.

21 See R.F. Foster, 'The Arch-Poet', in *W.B. Yeats: A Life,* 2 vols. (Oxford: Oxford University Press, 2003), Vol. II, pp. 11–13.

22 Michael Wood, *Yeats and Violence* (Oxford: Oxford University Press, 2010), pp. 6 and 27 and 28.

23 W.B. Yeats, 'A General Introduction for my Work' (1937), in *Essays and Introductions* (London: Macmillan, 1961), p. 509.

24 Yeats, 'The Tragic Generation', in *Autobiographies* (London: Macmillan, 1956), p. 341.

25 Yeats, 'Coole Park and Ballylee, 1931', *Variorum*, p. 491.

26 Yeats, 'Per Amica Silentia Lunae' (1917), in *The Collected Works of W.B. Yeats*, Vol. V; *Later Essays*, ed. William H. O'Donnell (New York: Scribner, 1994), pp. 1–16.

27 Helen Vendler, *Our Secret Discipline: Yeats and Poetic Form* (Oxford: Oxford University Press, 2007), pp. 253 and 254.

28 Denis Donoghue, 'Yeats, Trying to be Modern', in *Irish Essays* (Cambridge: Cambridge University Press, 2011), p. 139. The Symons reference is to the introduction to *The Symbolist Movement in Literature* (1899).

29 Michael O'Neill, *The All-Sustaining Air: Romantic Legacies and Renewals in British, American and Irish Poetry since 1900* (Oxford: Oxford University Press, 2007), p. 35.

30 Harold Bloom, *Yeats* (New York: Oxford University Press, 1970), p. 203.

31 Yeats, 'Modern Irish Poetry' (1899 title), in *Collected Works of W.B. Yeats*, Vol. IV; *Prefaces and Introductions*, ed. William H. O'Donnell (New York: Scribner, 1989), p. 104.

32 Notes to *Book of Irish Verse*, in *Prefaces and Introductions*, p. 219.

33 Mangan, *The Collected Works of James Clarence Mangan*, 6 vols., eds. Jacques Chuto, Rudolf Patrick Holzapfel, Ellen Shannon-Mangan and Peter Van de Kamp (Dublin: Irish Academic Press, 1997–2002), Vol. IV.

34 See Chapter 5, pp. 165–166.

35 Yeats, 'Clarence Mangan (1803–1849)', in *Uncollected Prose,* ed. John P. Frayne, 2 vols. (London: Macmillan, 1970), Vol. I, p. 117. See also Chapter 5, pp. X.

36 Shelley, *Laon and Cythna,* canto 7, 3111–3114. Cythna draws 'clear elemental shapes, whose smallest change/A subtler language within language

wrought: The key of truths which once were dimly taught', in Percy Bysshe Shelley, *The Major Works*, ed. Zachary Leader and Michael O'Neill (Oxford: Oxford University Press, 2003), p. 175.

37 On the connection between 'Ego Dominus', *Per Amica* and Leo Africanus, see, for instance, Foster, *The Arch-Poet*, pp. 71–80.

38 Bloom, *Yeats*, pp. 199 and 200.

39 O'Neill, *All-Sustaining Air*, p. 42. See also, Bloom, *Yeats*, pp. 196–204; and George Bornstein, *Transformations of Romanticism in Yeats, Eliot and Stevens* (Chicago: University of Chicago Press, 1976), pp. 41–44.

40 Quoted in O'Neill, *All-Sustaining Air*, p. 40.

41 See Yeats, *Variorum*, p. 177.

42 Wallace Stevens, 'The Noble Rider and the Sound of Words', in *The Necessary Angel* (London: Faber, 1984), p. 36.

43 Brearton, *Great War in Irish Poetry*, p. 64.

44 Heaney, 'The Redress of Poetry', in *Finders Keepers*, p. 257.

45 David Bromwich, 'Destruction and the Theory of Happiness in the Poetry of Yeats and Wallace Stevens' *Essays in Criticism*, Vol. 60, No. 2 (April 2010), p. 115.

46 Yeats, *Variorum*, p. 138.

47 Declan Kiberd, *Inventing Ireland: The Literature of the Modern Nation* (London: Cape, 1995), pp. 119–120.

48 Yeats to Dorothy Wellesley, 8 September 1935, in *The Collected Letters of W.B. Yeats, Electronic Edition, Unpublished Letters (1905–1939)*, ed. John Kelly et al. (Charlottesville: Intelex, 2002).

49 Yeats, *Variorum*, p. 138.

50 Matthew Arnold, *The Study of Celtic Literature* (1867), repr. (Port Washington: Kennikat, 1970), pp. 102–013

51 Matthew Campbell, 'Yeats in the Coming Times', *Essays in Criticism*, Vol. 53, No. 1 (January 2003), pp. 10–32.

52 Yeats, 'A General Introduction for my Work', *Essays and Introductions*, p. 524.

53 Yeats, 'Modern Poetry: A Broadcast', *Later Essays*, p. 100.

54 Yeats, *Unpublished Letters*, 6–13 November 1924.

55 Yeats, *Variorum*, pp. 131–132.

Bibliography

Allingham, William *Nightingale Valley. A Collection, Including a Great Number of the Choicest Lyrics and Short Poems in the English Language*, ed. Giraldus, London: Bell and Daldry, 1860.

Laurence Bloomfield in Ireland: A Modern Poem, London: Macmillan, 1864.

A Diary, 1824–1889 (1907), ed. John Julius Norwich, Harmondsworth: Penguin, 1985.

Aristotle, *Poetics* in *Classical Literary Criticism*, trans. T.S. Dorsch, Harmondsworth: Penguin, 1965.

Arnold, Matthew, *On Translating Homer*, London: Longman, 1861.

The Study of Celtic Literature (1867), repr. Port Washington: Kennikat, 1970.

The Poems of Matthew Arnold, ed. Kenneth Allott, 2nd edn., ed. Miriam Allott, London: Longmans, 1979.

Beckett, Samuel, *Disjecta: Miscellaneous Writings,* ed. Ruby Cohn, London: John Calder, 1983.

Murphy (1938), London: Picador, 1973.

Behan, Brendan, *Brendan Behan's Island: An Irish Sketch-Book*, London: Random House, 1982.

Benson, Adolph B., 'English Criticism of the "Prologue in Heaven" in Goethe's *Faust*', *Modern Philology*, Vol. 19, No. 3. (Feb. 1922), 225–243.

Bevis, Matthew, 'Tennyson, Ireland and "The Powers of Speech"', *Victorian Poetry*, Vol. 39, No. 3 (Fall 2001), 345–364.

Bhabha, Homi K., 'Interrogating Identity: Frantz Fanon and the Postcolonial Prerogative', in *The Location of Culture*, London: Routledge, 1994, 57–93.

Bloom, Harold, *Yeats*, New York: Oxford University Press, 1970.

Bornstein, George, *Transformations of Romanticism in Yeats, Eliot and Stevens*, Chicago: University of Chicago Press, 1976.

Brearton, Fran, *The Great War in Irish Poetry: W.B. Yeats to Michael Longley*, Oxford: Oxford University Press, 2000.

Brennan, Timothy, 'The National Longing for Form, in *Nation and Narration*, ed. Homi K. Bhabha, London: Routledge, 1990, pp. 44–70.

Bridges, Robert, *Milton's Prosody* (1889–1921), revd. edn., Oxford: Oxford University Press, 1921.

Bromwich, David, 'Destruction and the Theory of Happiness in the Poetry of Yeats and Wallace Stevens', *Essays in Criticism*, Vol. 60, No. 2 (April 2010), 105–128.

Brooke, Charlotte, *Reliques of Irish Poetry* (1789), ed. Aaron Crossley Seymour, Dublin: Christie, 1816.

Brooke, Stopford A., *Tennyson: His Art and Relation to Modern Life*, London: Isbister, 1894.

Brown, Malcolm, *The Politics of Irish Literature*, London: Allen Unwin, 1972.

Brown, Terence and Nicholas Grene (eds.), *Tradition and Influence in Anglo-Irish Poetry*, Totowa, NJ: Barnes and Noble, 1989.

Bunting, Edward, *The Ancient Music of Ireland: The Bunting Collections*, Dublin: Waltons, 2002.

Burke, Edmund, *Reflections on the Revolution in France* (1790), ed. Conor Cruise O'Brien, Harmondsworth: Pelican, 1968.

Burns, Robert, *The Letters of Robert Burns*, ed. J. De Lancey Ferguson, 2 vols., Oxford: Oxford University Press, 1931.

Poems and Songs, ed. James Kinsley, Oxford: Oxford University Press, 1969.

Callanan, Jeremiah Joseph, *The Recluse of Inchidony and Other Poems*, London: Hurst, Chance, 1830.

The Irish Poems, ed. Gregory A. Schirmer. Gerrads Cross: Colin Smythe, 2005.

Campbell, Matthew, 'Davis, Mangan, Ferguson', in *The Blackwell Companion to Irish Literature,* ed. Julia M. Wright, 2 vols., Oxford: Blackwell, 2010, 427–443.

'Poetry in the Four Nations', in *A Companion to Victorian Poetry*, eds. Richard Cronin, Alison Chapman and Anthony H. Harrison, Oxford: Blackwell, 2002, 438–456.

'Yeats in the Coming Times', *Essays in Criticism*, Vol. 53, No. 1 (Jan. 2003), 10–32.

Campbell, Matthew and Michael Perraudin (eds.), *The Voice of the People: Writing the European Folk Revival, 1760–1914*, London: Anthem, 2012.

Carlyle, Thomas, *Chartism*, London: Fraser, 1839.

Sartor Resartus, Fraser's Magazine, Vols. VIII–IX (November 1833–June 1834).

Chuto, Jacques, 'The Sources of James Clarence Mangan's Oriental Writings', *Notes and Queries*, New Series, Vol. 29, No. 3 (June 1982), 224–228.

Clarke, Austin, *Poetry in Modern Ireland*, Cork: Mercier, 1951.

Connolly, Claire, *A Cultural History of the Irish Novel, 1790–1829*, Cambridge: Cambridge University Press, 2012.

Corbett, Mary Jean, *Allegories of Union in Irish and English Writing, 1790–1870*, Cambridge: Cambridge University Press, 2000.

Corkery, Daniel, *The Hidden Ireland* (1924), Dublin: Gill and Macmillan, 1967.

Crawford, Robert, *Devolving English Literature*, 2nd edn., Edinburgh: Edinburgh University Press, 2000.

Cronin, Michael, *Translating Ireland: Translation, Languages and Identity*, Cork: Cork University Press, 1996.

Cullen, L.M., 'The *Hidden Ireland*: Re-Assessment of a Concept', *Studia Hibernica*, No. 9 (1969), 7–47.

Curran, William Henry, *The Life of the Right Honourable William Philpot Curran*, 2 vols., London: Constable, 1819.

Davis, Leith, *Music, Postcolonialism and Gender*, South Bend: University of Notre Dame Press, 2006.

Davis, Thomas, *Literary and Historical Essays,* Dublin: James Duffy, 1847.

    Selections from His Prose and Poetry, ed. T.W. Rolleston, Dublin: Talbot, 1914.

Davis, Thomas (ed.), *The Spirit of the Nation* (1845), repr. Otley: Woodstock, 1998.

Deane, Seamus, *Celtic Revivals,* London: Faber, 1985.

    Strange Country: Modernity and Nationhood in Irish Writing since 1790, Oxford: Oxford University Press, 1997.

Deane, Seamus and Seamus Heaney, 'Unhappy and at Home', *The Crane Bag*, Vol. I, No.1 (Spring 1977), 61–67.

Deane, Seamus (ed.), *The Field Day Anthology of Irish Writing*, 3 vols., Derry: Field Day, 1991.

Denman, Peter, *Samuel Ferguson, The Literary Achievement*, Gerrards Cross: Colin Smythe, 1990.

De Vere, Aubrey, Preface to *Inisfail, A Lyrical Chronicle of Ireland*, new ed., London: Macmillan, 1897.

    Selections from the Poems of Aubrey de Vere, ed. George Edward Woodberry, New York: Macmillan, 1894.

Donoghue, Denis, *Irish Essays*, Cambridge: Cambridge University Press, 2011.

Dorson, Richard M., *Folklore and Fakelore,* Cambridge, MA: Harvard University Press, 1976.

Dougherty, Adelyn, *A Study of the Rhythmic Structure in the Verse of William Butler Yeats*, The Hague: Mouton, 1973.

Duffy, Charles Gavan (ed.), *The Ballad Poetry of Ireland*, Dublin: James Duffy, 1845.

Eagleton, Terry, 'Cork and the Carnivalesque', in *Reviewing Ireland*, eds. Sarah Briggs, Paul Hyland and Neil Sammells, Bath: Sulis, 1998, 20–29.

    Heathcliff and the Great Hunger, London: Verso, 1996.

Ebbatson, Roger, *Tennyson's English Idylls,* Tennyson Society Occasional Paper 12, Lincoln: Tennyson Society, 2003.

Farren, Robert, *The Course of Irish Verse,* London: Sheed and Ward, 1948.

Fegan, Melissa, *Literature and the Irish Famine, 1845–1919*, Oxford: Oxford University Press, 2002.

Ferguson, Samuel, 'A Dialogue Between the Head and Heart of an Irish Protestant', *Dublin University Magazine*, Vol. 2, (Nov. 1833), 586–593.

    'The Fairy Well of Lagnanay', *Blackwood's Edinburgh Magazine*, Vol. XXXIII, No. CCVII (April 1833), II, p. 667.

    'Hardiman's *Irish Minstrelsy*', 4 parts, *Dublin University Magazine*, Vols. 3–4 (April–November 1834).

    Lays of the Western Gael, London: Bell and Daldy, 1865.

    Poems, New York: Magee, 1880.

    'Robert Burns', 2 articles, *Dublin University Magazine*, Vol. 25, (January and March, 1845), 66–81; 289–305.

'Thomas Davis', *Dublin University Magazine*, Vol. 29, No. 170 (February, 1847), 190–199.

Fleischmann, Aloys, *Sources of Irish Traditional Music, c. 1600–1855*, 2 vols., New York: Garland, 1998.

Flint, Kate, *The Victorians and the Visual Imagination*, Oxford: Oxford University Press, 2000.

Foster, R.F., *W.B. Yeats: A Life*, 2 vols., Oxford: Oxford University Press, 1997–2003.

Gaynor, Feargal, '"An Irish Potatoe Seasoned with Attic Salt": *The Reliques of Fr Prout* and Identity before *The Nation*', *Irish Studies Review*, Vol. 7, No. 3 (1999), pp. 313–323.

Gibbons, Luke, *Transformations in Irish Culture*, Cork: Field Day, 1996.

Gibbon, Monk, *The Masterpiece and the Man*, London: Hart Davis, 1959.

Goethe, Johan Wolfgang von, *Faustus, A Dramatic Mystery*, trans. John Anster, London: Longman, 1835.

Graham, Colin, *Deconstructing Ireland: Identity, Theory, Culture*, Edinburgh: Edinburgh University Press, 2001.

'Hireling Strangers and the Wandering Throne: Ireland, Scotland and Samuel Ferguson', *Estudios Irlandeses*, No. 4, (2009), 21–35.

'Hopkins, Yeats and the Death of Samuel Ferguson', *Notes and Queries*, 40.4 (1993), 493–494.

Gray, Thomas and William Collins, *Poetical Works*, ed. Roger Lonsdale, Oxford: Oxford University Press, 1977.

Hardiman, James (ed.), *Irish Minstrelsy: Or Bardic Remains of Ireland, with English Poetical Translations,* 2 vols., London: Robins, 1831.

Hart, Matthew, *Nations of Nothing but Poetry: Modernism, Transnationalism and Synthetic Vernacular Writing,* New York: Oxford University Press, 2010.

Hazlitt, William, *The Spirit of the Age*, ed. E.D. Mackerness, London: Collins, 1969.

Heaney, Seamus, *Finders Keepers: Selected Prose, 1971–2001,* London: Faber, 2002.

Hemans, Felicia, *Records of Woman* (1828) repr. Woodstock: Woodstock Books, 1991.

Works, 7 vols., Edinburgh: Blackwood, 1839.

Hickey, Raymond, *Irish English: History and Present-Day Forms*. Cambridge: Cambridge University Press, 2007.

Hollander, John, 'Breaking into Song: Some Notes on Refrain', in *Lyric Poetry: Beyond New Criticism*, eds. Chavia Hošek and Patricia Parker, Ithaca: Cornell University Press, 1985, 73–89.

Hopkins, Gerard Manley, *The Correspondence of Gerard Manley Hopkins and Richard Watson Dixon*, ed. C.C. Abbott, 2nd edn., London: Oxford University Press, 1955.

Further Letters of Gerard Manley Hopkins, ed. C.C. Abbott, Oxford: Oxford University Press, 1971.

The Later Poetic Manuscripts of Gerard Manley Hopkins, ed. Norman H. MacKenzie, New York: Garland, 1991.

The Letters of Gerard Manley Hopkins to Robert Bridges, 2nd. edn., ed. Claude
Colleer Abbott, London: Oxford University Press, 1955.
Poetical Works, ed. Norman H. MacKenzie, Oxford: Oxford University
Press, 1990.
The Sermons and Devotional Writings of Gerard Manley Hopkins, ed. Christopher
Devlin, London, 1959.
Houghton, Walter A., ed. *The Wellesley Index of Victorian Periodicals*, 5 vols,
University of Toronto Press: Toronto, 1965–1988.
Hyde, Douglas, *Abhráin grádh chúige Connacht: The Love Songs of Connacht*,
Baile-Ath-Cliath: Gill, 1893.
Inglis, Henry David, *A Journey Throughout Ireland during the Spring, Summer and
Autumn of 1834*, 2 vols., London: Whittaker, 1835.
Jędrzejewski, Jan, 'Between Dublin and Siberia: Poland in *The Nation* Newspaper,
1846', *Dimensions and Categories of Celticity: Studies in Literature and Culture*,
ed. Maxim Fomin et al., Lodz: Lodz University Press, 2010, pp. 13–28.
Jeffares, A. Norman, *W.B. Yeats, Man and Poet*, third edn., New York:
Macmillan, 1996.
Johnson, James (ed.), *The Scots Musical Museum*, 6 vols., Edinburgh: Johnson,
1787–1803.
Joyce, James, *Occasional, Critical, and Political Writing*, ed. Kevin Barry, Oxford;
Oxford University Press, 2000.
Poems and Exiles, ed. J.C.C. Mays, London: Penguin, 1992.
Stephen Hero, ed. T. Spencer, revd. J.J. Slocum and H. Cahoun, London:
Jonathan Cape, 1956.
Ulysses, London: Bodley Head, 1960.
Joyce, P.W., *English as We Speak It in Ireland*, Dublin: Wolfhound, 1988.
Old Celtic Romances, London: C. Kegan Paul, 1879.
Kavanagh, Patrick, *Collected Pruse*, London: McGibbon and Kee, 1967.
Keats, John, *The Complete Poems*, ed. Miriam Allott, London: Longman, 1970.
Kelly, Ronan, *Bard of Erin: The Life of Thomas Moore*, Dublin: Penguin, 2008.
Kenner, Hugh, *A Colder Eye*, London: Allen Lane, 1983.
Kerrigan, John, *Archipelagic English*, Oxford: Oxford University Press, 2008.
Kiberd, Declan, *Inventing Ireland: The Literature of the Modern Nation*, London:
Cape, 1995.
Kinsella, Thomas, *The Dual Tradition: An Essay on Poetry and Politics in Ireland*,
Manchester: Carcanet, 1995.
'The Irish Writer', in *Davis, Mangan, Ferguson: Tradition and the Irish Writer*,
eds. W.B. Yeats and Thomas Kinsella, Dublin: Dolmen, 1970, 57–66.
Kirkland, Richard, 'Questioning the Frame: Hybridity, Ireland and the Institution',
in *Ireland and Cultural Theory: The Mechanics of Authenticity*, eds. Colin
Graham and Richard Kirkland, London: Macmillan, 1999, 210–228.
Larminie, William, 'The Development of English Metres', *Contemporary Review*,
LXVI (November, 1894), 717–736.
Ledwidge, Francis, *Selected Poems*, ed. Dermot Bolger, Dublin: New Island, 1992.
Leerssen, Joep, *Hidden Ireland, Public Sphere*, Galway: Arlen House, 2002.

'Ossianic Liminality: Between Native Tradition and Pre-Romantic Taste', *From Gaelic to Romantic: Ossianic Translations,* eds. Fiona Stafford and Howard Gaskill, Amsterdam: Rodoipi, 1998, 1–16.

Remembrance and Imagination: Patterns in the Historical and Literary Representation of Ireland in the Nineteenth Century, South Bend: University of Notre Dame Press, 1997.

Leighton, Angela, *On Form: Poetry, Aestheticism, and the Legacy of a Word*, Oxford: Oxford University Press, 2007.

Lennon, Joseph, *Irish Orientalism*, New York: Syracuse, 2004.

Lloyd, David, *Anomalous States: Irish Writing and the Post-Colonial Moment,* Dublin: Lilliput, 1993.

'James Clarence Mangan's Oriental Translations and the Question of Origins', *Comparative Literature*, Vol. 38, No. 1 (Winter, 1986), 20–35.

Nationalism and Minor Literature: James Clarence Mangan and the Emergence of Irish Cultural Nationalism, Berkeley: University of California Press, 1987.

Lucy, Sean, 'Metre and Movement in Anglo-Irish Verse', *Irish University Review* (1978), p. 158.

McBride, Ian (ed.), *History and Memory in Modern Ireland*, Cambridge: Cambridge University Press, 2001.

McCarthy, Denis Florence, *Ballads, Poems and Lyrics, Original and Translated,* Dublin: McGlashan, 1850.

McCarthy, Denis Florence (ed.), *The Book of Irish Ballads*, Dublin: Duffy, 1846.

McCormack, W.J., *From Burke to Beckett: Ascendancy, Tradition and Betrayal in Literary History,* Cork: Cork University Press, 1994.

McDiarmid, Hugh, *Complete Poems*, 2 vols., London: Martin Brian and O'Keefe, 1978.

McDonald, Peter, *Mistaken Identities,* Oxford: Oxford University Press, 1997.

McLane, Maureen, *Balladeering, Minstrelsy, and the Making of British Romantic Poetry,* Cambridge: Cambridge University Press, 2008.

MacDonagh, Oliver, *States of Mind: A Study of Anglo-Irish Conflict, 1780–1980,* London: Allen Unwin, 1983.

MacDonagh, Thomas, *Literature in Ireland* (1916), Nenagh: Relay, 1996.

Thomas Campion and the Art of English Poetry, Dublin: Talbot, 1912.

MacKenzie, Norman H., 'Hopkins, Yeats and Dublin in the Eighties', in *Myth and Reality in Irish Literature*, ed. Joseph Ronsley, Waterloo: Wilfrid Laurier University Press, 1977, pp. 77–97.

Maclise, Daniel, *Daniel Maclise: Romancing the Past, 1806–1870,* ed. Peter Murray, Cork: Crawford Art Gallery, 2008.

[Maginn, William], 'Parody' ['Tis the Last Glass of Claret'], *London Literary Gazette*, No. 183 (July 22, 1820).

Mahony, Francis Sylvester, *The Reliques of Father Prout,* 2 vols., London: Fraser, 1836.

The Reliques of Father Prout, London: George Bell, 1894.

Mangan, James Clarence, *Collected Works of James Clarence Mangan*, 6 vols., eds. Jacques Chuto, Rudolf Patrick Holzapfel, Ellen Shannon-Mangan and Peter Van de Kamp, Dublin: Irish Academic Press, 1997–2002.

Selected Poems, ed. Jacques Chuto Rudolf Patrick Holzapfel, Ellen Shannon-Mangan and Peter Van de Kamp, Dublin: Irish Academic Press, 2003.

James Mangan Selected Writings, ed. Sean Ryder, Dublin: University College Dublin Press, 2004.

Poems, ed. John Mitchel, New York: Haverty, 1859.

Poems, ed. David Wheatley, Oldcastle: Gallery, 2003.

Mannin, Ethel, *Two Studies in Integrity: Gerald Griffin and the Rev. Francis Mahony ('Father Prout')*, London: Jarrolds, 1954.

Markey, Anne, 'The Discovery of Irish Folkore', *New Hibernia Review* 10.4 (2006), 21–43.

Miller, Christopher R., *The Invention of Evening: Perception and Time in Romantic Poetry*, Cambridge: Cambridge University Press, 2006.

Milton, John, *Poetical Works,* ed. Douglas Bush, Oxford: Oxford University Press, 1966.

Moore, Thomas, *Irish Melodies*, 8 vols., Dublin and London: Power, 1808–1821.

Melodies, Songs, Sacred Songs and National Airs, New York: George Long, 1821.

Memoirs of Captain Rock, the Celebrated Irish Chieftain, with some Account of His Ancestors, Written by Himself, London: Longman, 1824.

Poetical Works, ed. A.D. Godley, Oxford: Oxford University Press, 1910.

'The Round Towers of Ireland', *Edinburgh Review*, Vol. LIX, No. CXIX (April 1834), 143–154.

Morash, Chris, 'The Little Black Rose Revisited: Church, Empire and National Destiny in the Writings of Aubrey de Vere', *Canadian Journal of Irish Studies*, Vol. 20, No. 2 (Dec, 1994), 45–52.

Writing the Irish Famine, Oxford: Oxford University Press, 1995.

Muldoon, Paul, *Poems, 1968–1998*, Faber: London, 2001.

To Ireland, I, Oxford: Oxford University Press, 2000.

O'Brien, Henry, *The Round Towers of Ireland*, 2nd edn., London: Parbury and Allen, 1834.

Ó Buachalla, Breandán, 'The Gaelic Background', in *Samuel Ferguson: A Centenary Tribute,* eds. Terence Brown and Barbara Hayley, Dublin: Royal Irish Academy, 1987.

Ó Ciosáin, Niall, *Print and Popular Culture in Ireland, 1750–1850*, London: Macmillan, 1997.

O'Connor, Frank, *The Backward Look: A Survey of Irish Literature*, London: Macmillan, 1967.

O'Daly, John (ed.), *The Poets and Poetry of Munster: A Selection of Irish Songs of the Poets of the Last Century*, trans. J.C. Mangan, Dublin: John O'Daly, 1847.

O'Donoghue, Bernard, 'The Translator's Voice: Irish Poetry Before Yeats', *Princeton University Library Chronicle*, Vol. LIX, No. 3 (Spring, 1998), 299–320.

O'Donoghue, D.J., *The Life and Times of James Clarence Mangan*, Edinburgh: Patrick Geddes, 1897.

O'Grady, Standish, *History of Ireland: The Heroic Period*, 2 vols., London: Sampson Low, 1878.

The Story of Ireland, London: Methuen, 1894.

O'Halloran, Clare, 'Historical Writings, 1690–1890', in *The Cambridge History of Irish Literature*, eds. Margaret Kelleher and Philip O'Leary, 2 vols., Cambridge, Cambridge University Press, 2006, 599–632.

O'Hegarty, P.S., *A History of Ireland Under the Union, 1801–1922*, London: Methuen, 1952.

O'Keefe, John, *The Poor Soldier*, Act II, sc. iii., retrieved from http://lion.chadwyck.co.uk.

Ó Lochlann, Colm, *Irish Street Ballads,* Dublin: Three Candles, 1939.

O'Neill, Michael, *The All-Sustaining Air: Romantic Legacies and Renewals in British, American and Irish Poetry since 1900*, Oxford: Oxford University Press, 2007.

Ó Tuama, Sean and Thomas Kinsella (eds. and trans.), *An Duanaire 1600–1900: Poems of the Dispossessed,* Dublin: Dolmen, 1981.

Omond, T.S., *English Metrists,* Oxford: Clarendon, 1921.

Paddy's Resource: Being a Select Collection of Original and Modern Patriotic Songs, Toasts and Sentiments Compiled for the Use of the People of Ireland (n.p. 1795).

Palgrave, F.T., 'English Poetry from Dryden to Cowper', *Quarterly Review* Vol. 112 (July 1862), 146–179.

Palgrave, Francis Turner, *The Golden Treasury*, ed. Christopher Ricks, Penguin: Harmondsworth, 1991.

Patten, Eve, *Samuel Ferguson and the Culture of Nineteenth-Century Ireland*, Dublin: Four Courts Press, 2004.

Pearce, David, *Yeats's Worlds: Ireland, England and the Poetic Imagination*, New Haven: Yale, 1935.

Perry, Seamus, *Tennyson*, Northcote: Tavistock, 2005.

Philips, Catherine, *Gerard Manley Hopkins and the Victorian Visual World*, Oxford: Oxford University Press, 2007.

Poe, Edgar Allen, *Selected Writings of Edgar Allan Poe*, ed. David Galloway, Harmondsworth: Penguin, 1967.

Pound, Ezra, 'Thomas MacDonagh as Critic', *Poetry*, 8 (Sep. 1916), pp. 309–312.

Ramazani, Jahan, *The Hybrid Muse: Postcolonial Poetry in English,* Chicago: University of Chicago Press, 2001.

Renan, Ernest, *The Poetry of the Celtic Races and Other Essays*, trans. William G. Hutchinson (1896), repr. Washington, NY: Kennikat, 1970.

Reynolds, Matthew, *The Realms of Verse: English Poetry in a Time of Nation-Building, 1830–1870*, Oxford: Oxford University Press, 2001.

Rodgers, W.R., *Collected Poems*, London: Oxford University Press, 1971.

Ruskin, John, *Complete Works*, eds. E.T. Cook and Alexander Wedderburn, 30 vols., London: George Allen, 1904.

Saintsbury, George, *A History of English Prosody from the Twelfth Century until the Present Day*, 3 vols., Macmillan: London, 1906–1910.

Schuchard, Ronald, *The Last Minstrels: Yeats and the Revival of the Bardic Arts,* Oxford: Oxford University Press, 2008.

Shannon-Mangan, Ellen, *James Clarence Mangan, A Biography*, Dublin: Irish Academic Press, 1996.

Shelley, Percy Bysshe, *The Major Works*, ed. Zachary Leader and Michael O'Neill, Oxford: Oxford University Press, 2003.

Shields, Hugh, 'New Dates for Old Songs, 1766–1803', *Long Room*, Vol. 18–19, (1979), 34–41.

Smith, Gregory G., *Scottish Literature, Character and Influence*, London: Macmillan, 1919.

Smyth, Gerry, '"The Natural Course of Things": Matthew Arnold, Celticism and the English Poetic Tradition', *Journal of Victorian Culture*, I, i (Spring, 1996), 35–53.

Stevens, Wallace, *The Necessary Angel*, London: Faber, 1984.

Stewart, Bruce (ed.), *Hearts and Minds: Irish Culture and Society Under the Act of Union*, Gerrards Cross: Colin Smythe, 2002.

Sullivan, Timothy Daniel, (1888), Dublin: Sullivan, n.d.

Swift, Roger, 'Thomas Carlyle, *Chartism* and the Irish in Early Victorian England', *Victorian Literature and Culture* Vol. 29, No. 1 (2001), 67–83.

Swinburne, Algernon, *Poems,* 6 vols., London: Chatto, 1904.

Taylor, Geoffrey, *Irish Poets of the Nineteenth Century,* London: Routledge, 1951.

Tennyson, Alfred, *The Poems of Tennyson*, ed. Christopher Ricks, 2nd Edn., 3 vols., London: Longman, 1987.

Tennyson, Hallam, *Tennyson: A Memoir*, London: Macmillan, 1899.

Tennyson, Hallam (ed.), *Tennyson and his Friends*, London: Macmillan, 1911.

Thrall, Miriam, *Rebellious Fraser's: Nol Yorke's Magazine in the Days of Maginn, Thackeray and Carlyle,* New York: Columbia University Press, 1934.

Tighe, Mary, *Psyche and Other Poems* (1811), repr. Woodstock: Oxford, 1992.

Trumpener, Katie, *Bardic Nationalism: The Romantic Novel and the British Empire*, Princeton: Princeton University Press, 1997.

Vaughan, W.E. (ed.), *New History of Ireland, Ireland Under the Union, 1801–1921,* Oxford: Oxford University Press, 1989.

Vendler, Helen, *Our Secret Discipline: Yeats and Poetic Form*, Oxford: Oxford University Press, 2007.

Walsh, Edward, *Irish Popular Songs,* Dublin: McGlashan, 1847.

Webb, J.F. (ed. and trans.), *The Age of Bede*, 2nd edn., Harmondsworth: Penguin, 1983.

Welch, Robert, 'Constitution, Language and Tradition in Nineteenth-Century Irish Poetry', in *Tradition and Influence in Anglo-Irish Poetry*, eds. Terence Brown and Nicholas Grene, Totowa, NJ: Barnes and Noble, 1989, 7–30.

A History of Verse Translation from the Irish, 1789–1897, Gerrard's Cross: Colin Smythe, 1988.

Irish Poetry from Moore to Yeats, Gerrards Cross: Colin Smythe, 1980.

White, Harry, *The Keeper's Recital: Music and Cultural History in Ireland, 1770–1970,* Cork: Field Day, 1998.

Music and the Irish Literary Imagination, Oxford: Oxford University Press, 2008.

White, Norman, *Hopkins in Ireland*, Dublin: University College Dublin Press, 2002.

Windele, John, *Historical and Descriptive Notices of the City of Cork and Its Vicinity*, London: Longmans, 1839.

Wolfson, Susan, *Formal Charges: The Shaping of Poetry in British Romanticism*, Stanford: Stanford University Press, 1997.

Wood, Michael, *Yeats and Violence*, Oxford, Oxford University Press, 2010.

Wordsworth, William, *Poetical Works*, eds. Thomas Hutchinson and Ernest de Selincourt, Oxford: Oxford University Press, 1969.

Wright, Joseph, *The English Dialect Dictionary*, 3 vols., London: Frowde, 1898.

Yeats, Grainne, *The Harp of Ireland: The Belfast Harpers' Festival, 1792 and the Saving of Ireland's Harp Music by Edward Bunting*, Belfast: Belfast Harpers' Bicentenary, 1992.

Yeats, W.B., *Autobiographies*, London: Macmillan, 1956.

Autobiography, ed. Denis Donoghue, London: Macmillan, 1972.

The Collected Letters of W.B. Yeats, Electronic Edition, Unpublished Letters (1905–1939), ed. John Kelly, Charlottesville, VA: Intelex, 2002.

Collected Plays, London: Macmillan, 1952.

The Collected Works of W.B. Yeats, ed. George Mills Harper, Richard Finneran and William H. O'Donnell, 14 vols, New York: Scribner, 1989–2006.

Essays and Introductions, London: Macmillan, 1961.

Fairy and Folk Tales of the Irish Peasantry, Gerrards Cross: Colin Smythe, 1973.

'Later Essays', in *The Collected Works of W.B. Yeats*, ed. William H. O'Donnell, New York: Scribner, 1994.

Prefaces and Introductions, ed. William H. O'Donnell, London: Macmillan, 1988.

Uncollected Prose, ed. John P. Frayne, 2 vols., London: Macmillan, 1970.

The Variorum Edition of the Poems of W.B. Yeats, eds. Peter Allt and Russell K. Alspach, New York: Macmillan, 1957.

Young, Robert J.C., *Colonial Desire*, Abingdon: Routledge, 1995.

Index

Adorno, Theodor, 12
aisling, 129
Allingham, William, 133–135
    Diary, 133, 147, 148, 162, 226
    Laurence Bloomfield in Ireland, 226
    Nightingale Valley, 142
    'The Fairies', 88, 137
amhrán, 41, 43, 198
ancien régime, 48, 82, 132
Anglo-Saxon, 147
Anon
    'Aisling an Oigfhir', 66
    'Castle Hyde', 63
    'Ceann Dubh Dílis', 9
    'last romantics', 197
    'Londonderry Air', 66
    'Molly My Dear', 37
    'Muna b'é an t-ól', 44
    'Páistín Fionn', 75, 198, 208
    'Slán le Máigh', 66
    'The Banks of Banna', 34
    'The Voyage of Maeldune', 133
Anster, John, 117, 118, 127
    Faust, 108
Apocalypse, 107
Aquinas, Thomas, 55
archipelagic, 186, 188
archipelago, 15, 25
Aristotle, 98
Arnold, Matthew, 1–5, 13–16, 31, 37,
    39, 72, 83, 98, 135, 141, 143,
    156, 172, 201
    'St. Brandan', 148, 155
    The Study of Celtic Literature, 2, 6,
    138, 205
ascendancy, 16
atavism, 149, 185, 206
Atlantis, 134
authenticity, 13, 18, 25, 30, 39, 41, 48, 52, 54, 56,
    59, 65, 70, 84, 86, 102, 104, 193

Bairéid, Riocard
    'Preab san Ól', 64
Bakhtin, Mikhael, 18, 52
Barthes, Roland, 56
BBC, 207
Beckett, Samuel, 26, 41, 46, 209
    Murphy, 21, 41
    'Recent Irish Poetry', 23
Beethoven, Ludwig, 68
Behan, Brendan, 62, 219
Belfast Harpers Festival, 1792, 4
Benthamism, 181
Bevis, Matthew, 133
Bhabha, Homi, 56, 58
Black and Tans, 195
Blackstone, William, 176
Blackwood's Edinburgh Magazine, 48,
    73, 88
Blake, William, 198
blarney, 63, 167, 168
Blarney Castle, 50, 62
Bloom, Harold, 198, 201
Bonaparte, Napoleon, 127
Bonaparte, Napoleon III, 138
Bornstein, George, 201
Boru, Brian, 113
Brearton, Fran, 188, 203
Brennan, Timothy, 2
Bridges, Robert, 27, 163, 166, 169, 170,
    172, 173, 176, 181
British Empire, 171, 172, 173
Brittany, 138, 139
Bromwich, David, 203
Brooke, Charlotte, 16, 83, 85
    Reliques of Irish Poetry, 8
Brooke, Stopford, 147
Brown, Malcolm, 160
    'Literary Parnellism', 159
Brown, Terence, 187
Browning, Robert, 114, 126, 200

Stevenson, John, 85
Stewart, Bruce, 213
Stonyhurst, 162
Sudan, 172
Sullivan, Timothy Daniel, 135
  'The Voyage of the Corras', 144
sunset, 162, 163, 170
Swift, Jonathan, 22, 48, 52
Swinburne, Algernon Charles, 16, 171, 172
  'An Appeal to England', 169
  'Apostosy', 169
  'Evening on the Broads', 170
  'The Commonweal', 168
Symons, Arthur, 197
Synge, John Millington, 42, 194
synthetic form, 5, 13, 14, 15, 18, 20, 25, 28, 30, 35,
    40, 44, 48, 52, 59, 66, 90, 104, 125, 130,
    135, 167, 191, 204, 207
synthetic Scots, 25, 86

Tasso, Torquato, 108
Taylor, Geoffrey, 63
Tennyson, Alfred, 3, 16, 39, 64, 126, 132,
    135–137, 162
  Idylls of the King, 3, 137
  in Ireland, 139
  'Locksley Hall', 115, 132, 146
  'Locksley Hall Sixty Years After', 132, 146
  In Memoriam, 98
  'Ode on the Death of the Duke of
    Wellington', 155
  The Princess, 140, 146, 150
  'Recollections of the Arabian Nights', 119
  on Robert Burns, 136
  'Tears, Idle Tears', 117, 136, 150
  'The Bugle Song', 139
  'The First Quarrel', 150
  'The Golden Year', 141
  'The Lady of Shalott', 8
  'The Lotos-Eaters', 122
  'The Voyage of Maeldune', 133, 144, 149,
    150, 154
  'Tomorrow', 155
terrorism, 134
Thackeray, William Makepeace, 63
Thompson, George, 68
  Select Collection of Scottish Airs, 86
Thrall, Miriam, 217
through-otherness, 18, 188, 191
Tighe, Mary, 135
  'Written at Killarney', 140
The Times, 169
Tír na nÓg, 134, 152, 185
Tone, Wolfe, 4
tourism, 137, 138, 139

translation, 9, 10, 16, 25, 31, 33, 44, 46, 59, 65,
    72, 80, 81, 83, 85, 88, 99, 107, 114, 116,
    121, 129, 136, 144, 147, 186
Trevelyan, Charles
  The Irish Crisis, 228
Trumpener, Katie, 7
Tynan, Katherine, 177, 181

Ulster Gaelic Society, 70
Ulster Scots, 43, 88
Union of England and Wales with Scotland
    1707, 4, 87, 164
Union of Great Britain and Ireland 1801, 6, 14
unionism, 168, 170
United Ireland, 159
United Irishmen, 5, 83, 128, 132

Vendler, Helen, 197
Verlaine, Paul, 197, 198
vers libre, 27, 187
Vico, Giambattista, 96
violence, 203, 206, 208
Von Hammer-Purgstall, Joseph, 118

Wales, 138, 167
Walsh, Edward, 40, 45, 46, 84, 115, 130
  'Mo craoibhin cno', 31
War of Independence, 1919, 87
Warton, Thomas
  The Union, 164
Weatherly, Frederick
  'Danny Boy', 66
Welch, Robert, 8, 33, 34, 41, 83, 98, 108
Wellesley, Dorothy, 205, 216
Welsh (language), 138, 167
Wheatley, David, 224
White, Harry, 29, 34
White, Norman, 166
Whitman, Walt, 204
William of Orange, 62
Windele, John, 140
Wolfson, Susan, 13, 17
Wood, Michael, 195
Wordsworth, William, 72, 85, 122, 135, 141, 143,
    153, 189, 190, 201
  The Excursion, 153
  'It is a beauteous evening', 168
  Lyrical Ballads, 7, 17, 83, 126
  'The Seven Sisters', 88
  'Tintern Abbey', 117, 136
  Yarrow poems, 136
Wright, Joseph, 167

Yeats, George, 207
Yeats, Grainne, 211

LIBRARY, UNIVERSITY OF CHESTER